RECOVERING THE PERSONAL

ÆR

American Academy of Religion
Studies in Religion

Editor
Lawrence S. Cunningham

Number 52
RECOVERING THE PERSONAL
Religious Language and the Post-Critical
Quest of H. Richard Niebuhr
by
R. Melvin Keiser

RECOVERING THE PERSONAL
Religious Language and the Post-Critical Quest of H. Richard Niebuhr

R. Melvin Keiser

Scholars Press
Atlanta, Georgia

RECOVERING THE PERSONAL

Religious Language and the Post-Critical Quest
of H. Richard Niebuhr

by
R. Melvin Keiser

Library of Congress Cataloging in Publication Data

Keiser, R. Melvin.
    Recovering the personal.

    (American Academy of Religion. Studies in religion ;
no. 52)
    Bibliography: p.
    1. Niebuhr, H. Richard (Helmut Richard), 1894-
1962. 2. Languages--Religious aspects--History--20th
century. I. Title. II. Series: Studies in religion
(American Academy of Religion) ; no. 52.
BX4827.N52K45   1987   230'.092'4   87-23354
ISBN 1-55540-185-6
ISBN 1-55540-186-4 (pbk.)

Printed in the United States of America
on acid-free paper

To H. Richard Niebuhr and William H. Poteat,

who in their own graceful ways have engaged in recovering the personal not only in thought but in the midst of their students' lives—as masters of the maieutic art.

CONTENTS

ACKNOWLEDGEMENTS   xi

LIST OF ABBREVIATIONS   xiii

INTRODUCTION   xvii

PART ONE: LINGUISTIC CONVERGENCE IN
          POSTCRITICAL THEOLOGY

CHAPTER

1. HEURISTIC METAPHORS AND RELIGIOUS
   GRAMMAR   1
   Language as Metaphor and Symbol System
   Heuristic Metaphors
   Theopoesis: A Fabric of Metaphoric Languages
   The Linguistic Exigence of Our Time: Resymbolization and
      Grammatical Analysis
   The Method of Grammatical Analysis
   Comparative Metaphor Analysis of Responsibility
   Earlier Grammatical Comparisons
   Conclusion

II. MEANING, MYTH, AND THE DIALOGICAL SELF   21
    Linguistic Meaning
    Religious Meaning
    Metamorphosis in Mythic Conception
    Niebuhr in Mythic Perspective
    History as Myth
    Niebuhr as "Homo Dialogicus"
    The Dialogical Self

Earlier Work from the Standpoint of Language
Conclusion

III.　A POSTCRITICAL AMBIENCE　　　　　　　45
　　　Critical Theology: Niebuhr's Contemporaries
　　　Postcritical Philosophers: Polanyi, Merleau-Ponty,
　　　　　Wittgenstein
　　　Postcritical Explorers of Symbolic Forms
　　　Conclusion

PART TWO: THE COMMITTED SELF'S THEOPOETICAL
　　　　　　　QUEST FOR INTEGRITY

IV.　HEURISTIC METAPHORS: HISTORY AND VALUE　　65
　　　History as Threat to Language and Integrity
　　　Inner and Outer History
　　　Recovering a Shared World: Revelation and Pattern
　　　Recovering a Real World: Animal Faith the Ground of
　　　　　Knowing
　　　Critical Ingredients in the Heuristic Metaphor of History
　　　Commitment in History and Beyond
　　　The Heuristic Metaphor of Value
　　　Relational Value: The Realm of Tacit Commitments
　　　History and Value in Comparison
　　　Residual Kantianism in the Metaphor of Value
　　　Conclusion

V.　HEURISTIC METAPHORS: FAITH AND FEELING　　85
　　　The Heuristic Metaphor of Faith
　　　Five Types of Faith
　　　Faith and the Theological Task
　　　Value within the Metaphor of Faith
　　　Historical Revelation within the Metaphor of Faith
　　　Integration and the Personlike Integrity of the One
　　　Beyond Critical Dichotomies to Personal Speech
　　　Noetic Faith: A Residual Dichotomy
　　　Symbolic Expression of Being in the World
　　　The Heuristic Metaphor of Feeling
　　　Feeling in a Critical Age
　　　Religion—An Affair of Emotion
　　　Jonathan Edwards on Feeling and Emotional Wildness
　　　Divine Election and the Objectivity of Emotion
　　　Parabolic Understanding and Emotional Truth

Our Task: An Affectional Awakening
Feeling—The Symbolic Layer
Conclusion

PART THREE: RESPONSIBILITY AS LINGUISTIC LIFE
            FORM: RELIGIOUS GRAMMAR OF THE
            COMMITTED SELF

 VI. SPEAKING OF AN ELUSIVE SELF   113
     The Irreducible "I" and Its First Person Grammar
     The Elusive Self—Irreducible and Committed
     I and Thou: A Distinction
     Radical Action in the First Person
     The Space of God's Appearing
     The Space of Our Appearing: The Divine-Human Dialogue
     The Third Person Mood of Modernity
     Divine Sovereignty in the First Person
     An Emergent First Person Perspective
     Inner and Outer History—A Grammatical Incipience
     Critical Categories and Postcritical Conclusions: A Tension
     Confessional Theology: A First Person Method
     Confessional Theology in Critical and Postcritical
        Perspectives
     Conclusion

VII. SPEAKING AND BEING TRANSFORMED: THE
     LOGIC OF RELIGIOUS DISCOURSE   133
     Language of Integrity and Divinity in Being
     Reflexiveness: Referential Language and the Objective
        Self—A Critical Recalcitrance
     Dialogical Transformation
     Elusive God and Elicited Faith
     Recovering the Personal

BIBLIOGRAPHY   149

ACKNOWLEDGEMENTS

I wish to acknowledge here my gratitude to my professors who encouraged over many years a concern for Niebuhr—Joe E. Elmore, Sydney E. Ahlstrom, Robert L. Calhoun, and William H. Poteat. There are others I wish to thank who as my teachers nurtured the intellectual life within a humane and richly fulfilling ethos—Thomas S. Brown at Westtown School, Kathleen Postle and Grimsley T. Hobbs at Earlham College. For a place to be, to think, and to write I am grateful to Helen G. Hole. For the insight and delight of convivial dialogue I am thankful to my colleagues and students at Guilford College. I wish as well to thank Guilford for typing support and two study leaves to work on Niebuhr. I have benefitted from the indefatigable typing assistance of Ibby Hunt and Alice Johnson, and from the proofreading care of David Teague. For access to, and permission to quote from, Niebuhr's unpublished writings, I am grateful to Richard R. Niebuhr. For the grace of family I am grateful to my parents, David S. and Marjorie H. Keiser, my children, Megan and Christopher, and my wife, Elizabeth B. Keiser. Finally, I am appreciative to the friends who have critically read and substantially improved this book—Elizabeth D. Kirk, John H. Stoneburner, and Elizabeth B. Keiser; to those who have encouraged me throughout—Carol Stoneburner, Jerry Godard, and Jane Caris; and to those others as well whose friendship is sustenance.

August, 1987

R. Melvin Keiser
Laurel Island, Squam Lake
Holderness, New Hampshire

LIST OF ABBREVIATIONS

CAW   THE CHURCH AGAINST THE WORLD, by H. Richard Niebuhr, Wilhelm Pauck, and F. P. Miller (Chicago, New York: Willett, Clark & Co., 1935). Niebuhr's contributions, "The Question of the Church" and "Toward the Independence of the Church," reprinted in THEOLOGY IN AMERICA: THE MAJOR PROTESTANT VOICES FROM PURITANISM TO NEO-ORTHODOXY, ed. by Sydney E. Ahlstrom (Indianapolis and New York: Bobbs-Merrill Company, 1967). All page references are to latter volume.

CC   CHRIST AND CULTURE, by H. Richard Niebuhr, Harper Torchbooks (New York: Harper & Brothers, 1956); originally published (New York: Harper & Brothers, 1951).

KGA   THE KINGDOM OF GOD IN AMERICA, by H. Richard Niebuhr, Harper Torchbooks (New York: Harper & Brothers, 1959); originally published (New York: Harper & Brothers, 1937).

MR   THE MEANING OF REVELATION, by H. Richard Niebuhr (New York: Macmillan Company, 1941).

PCM   THE PURPOSE OF THE CHURCH AND ITS MINISTRY: REFLECTIONS ON THE AIMS OF THEOLOGICAL EDUCATION, by H. Richard Niebuhr, in collaboration with Daniel Day Williams and James M. Gustafson (New York: Harper & Brothers, 1956).

RMWC   RADICAL MONOTHEISM AND WESTERN CULTURE, WITH SUPPLEMENTARY ESSAYS, by H. Richard Niebuhr (New York: Harper & Brothers, 1960).

RS   THE RESPONSIBLE SELF: AN ESSAY IN CHRISTIAN MORAL PHILOSOPHY, by H. Richard Niebuhr, with a Preface by Richard R. Niebuhr, and an Introduction by James M. Gustafson (New York, Evanston, and London: Harper and Row, 1963).

SSD   THE SOCIAL SOURCES OF DENOMINATIONALISM, by
             H. Richard Niebuhr, Living Age Books (New York: Meridian
             Books, 1957); originally published (New York: Henry Holt and
             Company, 1929).

Ac Theologie hath teened me ten score times,
For the more I muse therInne the mistloker it seemeth,
And the deeper I devined the darker me thoughte.
It is no science, forsoth, for to subtile Inne.
Ne were the love that lieth therinne a wel lewid thyng it were.
Ac for it leteth the best be love, I love it the better,
For where that love is ledere lackith never grace.
(William Langland, PIERS PLOWMAN)

And therefore the thing may possibly be better understood, by using many words and a variety of expressions, by a particular consideration of it, as it were by parts, than by any short definition.
(Jonathan Edwards, DISSERTATION CONCERNING THE
END FOR WHICH GOD CREATED THE WORLD)

We keep coming back and coming back
To the real: to the hotel instead of the hymns
That fall upon it out of the wind. We seek . . .
Nothing beyond reality. Within it,
Everything, . . .
So that morning and evening are like promises kept,
So that the approaching sun and its arrival,
Its evening feast and the following festival,
This faithfulness of reality, this mode,
This tendance and venerable holding-in
Make gay the hallucinations in surfaces.
(Wallace Stevens, "An Ordinary Evening in New Haven")

And be ware thou take not on[e] thing after thy affection and liking and leve another, . . . but take every thing with other, and trewly vnderstonden.
(Julian of Norwich, A BOOK OF SHOWINGS)

The knowledge imposes a pattern, and falsifies,
For the pattern is new in every moment
And every moment is a new and shocking
Valuation of all we have been.
(T.S. Eliot, "East Coker")

INTRODUCTION

Like a great poem, quartet, or conversation the theology of H. Richard Niebuhr has a richness of insight, thematic and temporal interweaving, and evocative depth. Within the plenitude of possible approaches to this complexity I am interested in Niebuhr's ongoing search for a fitting theological method. His is a theology of human experience; while culturally sophisticated and intellectually subtle, it nonetheless bears the imprint of a unique self involved in a profound struggle in the midst of the joys and sorrows of human existence, groping for patterns of meaning that will recover the personal in our life and thought. Exploring the reflections of his last years, I have been struck by the "postcritical" nature of his methodological preoccupation.

Evident in THE RESPONSIBLE SELF and other literary remains of the early 1960's, he immerses himself in phenomenology, Michael Polanyi, and the interdisciplinary exploration of symbolic forms; he begins to find common ground with Wittgenstein; and he draws afresh from his long-standing interest in existentialism. In Polanyi's words, the point of view coming to full expression in this preoccupation at the end of his life is, in several ways, "postcritical."

First, Niebuhr begins with a committed self. Rather than the doubting and detached self of Cartesianism and Kantianism, the self as responder is committed to, actively involved in, multiple aspects of reality—natural, social, cultural, religious. Beneath all knowing and doing, which depend upon it, is the responsive agency of these interactions. Secondly, these commitments are fundamentally tacit or unconscious. As we know or do anything, we rely on the whole network of commitments in our response relations without being explicitly aware of them. Our lives rest, therefore, irrevocably on the unknowable, on mystery. Thirdly, the self is not isolated but dwells in a world sustained by these multiple tacit relations to various aspects of reality. Fourthly, while he masterfully used dualisms earlier, responsive relating goes beyond the dichotomies of mind/body, fact/value, subject/object, theory/practice, religion/science, and reason/feeling—all of which seek to preserve some part of our being or doing immaculate from the commitment and personal agency of responsiveness. Response, fifthly, involves the body in the mind's creativity and the mind in the body's agency.

Sixthly, the search of a responsible self, committed to and indwelling a world, is for integrity—the integration of ourselves within our world and the ultimate environment that encompasses us. What Niebuhr finds in our modern world, pervasively shaped by the "critical" thought of Kantianism and Cartesianism, is rather a fragmentation of self, the loss of a real and shared world, and a fundamental distrust and disbelief in any circumambient mystery. As he takes up the challenge and works toward a resolution of integrity as the central problem of modernity, he comes to see, seventhly, that both problem and solution lie in our understanding and use of language. We live our lives within the paradigmatic responses of words which express and shape self and world. The loss of integrity he discovers is the result of our loss of confidence in certain forms of speech and of understanding how language functions. His quest for integrity becomes, therefore, a methodological exploration of the nature of language—both its logic or grammar and poetic-like creativity and communication of meaning through metaphor and myth—as an effort to recover and fashion anew those forms of speech we call religious.

Niebuhr's final thought is explicitly postcritical, in a word therefore, because it presents the self as *committed* and *linguistic*. As committed it is: tacit, dwelling in a world, non-dualistic, embodied, and seeking within being for integrity. As linguistic it uses religious language as that which shapes, expresses, and transforms self and world. It is postcritical, therefore, because it is personal—grounding all knowing, doing, being in *trust* in the unknowable and uncontrollable depths, in *passion* that weaves us into the fabric of a world, and in *creativity* that dwells amidst ambiguity and gropes toward clear patterns of meaning. We exist and think personally in *connectedness*—to our social and natural contexts, and to the flow of time. We are not isolated individuals but particular configurations of, and unique ways of being in, unlimited response relations. Nor do we inhabit time as a succession of infinitesimal points but dwell in the fullness of a present that includes the bodily and sometimes conscious reaches of memory and expectation.

That we dwell within such spatial and temporal connectedness means we are immersed in a matrix of meaning. Doubt can obstruct or ignore it; critical reason can reject or attempt to erode it; our own dogmatic affirmations can distort or truncate it. But it endures; every act of violence against it depends on it. We can open to and live and think out of this fullness. Then our religious language is empowered as it gives incarnate shape to inchoate commitments, bearing on reality and transforming selves.

Following, in Part One we shall explore the multifaceted centrality of language; in Part Two, the nature of the committed self in its search for integrity through heuristic metaphors; and in Part Three, the grammar of the committed self's religious language.

While his method is usually taken to be critical, a historicized Kantianism, when viewed from the perspective of his final theological explorations in the early 1960's, it can be seen clearly as postcritical and as the culmination of the central concern of his mature years. There is, however, a density in his thinking which makes it difficult to comprehend what he is really doing. He can be read on many levels both by the technical theologian and layperson—there is information for the beginner, insight for the experienced, and wisdom for the mature. In addition to this density there is difficulty in reaching the marrow of his methodological mind because, as we can see from the vantage point of his final years, his method is emergent, dialogical, and radical.

Nurtured among the ideals of nineteenth and early twentieth century theological liberalism and philosophical idealism, evident in his writings up to 1929,[1] he underwent a profound turning at the end of 1929 just after the publication of his first book, THE SOCIAL SOURCES OF DENOMINATIONALISM. In the early 1930's he exhibits this as a turning to "theological realism"[2]—from spirituality of ideals to the actuality of being. In his last years he speaks of it as coming to affirm divine sovereignty and as a change in his personal trust in being.[3]

Born out of the depth of experience, the entirety of Niebuhr's mature theology is a gradual realization of the postcritical orientation implicit in this conversion. Originating in this turning are what he at the end of his life calls "root metaphors," (which, in order to call attention to their capacity for discovery, we will call "heuristic metaphors")—general patterns of meaning, issuing from the interaction of the self with a second term, which open up insight into, and shape, the self and its world.[4] The entirety of his mature theology is the development, the dense and intricate weave, of five root metaphors: history, value, faith, feeling, and responsibility.

The seeds of the first four root metaphors are visible in the "conversion essay" even though they ripen at different times, and the fifth and consummate metaphor of responsibility becomes visible shortly thereafter.[5]

---

[1]. This period of Niebuhr's liberalism and idealism is evident in his M.A. thesis on a late nineteenth century German poet (Helmut Niebuhr, "The Problem of the Individual in Richard Dehmel" [unpublished M.A. thesis in the Department of Germanics, Washington University, June, 1917]) through SOCIAL SOURCES.

[2] For Niebuhr's exploration of "theological realism" see H. Richard Niebuhr, "Can German and American Christians Understand Each Other?," in *Christian Century*, XLVII (July 23, 1930); "Religious Realism in the Twentieth Century," in RELIGIOUS REALISM, ed. D. C. Macintosh (New York: The Macmillan Company, 1931); and "Translator's Preface," of THE RELIGIOUS SITUATION, by Paul Tillich, Living Age Edition (New York: Meridian Books, 1956) (originally published New York: Henry Holt & Co., 1932).

[3] H. Richard Niebuhr, "Reformation: Continuing Imperative," in HOW MY MIND HAS CHANGED, ed. with an intro. by Harold E. Fey, Meridian Books (New York: World Publishing Company, 1961), p. 72 (originally published in *Christian Century*, LXXVII [1960]).

[4] An idiosyncratic use, perhaps, of metaphor, it will be explained in detail in chapter one. See RS p. 153 for Niebuhr's use of "root metaphor" and acknowledgement of its source in Stephen Pepper, WORLD HYPOTHESES (Berkeley: University of California Press, 1961).

[5] In H. Richard Niebuhr, "Moral Relativism and the Christian Ethic" (New York: International Missionary Council, 1929. Address given at a Conference of Theological Seminaries, meeting at Drew Theological Seminary, Madison, New Jersey, November 29–December 1,

Throughout their development Niebuhr is groping for a fitting theological method. As his thought matures, he passes on consciously from one metaphor to another. After working with the metaphor of history from THE KINGDOM OF GOD IN AMERICA of 1937 through THE MEANING OF REVELATION to CHRIST AND CULTURE of 1951 and THE PURPOSE OF THE CHURCH AND ITS MINISTRY of 1956, he explicitly discards it in order to inquire into faith as the metaphoric milieu for theology. In its climactic development in RADICAL MONOTHEISM AND WESTERN CULTURE he says of theology:

> As an effort of disciplined thinking in this context it cannot easily be classified under one of the current great categories of human inquiry: as a science, or as one of the humanities, or as history, or as a *Geisteswissenschaft,* or as a critique or a philosophy. It must develop its own methods in view of the situation in which it works and of the object with which it deals, without becoming the vassal of methodologies developed by rational inquiries directed toward other objects and existing in connection with other nonrational activities of men [sic] besides faith.[6]

1929, on "Theological Education and the World Mission of Christianity"), history is present in the recognition that it not only means the threat of historical relativism but the promise of "the revelation of ultimate reality" (p. 9); value in the affirmation of the inseparability of value and being, in that the "pattern of ultimate goodness" is dependent upon "the pattern of existence" which is "the will of God" (p. 10); faith as "trust" in and "loyalty" to "the pattern of existence" as "the will of God" (pp. 9 & 11); and feeling as "conviction of" and "trust in the actuality of God's *love*" (p. 11; my italics). Finally, there is the fifth and consummate metaphor of responsibility which similarly takes its origins in Niebuhr's conversion but does not become visible until 1933 in an unpublished essay, "The Social Gospel and the Mind of Jesus." There he distinguishes a third type of ethics that focuses neither upon "oughts" (as in what he will later call "deontological ethics"; see RS chapter one) nor "ends" (as in what will be "teleological ethics") but upon the realism of "what God is doing" (H. Richard Niebuhr, "The Social Gospel and the Mind of Jesus" [unpublished lecture, handwritten, read before the American Theological Society, in New York City, April 21, 1933, Niebuhr Folder VIII], p. 11). The word itself does not appear for another two years and then, interestingly enough, the phrase used is the same as the title of his last book—the "responsible self" (CAW p. 593).

The first two metaphors predominate from the 1930's into the beginnings of the 1950's. Faith becomes dominant in the 1950's reaching its culmination in 1960 with publication of RADICAL MONOTHEISM. Much less visible in its origins and much less developed than the others, feeling is attended to briefly but significantly in the early 1960's. While responsibility is being developed in his lectures on "Christian Ethics" throughout the 1950's, it achieves its consummation in the Robertson and Earl lectures delivered in the 1960's and posthumously published in 1963 as THE RESPONSIBLE SELF. Through the emerging and overlapping development of these root metaphors Niebuhr is groping for ways of affirming that the pattern of our lives dwelling within the pattern of existence and of ultimate goodness becomes articulate, and is therefore nourished and transformed, within religious language, which he brings to culminating expression in THE RESPONSIBLE SELF.

[6]RMWC p. 15. Niebuhr's use of masculine pronouns and nouns now jars the ear. It is true he

At the very end of his life, as he is developing the concluding metaphor of responsibility, he criticizes even more directly the theoretical/practical distinction that had been fundamental to his exploration of outer and inner history in THE MEANING OF REVELATION. To this reassessment of history he now adds a critique of value. Both perspectives, he argues, issue in misleading dualities, like the body/mind distinction, that dichotomize, rather than integrate, the self. In this light he proposes working with the metaphor of responsibility to solve the problem of the unity of the self, although even here, with typical humility, he is not sure this new perspective will succeed:

> The responsive self, however, exists in another triadic, dialectical interaction. Traditionally we have distinguished this second situation from the first by saying that in it we exercise practical reason, while in the other we use speculative or observing reason. Useful and unavoidable as this distinction is, it tends to lead us somewhat astray by dissolving the unity of the self, somewhat as the similar, useful, but also misleading distinction between body and mind does. Equally serious has been the consequence that the separation has often led us to ignore the practical or ethical elements in our knowing as well as the observing, interpreting elements in our doing. Instead of distinguishing the two situations by reference to the subjective activity of reason as contemplative or practical, we have more recently tended to distinguish them by reference to their objects as *facts* and *values*. But it is notorious that it is difficult to give definite meaning to either of these words, or even to correlate them as designating species of one genus, for instance, of being. It may be that the general problem which we have tried to solve with the use of these two familiar distinctions can be brought to our attention in a slightly different perspective with this view of ourselves as responsible beings, though it remains doubtful whether the ultimate problem of the unity of the self can be solved by means of this approach entirely more satisfactorily than it has been by means of the older distinctions.[7]

---

wrote prior to the recent rise in feminine consciousness of our pervasive use of masculine grammatical forms. We can only guess at his response. He might have observed the ambiguity of generic and specific in "men" and "he," and made clear he meant the generic. Even so he probably would have taken it as an opportunity for confession of his and our society's participation in the injustices between the sexes. To his credit, he was instrumental in opening Yale Divinity School admissions in the 1950's to women. His frequent use, for other reasons, of the first person, singular and plural, suggests a way of avoiding what now, once our ears become attuned, sounds like blatant sexism. The metaphor of responsibility possesses, I believe, a fruitfulness as yet unrealized for the development of a feminist theology; indeed, Niebuhr's theology creates a human space beyond the dichotomizing and truncating characteristics of sexist theology.

[7] RS pp. 82–83; his italics.

The gradual emergence of methodological clarity is like the dawning of understanding in a dialogue. In a conversation we take up one theme and then another only to return to the prior theme enriched by the perspective offered by the second, and then in taking up a third theme find both transformed as we see them in a new light. We begin a conversation from no planned starting point but *in medias res,* and move toward no set goal, even though there is a direction. Its beginning is fraught with intimations of potential meaning; as it unfolds, that which has been hidden, yet actually shaping the entire course of conversation, emerges into consciousness. The movement from where we are, with a sense of latent meaning, to emergent awareness also occurs in responsiveness to the initiation of the conversation, to the various contributions of fellow conversationalists and the situation, and to the direction in which we think the talk is moving and think our fellow speaker thinks it is moving.

So it seems to me is Niebuhr's manner of doing theology. Developing one of these metaphors, he draws the interwoven threads of the others with him so as to bring a richness of metaphoric perspectives to bear on a given subject, which is enhanced by taking up another metaphor, returning to the first, moving on to yet another that embraces and transcends from a different angle much that was present in the earlier two. He begins each theological effort from no explicit starting point, no adopted systematic principle, but from the complexity and depth of self-transforming experience, and moves in a direction, not toward the goal of a solution to a clearly defined problem, but toward increased awareness of the actuality intimated and emerging in his reflective experience. What he finds true at the end of his career about the emergent quality of God's divine rule is true as well of the nature of his own religious reflection:

> The divine rule, the divine action in all things, which now men only dimly perceive and understand in their encounter with creative and destructive events, will be clearly revealed at last, in the end. What is to become clear in the end, however, is not something new. It is now an emergency that is coming. The actuality of the present is to become emergent. God whose rule is hidden and whose rule will become manifest is ruling now, despite all hiddenness. Realized eschatology is realized theology.[8]

There is an "emergency" coming in Niebuhr's own thinking, a "realized theology" that recognizes the actuality present in his thought latent from the time of his conversion but at the last becoming clearly revealed.

But the conversation is ongoing, always responsive to new ingredients

---

[8]RS p. 167.

and occurrences, forever reaching toward greater clarity and depth of understanding: it is irrepressible. With characteristic wit and modesty he calls this indefatigability "recalcitrance." In dedicating RADICAL MONOTHEISM to the authors of his *festschrift*, FAITH AND ETHICS, and to his other students, he says: "I apologize to them for being as recalcitrant in hewing to my own line as I often found them to be in following their own bent."[9] In the medieval phrase he found in Gabriel Marcel, we can say Niebuhr as theologian is a *homo viator*—a thinker always "on the way."[10] And in his own words, what he says of human nature as such is especially true of himself—he is a man in dialogue, a *"homo dialogicus."*[11]

The process is never completed. Death came as an interruption to growing understanding; had Niebuhr lived into old age, death would still have caught him "on the way." It is not that he leaves us an uncompleted system; he leaves us no system, whether complete or incomplete. There is certainly a comprehensiveness and integrity to his thought but it is the wholeness of an emergent dialogue in which he is forever groping for new insight, new patterns of meaning, as the center of his concern achieves explicit form. It is the nature of such groping that not only is completion never achieved, but there are residual elements retained from conflicting points of view that have been embraced as means of growth but then superseded. This is especially true of the historicized Kantianism which he uses and then transcends, but nevertheless retains from it some mortgages to the past.

The problems of understanding such an unusual dialogical approach are further compounded by its breadth. All too often the diverse thinkers go unnamed making the extraordinary scope hard to comprehend. He is responsive to many of the intellectual currents of the day as well as to what is emerging within his own experience and that of his theological generation. In his theological conversation he engages not only theologians and ethicists, but natural and social scientists, poets and historians, literary and art critics, and philosophers of many different persuasions—especially Kantian, neo-Kantian, and existentialist, and toward the end of his life, phenomenological and analytic. Through the richness of his responsiveness Niebuhr develops several diverse linguistic perspectives: resonant with central themes in neo-Kantian, phenomenological, and analytic philosophy, he investigates the meaning and grammar of language; with the symbolist in poetry and literary criticism, he shares an interest in the nature of symbol and metaphor; and with the historian of religion, he pursues the meaning of myth. These four

---

[9] RMWC p. 10.

[10] This phrase and its interpretation, which Niebuhr liked and used in seminars, he drew from the title of a book by Gabriel Marcel, HOMO VIATOR: INTRODUCTION TO A META-PHYSIC OF HOPE, trans. by Emma Craufurd (Chicago: Henry Regnery Company, 1951).

[11] RS p. 160.

perspectives—linguistic meaning, grammar, symbol, and myth—converge upon the task of his dialogical theology: recovering the personal.

A final difficulty for the interpreter is that Niebuhr's thought is radical: his thought reaches to the roots, not only of our present religious situation, but of our modern age. Beneath the theological constructions of the first half of the twentieth century, to which he has made now classic contributions through his incisive clarity and imaginative grasp, he is doing nothing less than wrestling with the foundations of modernity. Through doubt the method of modernity erodes the personal by objectifying, dichotomizing, and disintegrating self, world, and God. In search for a fit habitation of the personal, Niebuhr explores our being as knowing, valuing, believing, feeling, responding, and discovers, contrary to the modern view, a fiduciary foundation underlying it. This postcritical exploration of our fundamental commitments becomes explicitly linguistic when he realizes that our fiduciary foundation both undergirds language, as forms of life which constitute us in our humanity, and comes to expression in language, as those particular linguistic life forms which integrate our existence.

These particular life forms are religious words, for in their nurturing commitment by articulation and transforming the self by integration, the personal is most fully displayed and primarily achieved. In the consummation of his thought he discovers that the logic of religious language is paradigmatically first personal: the personal comes to expression and achieves wholeness on the logical level of the "I" and "We." Through the use of the first person in religious language the fiduciary foundation of our linguistic meaning and being becomes evident, and we become open to the personal appropriation of elements that before resisted integration. This does not mean a rejection of second and third person speech, but a recognition of their dependence upon the fiduciary foundation most evident in first person speech. In our modern world we have taken third person speech as paradigmatic. Only by overcoming the excessively third person style of modernity by a shift from third to first person can we recognize the presence of the personal in all our modes of speech and open our being to its integrative efficacy. Niebuhr's theology is radical, therefore, because it seeks in the face of the impersonal perspective of the modern world to recover the roots of the personal in our speaking and being from which integrity grows.

As a result of the difficulties of the emergent, dialogical, and radical nature of his thought, Niebuhr's theology elicits as primary response neither *criticism* nor *defense* but *inquiry*, as he would say, into "what is going on."[12] He speaks of "imaginative interpretation" in THE MEANING OF REVELATION and "fitting interpretation" in THE RESPONSIBLE SELF. To understand Niebuhr, then, we need to grasp his thought in an imaginative way

---

[12] RS p. 60.

fitting to its direction, density, and depth. In response to the emergent character of his thought, we will look back over his mature work, which begins with KINGDOM OF GOD, from the perspective of the consummate end where the linguistic actuality is most fully realized in THE RESPONSIBLE SELF and other literary remains of the early 1960's. In response to its dialogical quality, we will need to ferret out the identity of his many conversationalists in order to flesh out the context, and therefore the meaning, of his thought. More importantly, his thought is an invitation to take up the dialogue he is engaged upon with the modern world. I am convinced that within the malaise of our modern theology, his work can be especially fruitful in carrying us beyond the fragmentation of our life and thought by providing us a milieu of meaning in which to discover our deep-lying commitments and to achieve self-integrity. To engage in the dialogue will mean in some cases to carry forward a conversation beyond the point reached by him in order to see what is coming to birth—and thus it can become a heuristic to belief. Finally, in response to its radical nature, we must understand the problem of modernity's foundations if we are to see why he is interested in language and postcritical thinking, and how this interest fructifies as a resolution of our problem—recovering the personal.

PART ONE:

Linguistic Convergence in Postcritical Theology

CHAPTER ONE
HEURISTIC METAPHORS AND RELIGIOUS GRAMMAR

The sensitive use and interpretation of metaphor is usually thought to belong to poets and their literary critics, while the analysis of the logic or grammar of ordinary language is presumed to inhabit another world, that of the philosophers of language. Neither, until very recently, has been considered the domain of theology. Nevertheless, H. Richard Niebuhr unites the metaphoric and grammatical traditions, activating them together in the postcritical use and understanding of religious language.

Metaphor for Niebuhr is indispensable to religious language and the theological task. Through metaphors language both shapes and grasps the different forms of living in our world. Within the general metaphoric richness of our ordinary language he is especially interested in the type he calls "root metaphors," that not only express some aspect of our actual existence but open up the meaning of an entire way of being in the world. In order to underscore their function of discovery, I prefer to call these "heuristic metaphors," although not without his prompting, as we shall see. While responsibility is the only one Niebuhr explicitly names a root metaphor, which is the most comprehensive, there are five root, or heuristic, metaphors that are the *modus operandi* of his theological reflections: history, value, faith, feeling, and responsibility. Each heuristic metaphor engenders a language of its own, which is intricately interwoven with the others. From his radical conversion in 1929 until his death in 1962, he fashions a theology that is a fabric of metaphoric languages richly interwoven: a "theopoesis."

The presence of the grammatical tradition in Niebuhr's work becomes explicit around 1960 when he calls for a method of theological investigation of the logic or grammar of religious language, and begins to rethink his theological heritage and his own writings from this perspective. While he did not live to flesh it out, he means in part what he goes on to do in THE RESPONSIBLE SELF. He compares heuristic metaphors: man-the-answerer over against man-the-citizen and man-the-maker. Although employment of this comparative method is methodologically clearer here, he has been using it in all his books beginning with KINGDOM OF GOD.

Metaphor and grammar, theopoesis and logic, are brought powerfully together. At the same time as his declared interest in an investigation of the logic of religious discourse, he calls for a resymbolization of our worn-out religious language, for the creation of new and the revivifying of old metaphors. We are not only to investigate metaphors through a comparative method, but are to use them; to understand afresh is to use anew—form and content are one.

We turn now to an investigation of Niebuhr's handling of heuristic metaphors and the comparative analysis of religious grammar. We should recognize, however, that these are but two of five aspects of his postcritical involvement with religious language. He also articulates a theory of meaning; explores a mythological conception of the ethos or environment within which we dwell; and is concerned with the dialogical nature of the self—that we are constituted in and transformed by dialogue. In chapter two we will consider these three other facets; in chapter three the context of his postcritical theology.

Language as Metaphor and Symbol System

The language of ordinary life is richly metaphoric. We perhaps are unaware of this until someone tries to deny it, to exorcise all metaphor from our talk as unnecessary and distracting embellishment. Ironically, Niebuhr remarks, the very effort to expunge metaphor—as in John Locke's efforts to establish a plain style of non-metaphoric language—invariably uses it. [1]

While not interested in giving a precise definition of metaphor, nor in distinguishing it from a multiplicity of other terms he uses interchangeably— such as symbol, image, analogy, parable, synecdoche—Niebuhr does speak of it in an unpublished fragment as a "likeness": "In all thinking as well as in all communicating we are dependent on the use of parable, metaphors, similes, analogies. Whenever we try to understand something we look for likeness." [2] This is what distinguishes metaphor from concept. Metaphors say what things "are like"; concepts attempt to say what things "really are." The difference is in "the way in which the heart uses it" [3] and consequent effect. Metaphor deals with particulars and events, concept with generalities and ideas. Insofar as to know by metaphor is to know one thing by another, metaphor locates us in the midst of multiple relations, concept in abstractions. Metaphor can, therefore, catch a moment of experience in its complexity and allow it to stand forth in its unique particularity, whereas a concept

---

[1] RS p. 152.

[2] H. Richard Niebuhr, [4.] "The Symbol of Structure," in "Adumbrations" (unpublished fragment written in connection with "Faith on Earth" [unpublished booklength manuscript originally titled, according to Richard R. Niebuhr, "Knowledge of Faith," later titled "Faith on Earth: An Inquiry into the Structure of Faith," begun in 1950, intended for a time prior to the publication of RADICAL MONOTHEISM in 1960 to be published with it under the altered title "Faith on Earth: Essays on Human Confidence and Loyalty," Niebuhr Folder III-B], probably after 1958, Niebuhr Folder III-P-A), marked as p. 9.

[3] MR pp. 110 & 125.

abstracts an idea from the event and subordinates its complexity and uniqueness to this general, repeatable pattern. A concept, therefore, uses a particular as illustrative of the general, whereas a metaphor expresses that particularity.[4]

Expressive or illustrative functions have differing effects. In metaphor reality is manifested and not simply categorized. In terms of revelation, metaphor, catching up the particularity and complexity of the actual event, makes the divine reality present, whereas concept categorizes it under some general rubric: "For what is revealed [in metaphor] is not so much the mode of divine behavior as the divine self." The effect of metaphor is transformation of self. Speaking now of revelation between friends, a moment of new understanding of their relationship through a particular event, he says: "But the revealing moment not only disclosed constant features of conduct which had previously been hidden; it also introduced a new relation between the persons and remains a unique point in their history." The effect is the growth of a self, the lived understanding of "how our present grows out of our past into our future," which is that work through which "the soul is reconstructed." For these reasons Niebuhr speaks of metaphor as personal—it seeks "understanding in terms of persons, communities, values [of] what we are doing and suffering"—and concept as impersonal—"From the great occasion we abstract general ideas of an impersonal character." Each has an important function to perform. While metaphor alone can express the actuality of an event, concepts through their generalizing and illustrative capacity provide needed "checks on the inner imagination."[5]

While Niebuhr is intent at one time on the differences between metaphor and concept, there are other times when he wishes to point out their commonality as two aspects of the creative capacity of all language. He does this by speaking of the entirety of language as a symbolic system:

> Our languages, we are reminded, are symbolic systems. Their very structures, their allocation of names to parts of our experience, their verbs, their tenses, their cases, their grammar and syntax, contain systems of forms with which we come to the multiplicity or chaos of our encounter with things. With the aid of these symbolic systems we distinguish and relate our pasts, presents, and futures; we divide up the world of nature into apprehendable, graspable entities; we relate these to each other in patterns that are intelligible and somehow manageable. The words we use in any language, moreover, are so richly metaphorical that we cannot even speak about metaphors or try to limit their use without employing metaphors.[6]

[4]See MR p. 127.
[5]Quotations are, respectively, MR pp. 130, 129, 128, 116, 128, 125, & 128.
[6]RS p. 152.

The world and our lives achieve a human form through the shaping and grasping capacity of the entire symbolic system of language. Here metaphor and concept are both symbols. It is important to note this broader use of symbol, where it is not used interchangeably with metaphor, but with language itself, so as to include metaphor, concept, and the other elements of speech in the universal creativity of language.

Heuristic Metaphors

In addition to the expressiveness and creativity of metaphor, there is a third characteristic important to Niebuhr, that of discovery. While all metaphors may have this quality, he is interested in a special type of metaphor that exhibits it dramatically. These are general patterns of meaning that have the power to discover in the interaction of mind and reality the meaning of an entire way of being in the world. There are several names he uses for this kind of metaphor: "root metaphor," "symbolic form," "master image."[7] I prefer to speak of "heuristic metaphor" so as to include the sense of discovery in the word itself. While he nowhere uses this word, he does speak of symbol, used interchangeably here with metaphor, in its loss of a heuristic capacity: "They are no longer heuristic in character, instruments for the discovery of meanings in the other man's mind and meanings in the object. They become definitions, determinations, things to be proclaimed."[8]

But how can a heuristic metaphor be a general pattern when it is expressive of a particular actuality? Implicit in Niebuhr's handling of metaphor is an interactional definition, like that of Charles Feidelson's: metaphor is "a meaning produced by the interaction of the two terms . . . if the two terms are seen under the aspect of each other."[9] The likeness Niebuhr discerns as essential to metaphor is the result of this yoking together of two terms. While he does not use the word "metaphor" in speaking of God as Father and our companion as Christ, he, nevertheless, exhibits the tension and multi-perspectivalism of Feidelson's interactional definition:

---

[7] For Niebuhr's use of "root metaphor" and "symbolic form" see RS pp. 151–154; "master image" he used in conversation in the early 1960's.

[8] H. Richard Niebuhr, Lecture II. "Toward New Symbols," in "Next Steps in Theology" (unpublished Cole Lectures delivered at Vanderbilt University, April 10–12, 1961), p. 18. I have no doubt that Niebuhr's use of the word "heuristic" is under the influence of Michael Polanyi, for it is introduced into philosophical discourse in the late 1950's by him; and it is used by Niebuhr only after he has discovered and immersed himself in the Gifford Lectures, published as PERSONAL KNOWLEDGE: TOWARDS A POST-CRITICAL PHILOSOPHY (London: Routledge & Kegan Paul, 1958).

[9] Charles Feidelson, Jr., SYMBOLISM AND AMERICAN LITERATURE, Phoenix Books (Chicago: The University of Chicago Press, 1953), p. 60.

[God is] the transcendent power that to all men of little faith seems anything but fatherlike. The word "Father" on the lips of Jesus is a greater, more faithful, and more heroic word than is evident when fatherhood and deity are identified.[10]

The needy companion is not wholly other than Christ, though he is not Christ himself. He is a Christomorphic being, apprehended as in the form of Christ, something like Christ, though another.[11]

Father and transcendent power are each seen under the aspect, or in the form, of the other. The metaphor's meaning is constituted through interaction of these two terms; so also with Christ and companion.

In light of this definition of metaphor implicit in Niebuhr, we can see that a metaphor can be, not only a specific figure of speech, but a general pattern of meaning, if it yokes two terms together in interaction. In fact, we can delineate several levels of general metaphor in Niebuhr's work: that which pervades a book, a linguistic community, and a cultural sphere.[12] Responsibility exhibits all three. Although general, it nevertheless retains a link to the concrete since one of the terms of interaction is the self. With responsibility the self is yoked to answering, evident in his depiction of the responsible self as "man-the-answerer." Self and answering are each seen under the aspect of the other; in the resulting tension something particular in our actual lives is made manifest through this general pattern—the ability of selves and myself to answer. It also retains a link to the concrete because it engenders an entire language of specific metaphors. While Niebuhr speaks of the generative influence of root metaphors on the construction of philosophic systems,[13] he nowhere describes metaphor as having as such this engendering capacity. Nevertheless, his handling of heuristic metaphors exhibits it. The self yoked with responsibility is spoken of as acted upon, addressed, reacting, and answering; with sin, as division and conflict within the multiple responses we are called upon to make; with salvation, as integrity, the whole-making that actualizes that seed of unity within the central self; and with God, as the radical act that acts upon us in every situation eliciting an answer.

Heuristic metaphors have, therefore, the following characteristics. They

---

[10] CC p. 17.

[11] RS pp. 154–155.

[12] For similar levels see Paul Ricoeur, INTERPRETATION THEORY: DISCOURSE AND THE SURPLUS OF MEANING (Fort Worth: The Texas Christian University Press, 1976), p. 65.

[13] See RS p. 153 and MR pp. 125–126 for Niebuhr's suggestion that the revelatory moment expressible in metaphor can generate a multiplicity of concepts. Note Ricoeur's clear discussion of this engendering capacity of root metaphors productive of both specific metaphors and concepts, in INTERPRETATION THEORY, p. 64.

obtain their meaning through a likeness constituted in the interaction of two terms joined together; they express, rather than illustrate, something of concrete actuality; they are instruments for discovery of self and world; and the more general forms engender a metaphoric language. These characteristics are most fully manifest in Niebuhr's self-conscious handling of responsibility as metaphor. But they are implicitly present in the other four themes. In each the self is joined to another term. In the style of the responsible self we could make this explicit, though inelegantly: self-as-historical-agent, self-as-valuer, self-as-faith-holder, self-as-feeling-possessor. And in each a metaphoric language is engendered of history, value, faith, and feeling through which we can discover different aspects of the actuality of self and world. Hence we have called all of them heuristic metaphors. But the metaphoric nature of these themes is clearest in the last one, evident in a closer look at what he names a root metaphor.

In THE RESPONSIBLE SELF Niebuhr discerns the recent emergence of a new heuristic metaphor by first investigating "responsibility" in its ordinary use:

> The word *responsibility* and cognate terms are widely used in our time when men speak about the phase of human experience to which they customarily referred in the past with the aid of such signs as *moral* and *good*. The *responsible citizen*, the *responsible society*, the *responsibilities of our office* and similar phrases are often on our lips.[14]

He locates it in the domain of moral language, where it is closely associated with such other words of moral discourse as duty, law, virtue, and goodness. It has not always been so, however. Drawing upon the OXFORD ENGLISH DICTIONARY, Niebuhr observes that "It is a relatively late-born child" within moral expression. Prior to the nineteenth century it "meant *correspondent* as in the statement 'The mouth large but not responsible to so large a body.'"[15] The word "responsibility" has been in the English language for some time but it has only recently taken on moral meaning.

It functions morally as a new symbol or metaphor:

> But it is also possible that the word gives us a new symbol with which to grasp and understand not a really well-known phenomenon or an old idea but the actuality of that human existence of which other aspects came into view when we employed the older symbols of *the mores*, or of *the ethos*, or of *what is due*, or of *being virtuous*, that is, being manly. I believe that this is the case; the symbol of responsibility con-

[14] RS p. 47; his italics.
[15] Ibid.; quote is from the OED; his italics.

tains, as it were, hidden references, allusions, and similes which are in the depths of our mind as we grope for understanding of ourselves and toward definition of ourselves in action.[16]

While he recognizes that many use this word in ways synonymous with the older terms of moral discourse, he finds in this metaphor a striking revelatory capacity that opens new facets of human actuality to discovery.

Since the self is dynamic, what he finds are styles of being a self manifest in action: "We shall be concerned rather with the style, or with the form, that comes to expression in specific actions. We shall address ourselves to the question about our *being*." Rather than articulating some ideal of the way human life ought to be, they "bring greater clarity to the self in its agency, not by supplying a theory on which practice may follow, but by illuminating the theory that is actually though unacknowledgedly present in practice."[17] There is a pattern in living life that lies deeper than our thoughts about life. Through "hidden references, allusions, and similes," a metaphor like responsibility brings to expression this underlying lived pattern, and is, therefore, a fruitful way to grope toward understanding of the self in action.

Searching for further ways to make clear his meaning, Niebuhr calls this a "synecdoche":

> men in isolating, defining, understanding, directing, explaining their life as agents, their moral existence, have made a manifold use of simile, metaphor and symbol. They have, in general, used synecdoche, that is, they have apprehended their total activity and their total existence as agents with the aid of some one of their many activities as representative of all. They have said the whole is like one of its parts; they have then analyzed the part and have interpreted the whole in the light of that analysis.[18]

By taking a part for the whole in synecdoche, we are able to grasp the self in its wholeness through a particular aspect of that whole. In our general moral symbolism we have used such partial activities as warfare, journey, and commerce synecdochically, as parts to interpret the whole.

> The active life of man has been understood as being *like* warfare. . . . We use the image of our journeyings toward destinations as pictures of what we are and what we are doing in all action. . . . From commerce we derive first similes, then

[16] RS p. 48; his italics.
[17] RS pp. 149 & 135; his italics.
[18] RS p. 159.

symbols, of indebtedness to one another, of punishment as a
payment of debt to society, of contract, of giving every man his
due, and perhaps even of all moral existence as an affair of
duties.[19]

As important as these three metaphors have been, "Two great synecdoches,
however, have established themselves in our Western world, as symbolic
forms with the aid of which we not only interpret a given actuality but define
its limits and apprehend its structure."[20] These are craftsmanship and political action. All of human action and life is seen under the aspect of one of
these parts of human existence, as *like* it. It is in relation to these last two
synecdoches that Niebuhr sees the heuristic metaphor of responsibility
newly emerging within our ordinary speech, and disclosing, he believes,
from the vantage point of its special partiality, some new aspect of the whole
self in its being, and in that, as we shall see, reconstructing the soul.

Theopoesis: A Fabric of Metaphoric Languages

The way in which a heuristic metaphor opens us to the discovery of self is
through engendering a "language." When we use the metaphor of craftsmanship heuristically, it pervades our speech and our being so that everything we
do and all that we know we see under the aspect of making. Not only ships
and houses, but mountains, babies, and the far flung stars are all *made*.
When we employ the political metaphor heuristically, we see not only
persons as citizens but planets, trees, stones, and the psyches of individuals
and of groups as living *under law*. Under the hegemony of one of these
heuristic metaphors, a multiplicity of other metaphors spring into use as
expressions and developments of the master symbol issuing in a pervasive
metaphoric language. In his exploration of responsibility Niebuhr is searching out the lineaments of just such a metaphoric language, trying to establish
that it is a viable and distinct alternative to the other two metaphoric
languages of craftsmanship and politics.

   While each metaphoric language has its own integrity, it does not
prohibit the simultaneous use of another. It is thus possible to mix the
metaphoric languages of making and political action, as has in fact often
occurred. Much of the dynamic and depth of Niebuhr's thought comes from
the intricate and multi-levelled weaving of five metaphors used heuristically
to open aspects of the self. Each metaphor reveals the whole from a certain
point of view; their meshing discloses, from several perspectives at once, self
and context in greater complexity. Much of his career he moves back and
forth between history, value, and faith. One will for a time become dominant

---

[19] RS pp. 159–160; his italics.
[20] RS p. 160.

receiving his direct attention, while the other two recede from view. Nevertheless, a development of the metaphor dominant for the moment carries further the tacit development of the others and provides an advanced position from which he can turn to the explicit extension of one of the others. Present with these three, yet remaining recessive through much of his career while they were developing, the metaphor of feeling only becomes important at the end of his life at the same time that responsibility emerges into dominance.

To describe the texture of such thinking, Niebuhr's own metaphor depicting the kingdom of God as a poem is apt.[21] While lacking spareness and metrical accouterments, his writing, nevertheless, has a poem-like density, craftedness, and evocative effect eliciting feelings and experiential background. The intent is to open otherwise inaccessible dimensions of our personal being, to draw us forth from behind our defenses to discover and respond to new, further reaches of self and world. Through heuristic metaphors offering a synecdochic perspective on the self, setting multiple relations to resonating within a metaphor, between metaphors of a linguistic cluster, and between several metaphoric languages woven together, a personal responsiveness is elicited, beyond the intellect alone, from the totality of our being. The metaphoric density of Niebuhr's theology in intent and effect is different from the intellectual clarity and succinctness of a Tillich. Beneath the ringing coins of Tillich's conceptual truth, Niebuhr is trying to entice the self forth from out of its defenses so as to make a personal response. It lures us in unprecedented ways, as he wrote at the end of his life, to "grope for understanding of ourselves and toward definition of ourselves in action."[22]

In weaving together metaphoric languages with the poetic intent of opening us to new aspects of our being in the world, Niebuhr's theology—to take a word from Amos Wilder and Stanley Hopper—is a "theopoesis."[23]

The Linguistic Exigence of Our Time: Resymbolization and Grammatical Analysis

Niebuhr develops a theopoesis in order to meet the linguistic exigence of our time. In his autobiographical essay of 1960, he acknowledges the

---

[21] Early in his career Niebuhr speaks of the kingdom of God as "like the pattern of a life, a poem or a New World symphony"; see KGA p. 164; see also MR p. 95.

[22] RS p. 48.

[23] See Amos N. Wilder's development of the intimate relation between the poetic and theological in THEOPOETIC: THEOLOGY AND THE RELIGIOUS IMAGINATION (Philadelphia: Fortress Press, 1976), and his acknowledgment in his Forward of Stanley R. Hopper's original use of the term "theopoesis." For such use by Hopper see his "Myth, Dream, and Imagination," in Joseph Campbell, ed., MYTHS, DREAMS, AND RELIGION (New York: E. P. Dutton & Co., Inc., 1970), p. 136.

erosion of our religious language and consequent impoverishment of our lives, and expresses his hope for reconstructing our lives through symbolization:

> I do not believe that we can meet in our day the need which the church was founded to meet by becoming more orthodox or more liberal, more biblical or more liturgical. I look for a resymbolization of the message and the life of faith in the One God. Our old phrases are worn out; they have become cliches by means of which we can neither grasp nor communicate the reality of our existence before God. Retranslation is not enough; more precisely, retranslation of traditional terms—"Word of God," "redemption," "incarnation," "justification," "grace," "eternal life"—is not possible unless one has direct relations in the immediacy of personal life to the actualities to which people in another time referred with the aid of such symbols. I do not know how this resymbolization in pregnant words and in symbolic deeds (like the new words of the Reformation and the Puritan movement and the Great Awakening, like the symbolic deeds of the Franciscans and the social gospelers) will come about. I do count on the Holy Spirit and believe that the words and the deeds will come to us. [24]

In his "Introduction to Theological Studies," a series of lectures given at Yale Divinity School in the fall of 1960, Niebuhr explores further the problem of resymbolization and calls it the main problem in theology for our time: "Resymbolization is the problem." [25] He links this process of resymbolizing directly with the function of the poet: "Our symbols are overly familiar—where is the poet's function here?" From the beginnings of Christianity this poetic process of resymbolizing was carried on. When Jesus first appeared to the Jews, Niebuhr remarks, the only description they employed was that of "Christ." But "Paul had to find another word for Roman, Hellenic Gentiles—*kyrios*." Then he queries "What must we call him today—why cannot Indians call him 'avatar'?"[26] In Luther we have another powerful example of the emergence of a resymbolized language. In "Toward New Symbols," Niebuhr speaks of a linguistic transformation created by Luther: "The secret of his success was that he broke through this sterile, antiquated, atomized, conceptual language and forced his way to the sources of a new proclamation. He made things new. He spoke a new language."[27] While Paul imported new

[24] Niebuhr, "Reformation: Continuing Imperative," pp. 79–80.

[25] H. Richard Niebuhr, "Introduction to Theological Study" (student lecture notes, handwritten by Elizabeth B. Keiser, delivered at Yale Divinity School, fall semester, 1960), November 30, 1960.

[26] Ibid., December 5, 1960.

[27] Niebuhr, "Toward New Symbols," p. 2.

words into Christianity from the Hellenic world, Luther took up old words already resident in the Christian tradition and revitalized them. Not only did he make words central that had been peripheral, such as "Word of God," "justification by faith," and "liberty,"[28] he used these as a means of reaching "direct relations in the immediacy of personal life to the actualities" formerly expressed by these symbols. He thus transformed them from mere counters in the tradition into articulate forms of life that could become the means for many others to achieve and dwell within the actualities of self and God.

In our own day, Niebuhr says, we have been groping with resymbolizing and have been trying out such new symbols as "encounter," "I-thou," "courage to be," "acceptance," "trust," and "maturity." In his typically interrogative form of lecturing he then inquires: "Why haven't we gone farther? Haven't we wrestled with reality like Luther? . . . Can we expect new forms of life to emerge when a new set of symbols grasps us?"[29] By these questions Niebuhr indicates his own uncertainty about these symbols, whether they embody new forms of life that issue from wrestling directly with the divine and human actualities. In his own wrestle with reality he has worked with various heuristic metaphors and has himself "gone farther" as he grasps the potency of the relatively new symbol of responsibility.

In the midst of the metaphoric fabric of his thought, however, we find a striking concern for the analysis of metaphor and religious language as such, issuing in an extraordinary methodological proposal that the theologian become grammarian. Not only do we need to speak religious language as theopoetic resymbolizers; we need as well to state the grammar of this language. As he says for the first time explicitly in THE MEANING OF REVELATION:

> theology can attempt to state the grammar, not of a univer-
> sal religious language, but of a particular language, in order
> that those who use it may be kept in true communication with
> each other and with the realities to which the language re-
> fers.[30]

When we ordinarily think of the word "grammar," we take it to mean the formal structure of verbs and nouns and the various other parts of speech and the way in which they are employed according to rules governing use. In his understanding Niebuhr includes all of this, as we have seen in his remarks about different aspects of the symbolic system of language, but he means as well the sum total of the relations between entities and of our ways of relating

[28] Niebuhr, "Introduction to Theological Study," (notes by Elizabeth B. Keiser), December 5, 1960.
[29] Ibid.
[30] MR p. 18.

to all realities that a language admits of and creates. If language were separate from, rather than expressive of, life, the analysis of its grammar would have no effect upon keeping selves in touch with community and reality, for it would be an abstract system rather than meaning ingredient in living itself. Grammar for Niebuhr is, therefore, not only the formal rules of linguistic use but the pattern of meaning inherent within the historical life of a people as expressed in their use of a particular language.

Such a pattern he calls a form of religious life, an intelligible pattern, and a reason in history:

> A critical historical theology cannot, to be sure, prescribe what *form religious life* must take in all places and all times beyond the limits of its own historical system. But it can seek within the history of which it is a part for an *intelligible pattern;* it can undertake to analyze the *reason* which is *in* that *history* and to assist those who participate in this historical life to disregard in their thinking and practice all that is secondary and not in conformity with the central ideas and patterns of the historical movement.[31]

Studying the historical life of a people, the task of theology, to state the grammar of a religious language, is to elucidate the form of religious life that comes to expression in our language.

It is astonishing in the 1940's to find a concern for metaphor and grammar, since the analysis of grammar by such philosophers as Bertrand Russell and A. J. Ayer, whom Niebuhr knew,[32] is alien to metaphoric intentions. They use grammar to deny, whereas Niebuhr uses it to affirm, the creativity of language, the different kinds of reality graspable through language, and the dynamic interrelation of speaker, speech, and reality—long before he and America become aware of Wittgenstein's nonreductive handling of philosophical grammar. Understandably resistant to Analytic philosophy for much of his career, he finally begins to recognize at the end of his life a kinship with at least some aspects of it as represented by Wittgenstein's later investigations.

While Niebuhr calls for a theology of religious grammar in THE MEANING OF REVELATION in 1941, it is not until about 1960, the same time as the call for resymbolization, that he talks a good deal about his concern for

---

[31] MR pp. 17–18; my italics.

[32] Niebuhr refers to Bertrand Russell in his first published article, H. Niebuhr, "An Aspect of the Idea of God in Recent Thought," *Theological Magazine of the Evangelical Synod of North America*, XLVIII (1920), p. 49; and to A. J. Ayer in H. Richard Niebuhr, "The Center of Value," in RMWC p. 101 (originally published in MORAL PRINCIPLES OF ACTION, ed. by Ruth Nanda Anshen [Harper & Brothers, 1952]).

the grammar or logic of religious language.[33] Just prior to 1960 he suggests somewhat reluctantly that, in working on the nature of faith, it would be good to begin with a linguistic analysis of the meaning of the word:

> One is tempted, in accordance with fashions of the day, to begin an inquiry into faith with a linguistic analysis. As logic has become the science of scientific language, ethics the study of moral language, so theology tends to become the study of religious language and of Biblical language in particular. Cannot the question about the meaning of faith be restated in the form of a question about the meaning of the word?[34]

By 1961 he is expressing this analytic concern without reluctance: "We speak of the problem of making our preaching and teaching relevant to modern men. . . . We engage in debates with philosophers about the meaning and the logic of religious language."[35] In another unpublished writing, entitled "An Introductory Essay on Language and Theology," possibly written in the spring of 1960, Niebuhr remarks on the absence of an explicit linguistic perspective in traditional theology:

> The traditional methods in theology have taken language more or less for granted. They have operated with words as instruments that needed frequently to be sharpened no doubt, that needed at times to be remade for particular purposes but which on the whole might be accepted without more question than the carpenter accepts his saw, hammer and plane. The theologian needed no more to give primary attention to his words than the carpenter to his tools.

He then goes on to speak, not only without reluctance, but in a programmatic and emphatic way of the necessity of investigating the logic of religious language:

---

[33] There is a point midway between these two dates where Niebuhr makes a further explicit statement about grammar, although unpublished and not on religious grammar but grammar as such, which indicates he is continuing to think about what he has broached in 1941. In the beginning of his "Christian Ethics" of 1952, he says: "The first inquiry of this sort to which we are exposed is Grammar. Of course, first we learned to speak; but then we noticed that our words went together in a certain pattern. There was structure, and therefore there was the possibility of right and wrong. Grammar is a critical inquiry into an activity that is continuous. It is the ethics of language" (H. Richard Niebuhr, "Christian Ethics" [student notes, transcribed by Robert Yetter, Gene Canestrari, and Ed Elliott, delivered at Yale Divinity School, spring semester, 1952], p. 1).

[34] Niebuhr, "Adumbrations," p. 1.

[35] Niebuhr, "Toward New Symbols," p. 3.

But method is in theology, at least, a matter of language, of symbols and symbol manipulation; it [is an] affair of logos and of logic. The problem of theology is the problem of theological language and theological logic. Until it solves this problem of its language and its logic theology cannot undertake to solve any of the objective problems to which it has addressed itself.[36]

At the same time he is beginning to rethink his own theological heritage from this linguistic perspective. In his own notes for "Christian Ethics Lectures," given in the spring of 1961, he speaks in a new way of Schleiermacher's feeling of absolute dependence. Earlier it had been important for him as a way of speaking of the relation of God and self from within the context of faith.[37] Now from a linguistic point of view it becomes the locus of the symbolic:

I have tried . . . to penetrate to that layer of our consciousness as selves lying beneath our conscious thoughts and our explicit intentions whence both thought and action flow. Schleiermacher—the realm of feeling: I will call it the symbolic layer where we are related to totalities, to ultimate contexts, to the circumambient, which modifies all our thinking and doing—which may not influence what we do so much as how we do it.[38]

As he begins to rethink major theological figures from his past, he similarly begins to see his own past theological work in this new light: earlier works would lend themselves to being rewritten from this explicit linguistic perspective. For example, Libertus Hoedemaker records this comment made by Niebuhr in a "Seminar on Theology and Language" taught in the spring of 1960:

---

[36] H. Richard Niebuhr, "An Introductory Essay on Language and Theology" (unpublished fragment, intended at one time, according to Richard R. Niebuhr, as introduction to "Faith on Earth: An Inquiry into the Structure of Faith," probably 1960 [certainly written after the reluctant embracing of linguistic analysis prior to 1960, evident in n. 34 above, perhaps written in connection with H. Richard Niebuhr, "Language and Theology" (seminar syllabus in possession of and student lecture notes handwritten by Libertus A. Hoedemaker, taught at Yale Divinity School, spring semester, 1960, Niebuhr Folder III-C); see n. 39 below for reference to and quotation from this seminar]), pp. 1 & 2. Within the brackets I am reading "is an" for "as" in the text.

[37] See MR pp. 23–28 where Niebuhr both praises Schleiermacher for holding God and faith together within his concept of the feeling of absolute dependence and criticizes him for making this feeling too much the object of his theological concern.

[38] H. Richard Niebuhr, "Christian Ethics Lectures" (Niebuhr's lecture notes, handwritten, for class in "Christian Ethics" at Yale Divinity School, spring semester, 1961, Niebuhr Folder X), March 15, 1961, p. 1.

Thus as Niebuhr once remarked in a seminar on Theology and Language (1960), the Christian community seeks to apply the *symbolic pattern of Jesus Christ* to its interpretation of encountered reality. With this remark Niebuhr simply restated the problem of THE MEANING OF REVELATION. He thought it necessary that theology should engage in reflections on language. Even CHRIST AND CULTURE "might be written today from the standpoint of language" (remark in the same seminar).[39]

While he is only beginning to glimpse the linguistic foundation of his theology, he, nevertheless, is drawing implicitly upon it as he now grasps with luminous clarity the linguistic exigence of our time for the resymbolizing and analysis of religious language. But what does Niebuhr mean by the logical or grammatical analysis of religious language?

The Method of Grammatical Analysis

This intense interest in grammatical analysis in the 1960's came too close to the end of Niebuhr's life to afford time to flesh out exactly what he meant. He nowhere presents a concerted answer to our question. Nevertheless, on the basis of his final work one of the things he means is comparative analysis of heuristic metaphors.

To analyze metaphors conceptually would miss their vitality, form, and meaning because it seeks to grasp what things "really are," abstracting general features that are static, unsituated, and not constituted in multi-perspectival relations. But metaphors have their meaning as forms of life through tension of two terms used in actual situations. Niebuhr uses a method of comparison that, rather than distorting their tissue by abstraction, lays one heuristic metaphor in its full richness alongside another, making possible a full-bodied sense of difference.

Comparative Metaphor Analysis of Responsibility

In THE RESPONSIBLE SELF the metaphor of responsibility is compared with two other dominant heuristic metaphors—the teleological image of "man-the-maker" and the deontological image of "man-the-citizen." By comparing their imaging of self-identity, reason, freedom, social relations, and time, the differences become clear.

[39] Libertus A. Hoedemaker, THE THEOLOGY OF H. RICHARD NIEBUHR (Philadelphia and Boston: Pilgrim Press, 1970), p. 185, n. 50; his italics. The undated fragment entitled "An Introductory Essay on Language and Theology" may have been written for this seminar or in its context as the introduction to "Faith on Earth."

In the metaphor of maker, developed by Aristotle and Thomas Aquinas into the most common symbol of humanity in the history of Western thought and practice, the self is seen as artificer. In all actions the self fashions something purposively, guided by an idea as an aim. Reason discerns general ideas in particulars, organizes life in terms of those which are most universal, and conceiving them as ends, searches among particulars for the best means to realize them. Freedom lies in the exercise of reason to fashion the self in terms of ends discerned.[40]

The self understands itself as basically rational; living in relation to ideas and ideals, bringing everything into relation to this universalizing capacity, the self makes itself. Other persons are subordinated to ideas, and are known only through their ideas, never directly. Time is not essential to being a self because it does not affect ideas or their actualizers, but primarily as future, simply provides the limits within which a self can strive to achieve ideals.[41]

In contrast, man-the-citizen, the second great heuristic metaphor, images us as self-legislator, ruling ourself according to laws we ought to obey. All existence is conceived in relation to law. Reason discerns or legislates law, and attempts to obey it. There is much less freedom in this political metaphor than in the technical or craftsman image. The materials and goals are chosen and relatively under control of the artisan, whereas the materials in political life are ourselves in our bodies, sensations, and impulses which are not finally subject to our control and choosing, since they are already given. While the artisan strives for the ideal, the politician deals with the possible. Other persons are secondary, not this time to ideas, but to laws. While ideas as ends are to be realized in the future, laws are to be obeyed in the present. For Kant and existentialists time past and future matters little.[42]

In contrast to moral agency articulate as striving and fashioning or obeying and legislating, the form of life expressed by the third metaphor, that of responsibility, is interaction and response. Drawing upon modern views in biology, psychology, sociology, and history, Niebuhr sees the responsible self as engaged in interaction with its entire spatio-temporal context.[43]

Attending to such interacting makes one aware that there are more than ends or laws in our ethos. Various actions affect us consciously and unconsciously all the time. Suffering and emergencies, two results of actions upon us, cut athwart our efforts. Striving for a goal or obeying law, responsible reason interprets what is happening, since how we respond depends upon our interpretation of the circumstance. It also depends upon anticipating responses to our responses. Both interpretation and anticipation within a

[40] See RS pp. 48 & 51.
[41] See RS pp. 49, 69, 70, & 91.
[42] See RS pp. 51–52, 70–71, & 91–92.
[43] RS pp. 56–57.

field of ongoing events depend upon continuity of self and community of agents.[44]

The responsible self defines itself in response to challenge. The question asked in living is neither teleological—"What is my goal, ideal, or telos?"— nor deontological—"What is the law and what is the first law of my life?"— but "What is going on?" In value language, the teleological form of life is oriented toward the good, the deontological toward the right, and the responsible form toward what Niebuhr calls "the fitting," to what fits into a total interaction adequately interpreted and anticipated.[45]

While the self responds to actions upon it within the natural environment, its relation to other selves is primary: we respond to responders. Law and goal, as well as all other actions, are interpreted in terms of the context of intentions of those who envisioned or enacted them. Time and self are correlative terms: the present is unthinkable apart from a self. Within the present as lived are past and future as extensions of the present: the past is within this "timeful" self as present memory and the future as present expectation and anxiety.[46]

Through analysis of a word in common speech, only recently gaining moral meaning, Niebuhr finds a third alternative to the two traditional heuristic metaphors of moral being. Each heuristic metaphor engenders a different linguistic form of life. When compared, the nature of and differences between them become apparent. Where the teleological maker exhibits the agency of realization, directed toward good ends according to guiding ideas, attentive to the future, and the deontological citizen exhibits the agency of obedience, directed toward right laws, attentive to the present moment, the responsible self engages in interpretative and anticipatory response, directed toward fitting answers to selves within the total field of interaction, attentive to the past, present, and future dimensions of human temporality.

Earlier Grammatical Comparisons

While most clearly understood within a grammatical, metaphorical theology in THE RESPONSIBLE SELF, this comparative method first makes its appearance in KINGDOM OF GOD. He explores how the historical theme (not yet recognized as metaphor) of the kingdom embodies the actual religious life form of Americans and compares three refractions of it developing sequentially from colonial times to the present: as rule of the sovereign God, reign of Christ, and coming kingdom on earth. After this first foray into

---

[44] See RS pp. 58, 60, 61, & 65.
[45] See RS pp. 59 & 61.
[46] See RS pp. 71 & 93.

theology of history he reflects in his next book, THE MEANING OF REVELATION, on the historical method he has used by comparing inner and outer history, two ways of relating self, world, and God. Even though he senses the linguistic heart of his theology of history in calling for a method that will state a religious grammar, he sees no connection there between this appeal to grammar and the use of a comparative method, nor does he recognize the metaphoric character of inner and outer history.

In CHRIST AND CULTURE he compares five historical forms of life expressed in five ways in which Christ (or religion) relates to culture—Christ against, of, above, in paradox with, and the transformer of culture. He calls these forms "ideal types," "motifs," "families," and "figures," rather than metaphors, and his manner of proceeding "typological" rather than metaphoric. While each type is a "construct" to which no person conforms completely, they are, nevertheless, abstractions from the rich complexity of life and so are five general forms of life inherent in Christianity.[47] Even though he does not yet understand these forms to be articulate as metaphors, he says the entire book is an effort "to analyze form in the manifold richness of historical life," and "to seek *logos* in *mythos*, reason in history, essence in existence."[48]

In his next book, PURPOSE OF THE CHURCH, Niebuhr finds in the confusing situation of theological education in the mid-1950's in North America "an emerging new conception of the ministry" as "pastoral director"[49] which he compares with the historical forms of pastoral rule, priest, preacher, and evangelist.

The theme of value is also treated comparatively. In "The Center of Value" he explores objectivist, subjectivist, and relational perspectives on value. In RADICAL MONOTHEISM he discovers within the contemporary life of faith in centers of value five different metaphoric forms of faithful being. "Polytheism" is life lived by faith in multiple centers of value; "henotheism" in some finite society; "supernaturalism" in a divine being separate from the world; "atheism" in some unacknowledged center of value while consciously denying the existence of a supernatural god; and "radical monotheism" in the One beyond the many, in the principle of being which is the principle of value.[50]

Unlike these four metaphors, however, the heuristic metaphor of feeling is not developed comparatively. This no doubt is due to the brevity of treatment it receives as he only begins to deal with it explicitly at the end of his life. Nevertheless, his early treatment of feeling in KINGDOM OF GOD is implicitly comparative. Feeling is central to the reign of Christ who

---

47 See CC pp. 40 & 43–44.
48 CC pp. 231 & x.
49 PCM pp. 57, 58, & 79ff.
50 See RMWC pp. 11, 28, & 32.

initiates a new affection in the self that flows forth in love, and is, therefore, implicitly compared with the other two metaphoric forms, faith in divine sovereignty and hope in the coming kingdom.

Conclusion

In our exploration of Niebuhr's use of heuristic metaphors and investigation of religious grammar we have begun to get a sense of the postcritical theology that is the root of his deep and broad ranging religious reflection. He attends to metaphors in our ordinary language. Among them he finds certain heuristic metaphors that open up a perspective on the entirety of our being in the world, that express a certain form of life. His theology is a densely woven fabric of five such heuristic metaphors—history, value, faith, feeling, and responsibility. Like a long poem these metaphors disclose and develop multiple themes which, when seen in their intricate interrelationships, embody and make accessible the self in much of its lived complexity.

Conjoined with this theopoetic weave throughout his mature work, he compares heuristic metaphors so as to catch their meaning in use. Initiating this method unself-consciously in KINGDOM OF GOD, Niebuhr employs it in a fundamental way in each of his subsequent books until his culminating comparison of three styles of being human in THE RESPONSIBLE SELF. In each of these forms of life, patterns of meaning inherent in the actuality of human existence come to complex expression in metaphor.

Midway in his mature work he calls for a method that will describe religious grammar, but it is not until the end of his life, around 1960, that he speaks extensively of theological investigation of the grammar or logic of religious language and of the resymbolization of our religious metaphors, and recognizes that his grammatical comparisons are of metaphors. Even then, however, he does not make explicit what we have: that one aspect of grammatical analysis is the comparative method. The first two linguistic aspects of Niebuhr's postcritical theology are, therefore, the theopoetic use of heuristic metaphors and their comparative analysis.

CHAPTER TWO
MEANING, MYTH, AND THE DIALOGICAL SELF

The linguistic lineaments of a postcritical theology have become visible in our exploration of Niebuhr's use and comparative analysis of heuristic metaphors. We turn now to three further linguistic strands: a theory of religious meaning, a use and conception of myth, and a portrayal of the linguistic nature of the self.

We have already touched on his fundamental affirmation of meaning as use and life form: on how words are forms of life whose meaning lies in their use or enacting by a self in a context.[1] Now we shall inquire more deeply into this affirmation and investigate the linguistic theory he builds upon it: how words mean and how their meaning is understood, the role of the self and its context as words have meaning, the bearing of language on reality, and the effect of these upon the nature of religious language.

Secondly, we shall trace his change from a negative to positive attitude toward myth and his use of several mythic functions in his presentation of history as myth. Finally, we shall explore his definition of the self as essentially linguistic. In the totality of its relations to its environment—to itself, other selves, nature, and God—the self is a being in dialogue. Since we can discern this pattern of dialogical existence not only in his concept of the self but in the actuality of Niebuhr's own reflective being, we shall look, as well, at how it is operative within his life as thinker and teacher.

Linguistic Meaning

At the heart of theology of history in THE MEANING OF REVELATION is a theory of linguistic meaning. In displaying the function of image and imagination, Niebuhr shows that the meaning of language is contextual

---

[1] As displayed in the first chapter, linguistic meaning as forms of life is evident in Niebuhr's talk of "the form religious life" takes in a particular history, according to THE MEANING OF REVELATION (p. 17), and of "the actuality of . . . human existence" expressed in metaphors, according to THE RESPONSIBLE SELF (p. 48). Linguistic meaning as the use of words is present in the dynamic conception of metaphor, the manner of distinguishing between metaphor and concept, investigating "responsibility" as it functions in ordinary language, and employing a comparative method to catch metaphors as they perform within actual contexts.

and performative: it is in a "context in which we look for the meaning of the word and in which the significant phrase performs its meaning-giving function."[2] A word or phrase has meaning as words relate to one another and to the larger linguistic and lived historical context in which they inhere, for only where there are relationships is there meaning. Situated in a context words are brought into relationship by being used, enacted, performed. Much like organs in the body whose proper significance lies in functioning, words do not mean except as they perform.

The performing of words requires an agent self to use and understand their use and to supply in part their context: "we do not hear isolated ejaculations, separate and therefore meaningless words but apprehend each sound in a context that we in part supply."[3] A context is supplied through an interpretative image. Niebuhr nowhere gives a definition of image. But we can say it is a gestalt or pattern embodying a context that organizes and comprehends some aspect of our experience and world. Like symbol it displays the creativity of shaping and grasping our world; like metaphor it exhibits relationships. Often used interchangeably, it nevertheless brings to light what is implicit in the other two terms: that patterning always involves situating in a context.

Not only are words situated in a context but the language-user is as well. Images are always wielded from a standpoint; to use and understand words properly requires apt images and appropriate standpoints.[4] Through images, whether of sensations in perceiving nature, affections in knowing other selves, or events in historical understanding, we both shape and grasp reality.[5] The real always extends inexhaustibly beyond the borders of an image so that in the language of THE RESPONSIBLE SELF, an image is a "synechdochic analogy," grasping the whole through a part.[6] Such grasping is a creative shaping. The self actively contributes to meaning in selecting which reality to grasp, taking a hold of it, orienting oneself towards the whole from the perspective of a certain part, and employing particular images to express it. The pattern which comes to expression is not, however, a mere projection from the self; it is rather a form of something which is really there, something that can be grasped.[7]

Niebuhr is denying both the copy theory of meaning, that sees what is spoken of as a structure or object independent of language and its shaping, and the view that claims an absolute creativity for language, where all its forms are entirely the product of the language-user and in no sense emergent

[2] MR p. 141.
[3] MR p. 96.
[4] See MR pp. 13, 22, & 96–97.
[5] See MR pp. 95–98 and RS pp. 48 & 161.
[6] See RS pp. 55–56.
[7] See RS p. 154.

from what is really given. Language, rather, brings to expression what is there but changes it. We might say language makes determinate, that is shapes, what it grasps as indeterminate, as inexhaustible.

This does not mean that what is grasped is formless, though Niebuhr sometimes suggests this by speaking of our ordering a chaos, suggesting the imposition of conscious forms on what otherwise is formless.[8] This is not, however, what Niebuhr finally means, for he says metaphoric patterns "are partly in his conscious mind but so largely in his unconscious mind"; "the symbol of responsibility contains, as it were, hidden references, allusions, and similes which are in the depths of our mind."[9] Such unconscious relatings belie the talk of a chaos in our depths or in the deeps of the world.

There is, we must acknowledge, an ambivalence on this point in Niebuhr: he speaks both of chaos and pattern in our unconscious depths. To speak of a less formed or indeterminate, inexhaustible reality encountered unconsciously which we make more formed, determinate, through the gestalt-engendering power of language would overcome this ambivalence. This is suggested in the way he speaks of patterns as the product of an "art of knowing in which subject and object interact," in which "Symbol and reality participate in each other."[10]

Symbols, images, and words are forms of life for Niebuhr, expressing, incarnating, something of reality and of the self. If words are the absolute creation of the speaker, they express the self but nothing of reality. If words are copies of reality, they mirror reality but nothing of the self. Mirroring or pointing, words function by themselves apart from the agency of self to use or enact them and without shaping self and reality. Language is either separate from reality, leading to scepticism and despair, or is separate from life, pointing to reality but itself empty of power and meaning.

The self that interacts with reality through the life forms of language is both social and individual. Symbols are social, the heritage of society. Through language we understand the system of nature and social interaction in terms of symbolic patterns of meaning born and maintained by society. Niebuhr rejects the notion that the self is a "radical doubter"[11] who can understand things anew without the linguistic heritage of society.

To say symbols are social is not for Niebuhr, however, to say that they are merely conventional. Symbols, whether scientific or artistic, are expressive, not only of societal meaning, but of that which is inescapably individual, not only of the "way" but of the "what" of expression: "The ways in which I shall formulate and justify and express . . . in words or ritual acts are largely dependent on the social and historical setting, but what is

[8] See RS p. 152.
[9] RS pp. 161 & 48.
[10] RS pp. 161 & 155.
[11] RS p. 8; see RS pp. 78–80.

formulated and expressed in such words is individual and personal."[12] Form and content are held necessarily together here; there are always social and individual dimensions at work in language. We always orient ourselves within society and nature through our social language so that what we say is expressive of the individual forms of our existence.

Niebuhr's theory of meaning, in summary, affirms that words and symbols have meaning in their use as forms of life enacted by selves in a context. From the first major statement of this position in THE MEANING OF REVELATION to its final presentation in THE RESPONSIBLE SELF there is a significant deepening, in showing how the use of words involves the enactment of forms of life that arise from the largely unconscious grasping and shaping interaction of self and world, and that are individual expressions through the social nature of language.

Religious Meaning

The general life form of religious language is faith. Beneath cognitive belief, faith is an existing self's lived orientation of trust or distrust toward all beings it exists among and their context, and therefore toward its ultimate environment, the "metahistory" of all histories, toward being itself. While this trust or distrust of being and our ultimate ethos is at work in every aspect of our interaction with the world, it becomes centrally articulate in religious language. Consider the language of creation. While it employs one or another theory of the formation of the world, it fundamentally expresses our trust or distrust in the "inscrutible power" that has called us and all things forth.[13] So also with the word "God." Within his earlier theology of history Niebuhr speaks of faith as the standpoint from which "God" is appropriately used. "God" is a value term so that "God" and faith belong together. To speak of God apart from faith is to speak about something other than God, something of the world.[14]

Now in THE RESPONSIBLE SELF faith is presented, not purely as the standpoint, but more profoundly as the life form itself. To use the word "God" fittingly is to enact the form of life of trust in the trustworthiness of being.[15] But there is no magic merely in speaking the words "God" and "creation." We can say the words and express distrust in being. It depends on how they are used: both on the "way," society's language of "God" and "creation," but more importantly, on the "what," the personal life form of trust or distrust enacted in that way.

The general function of religious language is integrative. The self as grasped/shaped through the metaphor of responsibility responds to actions

[12] RS p. 120; see RS p. 81.
[13] See RS pp. 106, 109, 118, & 119.
[14] See MR pp. 23–25.
[15] See RS p. 119.

upon it on many levels. Each dimension, however, calls forth a different aspect of or role for the self, so the self experiences itself as many selves. In response to the physical environment I am a cloud of subatomic particles, a compound of chemical reactions, a complex metabolic organism, an evolute from lower life forms. In response to the political sphere I am a democrat, aristocrat, or communist; to the economic I am a capitalist or Marxist; to the scientific a Newtonian or Einsteinian; and to the artistic a classicist or romantic. The basic problem of human existence here is that of personal integrity; can one amidst the many roles find a unified self?[16]

For the answer to this question Niebuhr turns to religious language: "In religious language, the soul and God belong together; or otherwise stated I am one within myself as I encounter the One in all that acts upon me." While there is a unity in each given role, none embraces the totality of roles and discerns within an underlying coherence of self. This function is unique to religious language. Only within the domain of religious language can this underlying integrity of self be discerned in the midst of multiple roles because only here does it come to expression. Within religious language the self responding to many different spheres of action discovers its unity in responding to One ultimate action present in each of these spheres. The self in its wholeness is the logical correlate of God's oneness. We cannot truly speak of the "central self"[17] underlying all of its cultural and natural manifestations without speaking of God, nor of God without speaking of this central self. Self and God inhabit the same logical realm of discourse.

Faith as the life form expressed in religious language is essential to this integrative function. To respond to the One in all that acts upon me is to trust by opening myself to ultimacy on every occasion and to every sphere of being within which it acts upon me. We can see here that the responsibility metaphor, more than that of history, involves us deeply with the phenomenon of death as the metahistory of our being. Many spheres threaten our lives and if we open to them because of God's active presence there, we must confront the threat. But there are resources in religious language to face the different threatening areas through the life form of faith and to assimilate them through its integrative function.

When in the above passage Niebuhr restates the ineradicable unity of soul and God, he exhibits what comes clear in THE RESPONSIBLE SELF— that the grammatical mode of religious language is first person speech: "I am one within *myself* as *I* encounter the One in all that acts upon *me*." The life form of faith manifest in religious language is expressed in the first person; integration of the self occurs in religious language as the human "I" responds to the divine "I." Personal integrity comes through responding to the personal God in the first person.

The plural form is used extensively in THE MEANING OF REVELA-

[16] See RS pp. 121 & 123.
[17] RS pp. 122 & 115.

TION's growing awareness of this grammatical mode as essential to religious discourse. Since the meaning of words is contextual, theology must present their context. Since the context is the life of faith of a people in history, theology of history is a theology of story-telling. Only through telling the story of a people's life in faith can the shape of their context, the pattern of meaning inherent in their form of life, come to expression. To look for the meaning of "God" and "Jesus" in the life story of a people is not to construct what these words ought to mean but to show what in fact they have meant—how they have been used within their proper context, what their logical grammar is. So the early church "turned at last to the story of their life, saying, what we mean is this event which happened among us and to us." The story form was not, however, merely illustrative; it was "irreplaceable and untranslatable." Abstract systems of metaphysics or morality have not been able to sustain the intellectual and spiritual lives of a people. Through story-telling alone can the context of our lives be bodied forth so as to make clear what is meant when Christians appeal to nature, the Bible, or inner religious experience. Revelation itself "provides us with an image"[18] which contains the story of the life, death, and resurrection of Jesus Christ that can clarify what has happened, is happening, and is to be expected to happen in the story of our own lives.

In moving from history to responsibility, Niebuhr becomes more attentive to the first person grammatical mode of religious language and shifts from a predominant plural to singular mode, as he deepens his understanding of the existing self and its religious discourse. One indication of this shift is the magnificent prologue of THE RESPONSIBLE SELF in which he gives reasons no longer simply why the church is Christian, but why he calls himself a Christian.[19]

We shall explore this further, but what we have seen so far is Niebuhr's presentation of the meaning of religious language in terms of meaning as use and form of life. Religious meaning, in its bearing on our ultimate context and in its use by a multi-leveled self, involves expression of the life form of faith, the function of self-integration, and the grammatical mode of first person speech. In turning to myth we focus on the cosmic context of these integrative and expressive, and other, ways of relating.

Metamorphosis in Mythic Conception

Niebuhr seldom speaks of myth but when he does his few remarks are especially suggestive. In THE MEANING OF REVELATION he presents a considered view, but it is negative: he rejects myth as an inappropriate and deceptive use of the personal. Gradually, however, he changes his mind, so

---

[18] See MR pp. 42, 45–52, & 109.
[19] See RS pp. 43–44.

that by the time of THE RESPONSIBLE SELF, he speaks positively: it is a way of using history to understand our existence. To see his thought from the perspective of myth, it will be helpful to follow this change in his explicit consciousness. This will bring us into initial contact with his wrestle with the problems of modernity, to be explored at length in Part Two, for the change is from his own use of some disintegrative dichotomies of modernity, toward their integrative resolution within a linguistic theology. Beneath his conscious view, however, there is already at work in THE MEANING OF REVELATION a profound fashioning of myth. As he recognizes in this book a linguistic method previously employed but unacknowledged in KINGDOM OF GOD, so he recognizes the significance of mythic language in THE RESPONSIBLE SELF. After looking at the changes in his manifest view, we will look at what latently in fact is going on in his writing, long before he embraces it. The mythic proportions of his thought are difficult to see because of his early negative view, the brevity of his later positive perspective, and the undramatic nature of the shift from one to the other. For these reasons we will compare his constructive point of view with several outstanding scholars of myth to illumine the various ingredients in his mythic perspective.

Niebuhr begins his negative appraisal by exploring the popular view that myth is identified with the inner fictions of imagination and opposed to the outer facts of reason:

> we are likely to regard the stories of our inner life as poetic in character, the product of fancy; so we call them myths, contrasting them with the surer knowledge of fact which we believe ourselves to possess as rational observers of external events. Then Christianity is classified with poetry not only in the true sense, as dealing with selves, values and enduring time, but also in the wrong sense as permitting poetic license and the use of fictions in its explanation of history.

Niebuhr hastens, however, to reject this dichotomy between imagination and reason:

> This allocation of reason and imagination to separate spheres is doubly false, for in our knowledge of the external world we must employ imagination and in our interpretation of inner history we cannot get along without reason. Reason and imagination are both necessary in both spheres.[20]

Insisting on the presence of imagination and reason in both inner and outer worlds, Niebuhr, one would suppose, would want to argue that myth similarly has a legitimate bearing on both self and external world. This is precisely, however, what he draws back from saying. Distinguishing the images used by imagination in inner knowledge of selves as personal from those used in outer knowledge of the external world as impersonal, he does not refer to these inner personal images as myth. Myth is the misapplication of personal images from inner to impersonal outer world.

> In this realm [of the inner knowing of ourselves] all our images seem to be personal. We cannot think here with the aid of impersonal ideas; we cannot use machines as our models or mathematical formulae as our patterns. Inevitably, though we be disciplined in our external knowledge never to use the images of persons, when we interpret affections of the soul we use subjects for our ideas. This use of imagination is something quite different from mythology, which is the employment of personal images in objective knowledge where it is always deceptive, leading to unfulfillable expectations and to inept actions on external objects.[21]

What he means by this is that figures of the gods and primordial heroes are not appropriate to scientific explanations of natural phenomena. While this is certainly true, what he has done is to define myth as having no legitimate bearing on either inner or outer knowing.

What lies behind this rejection of myth, we can see, is Niebuhr's use of Kantian dichotomies. He divides reality in two: the personal world of the subjective, practical, or moral knowledge of selves, and the impersonal world of the objective, theoretical, or scientific knowledge of the external world. Between these he cannot locate a place for myth. To locate myth in the subjective is for it to become a means of knowing selves through personal involvement, but this would be to overlook the bearing myth traditionally has on the external world, such as dealing with the creation of the world or of mankind. To locate it in the objective is to make it a means of knowing things impersonally by a disengaged self, but this would be to overlook the personal involvement myth traditionally has through its portrayal of personal figures, whether human or divine. Myth does not belong in either to the exclusion of the other. Niebuhr resolves this by locating it in the juncture of these two essentially disparate spheres as the misapplication of the personal from the subjective to the objective.

The mythological is, however, neither subjective and practical nor objective and theoretical; it offers a third, postcritical, possibility not envisioned by the Kantian dichotomous view of reality. Myth does bear on the external world, but is not "objective"; and it is expressive of the personal of the inner

[21] MR pp. 98–99.

world, but is not "subjective." Under the influence of Kant Niebuhr has defined external knowing as impersonal and internal knowing as personal, both in terms of the known—as mechanism or self—and the knower—as impersonally detached or personally involved. It is possible, however, to understand "personal" differently, no longer identified with subjective, but as present in both inner and outer knowing inasmuch as the knower is personally involved in knowing either thing or self. What Niebuhr fails to see in THE MEANING OF REVELATION is that the mythological is personal—neither opposed to external knowing nor restricted to inner knowing, but a third, yet involved in both. To recognize such a third would be to give up these Kantian dichotomies used here so fruitfully. This is, in fact, what he does in RADICAL MONOTHEISM.

In this later work he distinguishes the personal, not only from the theoretical, which he has already done earlier, but from the practical as well, which earlier was identified with it. First, he distinguishes the personal from theoretical reasoning:

> When we try to think and speak intelligibly and rationally, from mind to mind, we abjure the use of personal pronouns, of "I" and "Thou." . . . We try to unify our experiences and our thoughts about them with the aid of impersonal symbols, among which mathematical symbols seem the least personal, most orderly, manageable, and unambiguous.

Then he distinguishes the personal from practical reasoning as well:

> When we reason practically as moral beings we try to deal with ideals to be actualized, with laws to be obeyed, and with abstract values to be honored or chosen.

The personal is neither theoretical nor practical, for they both employ impersonal symbols, whether theoretical mathematics or practical ideals, laws, and abstract values.

Preoccupation with impersonal symbols is similarly the case with traditional theology. It is given to reasoning about impersonal ideas and theories: "When we reason as theologians we undertake to define *ideas* of God, *forms* of faith, *notions* of the soul, *theories* of salvation." Placed within the dichotomy of theoretical and practical, theology is thus classified with the practical acknowledged as impersonal. But now he proposes the third category of "mythological," and calls attention to its personal grammar: "To reason so oriented and employing such instruments there is something animistic, prelogical, or mythological in all speech and thinking that use personal pronouns as ultimate terms of reference."[22]

---

[22] RMWC p. 45; his italics. This positive identification of myth with the personal is already present in Niebuhr's mind in 1951, although not in print nor understood in terms of the

"Personal" here no longer allies the involvement of the knower with the self as the known. It means rather that the knower as person is involved in all types of knowns—religious, political, scientific. There is a multiplicity of knowns, not just inner and outer, and the knower is personally involved in each. And this involvement is spoken of in grammatical terms: the personal-mythological third differs from theoretical and practical in its use of language, of particular grammatical forms. There is a significant difference between all forms of speech that employ personal pronouns and those that do not. Niebuhr is now distinguishing a family of grammatical forms that use personal pronouns from a much larger variety of impersonal grammatical forms. But this is not just a new name for an old dichotomy. The exploration of the grammatical forms of personal speech, not only illustrates the personal involvement of the knower in personal speech, it reveals it in all speech, including the impersonal modes of scientific discourse, inasmuch as all language can now be seen as having its meaning as used by persons. Undramatically, Niebuhr is suggesting a revolution in theology that shifts its foundation from Kantian disjunctions to the personal, to what is mythological and linguistic.

Niebuhr offers us no redefinition of myth in RADICAL MONO-THEISM. If he had, it would no longer be defined negatively as the misapplication of personal images to impersonal knowing. Rather it would be defined positively in some manner as the personal framework of all our knowing. While not present in this book, we find him, nevertheless, in THE RESPONSIBLE SELF defining myth positively as the "metahistory" of our existence as knowing selves living in our world: "Deep in our minds is the myth, the interpretative pattern of the metahistory, within which all our histories and biographies are enacted."[23]

The explicit discussion of myth in THE RESPONSIBLE SELF is brief but dense.

> To insist in this fashion on the symbolic function of the Christ-figure and the Christ-story does not beg the question of the historical actuality of that figure and story. For history may function as myth or as symbol when men use it (or are forced by processes in their history itself to employ it) for understanding their present and their future. When we grasp our present, not so much as a product of our past, but more as

---

grammar of pronouns, as evident in student class notes from that year: "Personality is selfhood, conscience, obligation; you can't talk about God without speaking *personally*. There is mythology here, but it's necessary. . . . Let us reflect and see what our language *means*! Let us see what all this mythology—which is necessary—is getting at" (H. Richard Niebuhr, "Protestant Theology Since Schleiermacher" [student lecture notes, handwritten by Joe E. Elmore, delivered at Yale Divinity School, fall semester, 1951], p. 37; italics in text).

[23] RS p. 106.

essentially revealed in that past, then the historical account is necessarily symbolic; it is not merely descriptive of what was once the case.

He illustrates this mythic function of actual history both from secular history, the American Civil War, and Christian history. With regard to the latter he says:

> It is impossible to describe with any adequacy the variety and richness of the imagery derived by Christians from the story of Jesus and employed by them not only in their descriptive language but in their apprehensions, evaluations, and decisions. From the recognition of an infant's value and destiny with the aid of images of manger and cross of Christ, to the acceptance of death as a dying with Christ, to the discovery of a quality of existence that like Christ's cannot be conquered by death, to the understanding of man's place and responsibility in the cosmos as a son of God, the symbolism of the gospel story pervades the Christian consciousness in all evaluation, action, and suffering.[24]

Niebuhr in Mythic Perspective

Within this passage we can discern myth at work in several ways that suggest affinities, unwitting to be sure, with myth scholars today. Myth according to Joseph Campbell orients our lives on several levels at once: "psychologically," present in Niebuhr's recognizing through the images of manger and cross the value of infancy and the destiny of adulthood; "cosmologically," locating through the image of Son of God the place of the self in the cosmos; "metaphysically," accepting through dying with Christ that death is a part of the nature of existence; and "sociologically," (not apparent in this particular passage but elsewhere in the book) defining our place within history.[25]

Myth also integrates. Like Mircea Eliade, Niebuhr presents the various levels of human existence as open to each other, as the Christian story pervades the entirety of Christian consciousness, affecting decisions, evaluations, action, and suffering. While he does not speak here of integration, he does elsewhere in THE RESPONSIBLE SELF in his concern, like Eliade's, to overcome the self's sense of alienation from the world. And like Eliade

---

[24] RS p. 156.

[25] See Joseph Campbell, THE MASKS OF GOD: CREATIVE MYTHOLOGY, vol. 4, Viking Compass Edition (New York: The Viking Press, 1970), pp. 4–6; see also his "Mythological Themes in Creative Literature and Art," in MYTHS, DREAMS, AND RELIGION, ed. by Joseph Campbell (New York: E. P. Dutton & Co., 1970), pp. 138–141.

speaking of the self being transformed in myth into a symbol, so Niebuhr conceives of the self as dialogical who thus becomes a symbol of the linguistic nature of the entire environment within which the self dwells in responsive relations.[26]

Finally, myth is a means of discovery. Elizabeth Sewell speaks of myth as the situation in which we unite with a figure or image to understand the world. Myth is not so much a kind of narrative content, as traditionally thought, as a method of inquiry, underlying both science and poetry.[27] Niebuhr's use of heuristic metaphors is in Sewell's sense mythological. Through uniting ourselves with the metaphor of responsibility within the Christian story, as in the above passage, we discover something about our world—the value and destiny of a child and a quality of existence accessible to us that in some way transcends death.

History as Myth

From these mythic perspectives we can see how Niebuhr's passage uses Christian history as myth—orienting, integrating, and discovering. Returning to THE MEANING OF REVELATION, we can now look for the latent actual functioning of history as myth beneath its manifest rejection, and then look again at its most powerful functioning within the manifestly affirmative attitude of THE RESPONSIBLE SELF.

The Christian story, in THE MEANING OF REVELATION, is a mythic means to discover the world. By it "The mind is freed to pursue its knowledge of the external world disinterestedly." Because the world is the creation of God, we are to use imagination and reason to understand it, employing whatever figures, such as mechanistic and mathematical models, can help. We learn as well about ourselves. Through the use of revelatory images, especially of Jesus—a self transformed into a symbol, as Eliade would have it—we come to know ourselves. This painful reasoning of the heart leads to what Niebuhr later will call history as myth, as it orients us within "a total picture of significant action" but in a world in which "the self no longer occupies the center."[28]

The Christian story not only orients but integrates us within both nature and history. Niebuhr makes an implicitly mythic effort to recover nature as the realm of divine action and human habitation, for it is just such a vital relation to nature that myth keeps alive and that the nineteenth and twentieth century denigrators of myth have sought to deny. Through Christian

[26] See Mircea Eliade, PATTERNS IN COMPARATIVE RELIGION, trans. by Rosemary Sheed, Meridian Books (Cleveland and New York: The World Publishing Company, 1970), pp. 452 & 455.

[27] Elizabeth Sewell, THE ORPHIC VOICE: POETRY AND NATURAL HISTORY (London: Routledge & Kegan Paul, 1960), p. 20.

[28] MR p. 124; see pp. 131, 173, & 174.

myth nature is not an alien realm of indifference, brutality, or impersonal mathematical design to be excluded from our being and triumphed over in self-defense, but is "our earthly home" to be dwelt in "kinship with" rather than lordship over all its creatures.[29]

Niebuhr achieves such a sense of kinship through a metaphoric fusion of God and nature: God is "Lord of Heaven and Earth; he is the descending rain and the shining sun, careless of the distinctions which men make between the good and evil"—he is the one "whose garment nature is." Then using natural images and those "subtler wonders" obtained by science's microscope and telescope and even more refined instruments,[30] we can feel at home in God's world.

Nature has a symbolic potentiality. Empowered by the Christian myth, "we can read words of God in nature's book."[31] Departing dramatically from nineteenth century views of nature as a mechanism devoid of spiritual value, Niebuhr is recovering a manner of speaking characteristic of the sixteenth century. Having passed, however, through the refining fires of historical relativism, he is not trying to revive their view of the univocity of nature's language, as if nature were inscribed with an articulated language apart from a self. Rather he is affirming the linguistic potentiality of nature which can be brought to religious articulateness through our uniting with the Christian myth.

As with nature, so also with history: through the Christian story we find ourselves oriented. We exist not simply within the history of our family or nation, or even of the West, where we might have thought of ourselves as at the center, but as part of a totality of mankind and of the world as a whole. What before had seemed alien or irrelevant, the Christian story integrates into our own lives: "the whole past is potentially a single epic" which mythic language actualizes as our own. The self and its parochial history is oriented within the entire history of humanity, the cosmic process of evolution, and the untold suffering and seeming meaninglessness of the metaphysical dimension of existence. Not only the scriptural history of Jesus and the Hebrews, but the history of Greeks and pagan empires, and "the long story of human ascent from the dust, or descent into the sloughs of brutality and sin, the nameless sufferings of untold numbers of generations, the groaning and travailing of creation until now"[32]—are now remembered as our own.

There is a dialectic at work in Christian myth that opens us from the circumscribed to the "inclusive process" of all being. Not only does this dialectic carry us outward to the limits of space, but as well forward to the limits of time, where this myth "prophesies our death" but also "the pos-

---

[29] MR p. 173; see pp. 48, 49, 175, & 186–187.
[30] MR pp. 186–187, 175, & 48.
[31] MR p. 49.
[32] MR p. 112.

sibility of the resurrection of a new and other self, of a new community, a reborn remnant."[33]

This inclusive mythic language is not, to be sure, in the archaic mode of primordial time and supernatural figures, but rather in the historical mode that speaks of particular peoples, natural processes, animate and inanimate phenomena of our ordinary world. The whole arrived at is more a lived than a conceptual totality, a "coincidence of opposites"[34]—the hanging together in experience of the diverse opposites of existence—than a systematic unity of rationalistic thought, which has eradicated disparities.

Niebuhr's language of mythic history has an extraordinarily evocative quality. When he speaks of a single epic, he not only talks about orienting and integrating, he evokes the whole vast panorama of human history and draws us into it, eliciting a "felt" knowledge, a "kynde knowyng,"[35] in medieval terms, that is an embodied wisdom, an incarnate knowing with the totality of oneself of this great dramatic unity and of our participation within it.

Perhaps in all that Niebuhr has written no passage better illustrates this evocative quality of mythic language than his affirmation of life and resurrection in the face of death and destruction in THE RESPONSIBLE SELF, which begins "Deep in our minds is the myth, the interpretative pattern of the metahistory, within which all our histories and biographies are enacted," and goes on to speak of "recurring cycles" or "infinite progress," "everlasting winter" or "all-destroying fire," and of "the image of myself as coming to that future when there is no more future."

What the Christian story can do is "challenge our ultimate historical myth" of death by questioning "the context into which we now fit our actions" and affirming "that we are surrounded in history by life and not by death, by the power of being and not by ultimate destructiveness." Death is here made vivid, the death of species, ages, empires, the cosmos itself, but most particularly my death. The depths of my own terror and sense of nothingness in this vast abysmal world are touched and made manifest in these images, but with them are evoked as well the springs of life and hope that water the hidden roots, if not the visible shapes, of our being in the world; these are conjoined so as to issue, not only in acceptance of death, but in the affirmation of unconquerable life. Here we clearly do not have a rational argument for immortality, but a "reasoning of the heart"—which is a reasoning in myth. The heuristic metaphor of responsibility evokes our

---

[33] MR pp. 112, 130, 131, & 167; cf. MR pp. 122–124, and RS pp. 124 & 157–158.

[34] See Eliade, PATTERNS OF COMPARATIVE RELIGION, pp. 419–420.

[35] See William Langland, PIERS PLOWMAN: THE A VERSION, ed. George Kane (London: Athlone Press, 1960), I. 127–132. For clarification of this term see Elizabeth D. Kirk, THE DREAM THOUGHT OF PIERS PLOWMAN (New Haven and London: Yale University Press, 1972), pp. 37–38 & 101–107.

depths, which are the depths of the world, and thereby engages in "revising our mythology of death into a history of life by transforming our responses so they become "fitting" to the circumambience of life.[36]

Niebuhr as "Homo Dialogicus"

In his irrepressible search for ever new metaphors Niebuhr suggests in the "Earl Lectures" of 1962 that the responsible self is "*homo dialogicus.*" The heuristic metaphor of responsibility reveals, not only mythic thinking, but the essential linguistic nature of the self: that the self is self in its use of words and metaphors, and is, therefore, a "symbolic animal,"[37] and that its language is fundamentally dialogical, used in ongoing conversation with the totality of its world. This metaphoric grasp of the self, so as to see its core and constitutive relations to the world under the aspect of dialogue, emerges from Niebuhr's own way of being in the world, for he was what he conceived the self to be—a *homo dialogicus.*

Evident in his publications, course syllabi, and students' notes, he carried on a wide-ranging dialogue in his reading that took him not only beyond religion into the humanities but into the social and natural sciences as well. Only Tillich among his theological contemporaries and Jonathan Edwards in his American theological past exhibit a similar breadth of cultural exploration. Niebuhr carried on a truly "interdisciplinary" exploration, before that word became popular, as he engaged in dialogue with the diverse elements in our culture, convinced that the world of dialogue is one—though not the oneness of a rational system—and that the method of dialogue would set imagination free from defensiveness to achieve new insight, new gestalts, new ways of knowing and therefore of being in our world.

As a teacher Niebuhr drew his students into this dialogue through class reading and seminar discussion—opening them to multiple perspectives coming to a focus on the subject of the religious emotions, faith, or Christian ethics, and drawing them forth into conversation with an expanding intellectual environment that was carrying them simultaneously, not only into greater complexity, but greater depth, demanding and eliciting the ongoing process of integration and self-transformation.

In lecturing he similarly employed a dialogical method: not only by encountering a multiplicity of thinkers from diverse perspectives, but by speaking often in an interrogatory mode—exploring a subject by asking questions, as if a many-faceted gem were caringly being turned so that each of its aspects could be seen—to engage his listeners in the dialogue he was carrying on with himself. At the beginning of what were to be his last lectures

[36] RS pp. 106–107.
[37] RS pp. 160 & 152.

in Christian Ethics, he invited students in the overflowing lecture hall to reflect *with* him and within themselves—"to retire to the laboratory which is the self," as he put it—in order "to reflect on the self in dialogue with community."[38] Inquiry and questioning, rather than assertion and proclamation, were the mode of his reflections. He would grope with a problem ranging afar into its many dimensions so that students were enticed into the quest themselves, even though, as in conversation, they had no idea where they were going to end up nor a certainty that the diverse phenomena inquired into were in fact multiple aspects of the same problem. But then towards the end of the hour these apparently disparate elements would be caringly gathered from the far ends of the world, through which they had been journeying, into a coherent whole, into a gestalt, that would leave one at the end of class with a heightened sense of discovery, a climactic sense of the fittingness of what had seemed alien and fragmentary. To listen to Niebuhr lecture was to witness and to become involved in an act of creative dialogue.

The Dialogical Self

Through comparing responsibility with the other heuristic metaphors of maker and citizen, Niebuhr displays the essentially linguistic nature of the self. As the citizen obeys and the maker strives, so the responder answers. An answerer exists definitively in speaking with and listening to another self. In this dialogical act it makes itself present, not as mind or will pursuing abstractions of law or goal, but as person relating to universals grounded in the act of interpersonal speech.

The responsibility metaphor not only discloses the self's fundamental use of dialogical language, it employs dialogue as a synecdochic analogy for the entirety of moral agency, non-verbal as well as verbal: "we think of all our actions as having the pattern of what we do when we answer another who addresses us."[39]

When all actions are seen as answers, they are viewed as parts of an entire conversation. All actions are reactions to events acting upon us and anticipations of events that will act upon us, just as what we say fits in with what has already been said and anticipates what will be said. Both responses, as reactions and anticipations, are moral actions because they are interpretations. As interpretations of meaning, all moral actions are, therefore, linguistic. While the citizen and maker are obeying and striving, the responder is trying, as Niebuhr says, to figure out what is going on,[40] to discern the

---

[38] H. Richard Niebuhr, "Christian Ethics" (student lecture notes, handwritten by R. Melvin Keiser, delivered at Yale Divinity School, spring semester, 1961), January 30, 1961.

[39] RS p. 56.

[40] See RS pp. 60–64; cf. also p. 97. While Niebuhr sometimes uses "reaction" and "response"

meaning of the action upon him or herself—i.e., to comprehend the intention of the action and the context within which it is occurring. Even where the action upon it is the claim of law or the attraction of a goal, the responder interprets it as symbolic of some larger pattern of meaning, as part of an ongoing conversation.

This larger pattern has both a social and natural dimension. The self lives within society seen as a "continuing discourse."[41] As an ongoing conversation society has a continuity as a constancy in the actions and responses of a community of agents. By participating in this conversation the self experiences its own continuity in the constancy of its interpretations of what is going on, both of its own response-relations to others and of the response-relations between those others.

Within society as conversation the self is intent, not upon abstractions of law or goal or "generalized other," but upon other selves. Yet others are not "atomic events" but "particular parts of a continuous discourse" who are "symbolic in [their] particularity of something general and constant." The general is encountered in the particular as the pattern of constancy of communal interaction, evident in the "constant meanings of a common language,"[42] met in the action and words of the other self.

Nature, as well as society, is seen as dialogue. The self exists in "triadic" relation to society and nature. They are not isolated spheres but exist together within a larger framework of meaning: each relation is seen as a simultaneous aspect of a larger "continuous dialogue."[43]

Our existence in time is also presented as dialogue. To exist in the present is to be in dialogue with, what Niebuhr calls, "compresence." To respond to the novel challenge of "those others or those actions" present with us is to interpret them. We do this in part by drawing upon the past, which is in my present as language learned in childhood, conscious and unconscious memory, habits of behavior, repressed emotions. The formation of this past is through encounters with others, so the language of memory used in interpreting the new challenge is rife with dialogues with past compresences. We also draw upon the future present in the now in anticipation. The future is filled with compresences whose questions, answers, and actions towards me I anticipate as I interpret the present challenge.[44]

These interpretations fraught with memory and anticipation employ images embodied in the language of our social past, shaped by its logic,

---

interchangeably, he prefers to distinguish them as non-interpretative and interpretative acts, respectively (see RS p. 64).

[41] RS p. 65.

[42] See RS pp. 77–78 for Niebuhr's rejection of G. H. Mead's "generalized other" or "impartial spectator" which he earlier embraced in "The Ego-Alter Dialectic and the Conscience," *Journal of Philosophy*, XLII (1945).

[43] RS p. 80.

[44] See RS pp. 93–95 & 64.

metaphors, names. Yet they are individual as well, as I use historic images in my particular complex of feelings, conscious or unconscious, of remembered and anticipated trust or distrust, fear or joy, hope or anxiety, importance or insignificance.[45]

To see our life in time, society, and nature as dialogue means that language is the matrix of our humanity. We not only become human by being born into an ongoing dialogue among selves and between selves and world, we mature into human fullness through the use of language. The different forms or styles of life we live are expressed in the varying metaphors of this complex dialogue. Citizen, maker, responder are all articulate forms of life within which we discover the further reaches of our humanity. But only one of these, the responder, reveals the self as person in dialogue—that human life is indispensably linguistic.

From this perspective new light is shed on Niebuhr's use of heuristic metaphors, comparative grammatical analysis, theory of meaning, and myth. The self uses heuristic metaphors and explores them through a comparative method in order to understand and carry further the ongoing dialogue of our being in the world. Meaning exists as it is used in a context which is that of dialogue. Forms of life enacted in language, imaginative interpretation, story-telling, grasping and shaping activity of language are carried on within dialogue through the self as speaker, so easily lost sight of in the written word. Religious language brings to expression the life form of faith within the totality of the self's dialogue with God and world, and effects ongoing integration of the self paradigmatically in the first person within the midst of the complexity of this interrelatedness. In myth the fittingness of our responses to the circumambient is understood as dialogue, and thus it is within dialogue that our mythology is revised from death to life.

Earlier Work from the Standpoint of Language

The fullness of Niebuhr's theory of meaning, myth, and dialogical conception of the self is achieved in THE RESPONSIBLE SELF, yet there are indications of the formation of linguistic foundations in his earlier work. Indeed, he himself suggests that his earlier work could be understood from the "standpoint of language."[46] We have already considered earlier handling of myth; following his lead, let us consider briefly, then, the presence of his affirmations of meaning and dialogue in earlier books.

We have already seen the emergence of an explicit theory of meaning in THE MEANING OF REVELATION, but it disappears from the light of day until its re-emergence, enriched, in THE RESPONSIBLE SELF. Between

---

[45] RS pp. 96–97.
[46] Hoedemaker, THE THEOLOGY OF H. RICHARD NIEBUHR, p. 185, n. 50.

these two books it has gone underground awaiting, as it were, the fructifying that comes as each specific interest, rooted in it, is cultivated. While the conception of the self's dialogical nature only first appears in THE RESPON-SIBLE SELF, there is already in THE MEANING OF REVELATION an explicit concern with dialogue, for the context of revelation is understood as dialogue. The revelatory images of Jesus are like a point in a conversation between friends to which they return in order to illumine where they have come in the confusion of the present.[47] So it is in the three intervening books that we look for the presence of linguistic foundations developing beneath the surface as concern for meaning and dialogue.

Underlying the five types of Christian life in CHRIST AND CULTURE is the issue of linguistic meaning: whether religious language has its meaning as forms of life and whether language is indispensable to being human. Approaching this comparative analysis as a "moralist," Niebuhr is interested in the biblical images of Jesus. Beneath concept and doctrine these present a coherent "form of a person." As a life form Jesus is in our actual history communicating his "virtues" or "excellences" of character—love, hope, faith, obedience, and humility, which inform, enliven, and pattern our own forms of life.[48]

The entire life of Christianity has been informed, given form, by the life form of Christ in five basic ways. In the first type, "Christ against culture," Christians see themselves as separated from and opposed to all of culture. Implicit in this type, made explicit in Niebuhr's criticisms, is the issue of opposing culture. These separatists oppose language, since culture is the "artificial, secondary environment" of language, and other non-linguistic patterns.[49] But they reject culture by relying upon it, for they use the language of the culture to articulate their rejection and to express their own positive beliefs whose meaning they have translated from the biblical culture into their own.

Present in Niebuhr's handling of the other four types is the issue of whether religious language is to be understood as forms of life. The second type, "Christ of culture," in which Christianity is equated with certain aspects of culture, he criticizes because it fails to affirm the life form character of the biblical language portraying Jesus. Attempting to make contact with its particular culture, it "distort[s] the figure of the New Testament Jesus," making it the "personification of an abstraction."[50]

The third type, "Christ above culture," in which Christianity is understood to perfect culture, denies the life form of Christ by absolutizing it. It sees the relationship between Christ and culture as hierarchical synthesis.

[47] MR p. 129.
[48] CC pp. 124 & 14; see CC p. 13.
[49] CC p. 32.
[50] CC p. 109.

But it fails to recognize that its hierarchical synthesis is "provisional and symbolic." Absolutizing relative structure, it denies the symbolic character of thought, and therefore that all of culture is "subject to continuous and infinite conversion."[51] And thus it rejects religious language as life form, for it is the vitality and dynamism of a form of life present in symbols which can undergo such continuous conversion that is denied.

Concerned to distinguish his own type, "Christ the transformer of culture," especially from the fourth type, "Christ and culture in paradox," Niebuhr locates the difference in their view of the presence or absence of a divine pattern of meaning in nature and culture. Implicit in this distinction is the issue of whether religious language has its meaning in the enactment of life forms or in pointing to a separate reality. For the "dualist" of the fourth type nature, nearly identified with the fall, does not adequately manifest the creative work of God, and culture manifests only the negative, restraining character of God's redemptive activity rather than his positive agency. For the "conversionist" of the fifth type, on the other hand, nature is the realm of God's creative activity and of Christ's rule, eliciting an affirmative and ordered response from the created self, and culture is the realm of God's presence in the "Now" offering the "divine possibility of a present renewal."[52] Rather than living as sinner within nature and culture while looking in faith beyond to God, as the dualist does, the conversionist sees a pattern of divine meaning present within nature and culture—"that faithfulness [which] is the moral reason in all things"[53]—and so responds to God within rather than beyond the entire creation. While the dualist speaks of divine meaning apart from, the conversionist speaks of it within, the actuality of human existence in the world.

Here the conversionist establishes a foundation for linguistic theology. If the presence of a divine pattern within human actuality in the world is affirmed, religious metaphor is seen to be expressive of this pattern as forms of life articulate in language; if it is denied, religious metaphor is no longer expressive of God in various forms of life but points to God beyond life.

Flowing with this undercurrent of affirmation of linguistic meaning is concern for dialogue. Introducing the five types Niebuhr presents the entire complex interaction between Christ and culture, the whole subject of the book, as "an infinite dialogue" in which the types are recurrent answers. Presenting his own answer he speaks of the context of companions, within which we know and make decisions, in terms of dialogue. Decision issues from ongoing dialogue in which we come to know the meaning for others of duty and Christ, and thus come to know what meaning they have for us and what then we must do.[54] While in no way the focus, a linguistic foundation of

[51] CC pp. 145 & 146.
[52] CC pp. 191–193 & 195.
[53] CC p. 255.
[54] CC pp. 39–40; see pp. 158 & 245.

concern for meaning and dialogue underlies this work. Recalling his remark, that "Even CHRIST AND CULTURE 'might be written today from the standpoint of language,'"[55] we can say that it has been; it only needs to be made more explicit.

While the subject of religious meaning recedes into the background, in his next book, PURPOSE OF THE CHURCH, dialogue becomes the central focus. Theological education is itself an ongoing dialogue within the Christian "community of discourse" through which "we learn the logic as well as the language" of the God-centered community.[56]

When this dialogue is entered upon in the 1950's what is discovered with respect to the aims of theological education is confusion. The context of theological education, the church—"the subjective pole of the objective rule of God"—is confused because it substitutes for its ultimate goal—"the *increase among men of the love of God and neighbor*"—various goals: in place of God a denomination, the church as a whole, the Bible, or Christ himself. But we also discover an emergent new form of ministerial life: the "pastoral director,"[57] who is a "responsible leader." He or she is "charged with the responsibility and given the authority to hold in balance, to invigorate and to maintain communication among a host of activities and their responsible leaders, all directed toward a common end."[58] This is a self devoted to dialogue.

In the book published just prior to his death, RADICAL MONOTHEISM, Niebuhr lets the metaphor of dialogue slip back into tacit thought as he turns to further exploration into the nature of religious language, suggesting that the life form of religious language is fundamentally that of faith. Discourse about God is inseparably linked with discourse about faith.[59]

In the inseparable linking of God and faith we have a turning point in the conception of religious meaning on the way from THE MEANING OF REVELATION to THE RESPONSIBLE SELF. In the earlier, faith is the context of religious language; in the later, faith is the life form itself of religious language. Now in RADICAL MONOTHEISM this latter recognition first achieves clarity: faith is that which is expressed through talk about God.

> Trust is, as it were, the passive aspect of the faith relation.
> It is *expressed in* praise or confessed in a creed that states the
> self-evident principle. Loyalty or faithfulness is the active

---

[55] Hoedemaker, THE THEOLOGY OF H. RICHARD NIEBUHR, p. 185, n. 50.
[56] PCM pp. 127 & 119; see pp. 112–3 & 117.
[57] PCM pp. 19, 31, & 79; his italics; see pp. 39–47 & 79.
[58] PCM pp. 90–91.
[59] See RMWC pp. 12 & 16.

side. . . . Faith-loyalty though it uses the same words as faith-trust *expresses itself in* a *sacramentum*, an oath of fealty, a vow of commitment.[60]

Conclusion

Emerging throughout his writings from THE MEANING OF REVELA-TION to THE RESPONSIBLE SELF are these three threads of religious meaning, myth, and dialogical self. Myth undergoes a seachange from negative conception in the earlier work to positive in the later by way of an evident but undeveloped transition in RADICAL MONOTHEISM. While the linguistic developments between THE MEANING OF REVELATION and THE RESPONSIBLE SELF do not present a theory of meaning with the comprehensiveness of either, nor grasp the self in its essentially dialogical nature as in the latter, nevertheless, we can see the linguistic foundations underlying Niebuhr's diverse investigations. After extensive treatment in THE MEANING OF REVELATION concern for religious meaning is implicit in CHRIST AND CULTURE as the underlying affirmation of the indispensability of language and meaning as life forms. In PURPOSE OF THE CHURCH religious meaning recedes into the background as dialogue becomes the explicit center of a newly conceived form of ministry, but re-emerges in RADICAL MONOTHEISM as faith is recognized as the life form of religious language. Dialogue in THE MEANING OF REVELATION is the context of revelation; in CHRIST AND CULTURE the context of decision-making and living in the diverse forms of interaction between Christ and culture; in the PURPOSE OF THE CHURCH the context within which the minister carries on his work; but in RADICAL MONOTHEISM it recedes from view as meaning re-emerges, except as it underlies the various communities considered—scientific, political, religious.

In the final analysis of meaning and dialogue in THE RESPONSIBLE SELF, we have seen that language has its meaning as words are used in a context by a speaker for whom they are forms of life enacted in his or her grasping/shaping interaction with reality. Religious language brings to articulateness paradigmatically the life form of faith, functions by integrating the self, and is expressed in the mode of first person discourse. The self who engages in the use of language and religious meaning is conceived as essentially linguistic in its nature as a being in dialogue. Seeing the self as a being existing in the midst of multiple relations to every aspect of reality, Niebuhr employs the metaphor of dialogue to catch the responsive character of all the interactions within these interrelations: we respond to all actions upon us as if they were questions to which we provide answers. Within this linguistic matrix we achieve maturity, but never in a final way, for the metaphor of

---

[60] RMWC p. 18; my italics except for *sacramentum*.

dialogue articulates the ongoingness and exploratory character of the integrative process.

We are now able to see that these three threads are interwoven with those investigated in chapter one. Niebuhr's linguistic theology is a complex weave of five threads: metaphor, grammatical comparison, religious meaning, myth, and dialogue.

CHAPTER THREE
A POSTCRITICAL AMBIENCE

In this convergence in Niebuhr's religious reflections of several fruitful perspectives on the nature of language, each of these perspectives has a freshness, originality, and integrity. While today there are advocates of each approach and some overlap between one or another, the convergence of five such widely different perspectives in a single theology is in our time unprecedented. One would have to go back to the seminal thinkers of our theological heritage—such as Jonathan Edwards, Thomas Aquinas, and Augustine—to find a similarly rich convergence of linguistic approaches.

While there is no doubt that Niebuhr spent his theological maturity in dialogue with Karl Barth, Rudolf Bultmann, Paul Tillich, Reinhold Niebuhr, and other twentieth century theologians, as well as deeply involved with the richness of the Western tradition, we must look beyond his theological contemporaries because their understanding of religious language is "critical." The ambience of his convergent thought as it emerges into linguistic clarity at the end of his life is postcritical: the exploration into symbolic forms within many different disciplines and the philosophical investigations, both analytical and phenomenological, into the nature of language as forms of life.

Who these dialogical companions of his last years are we will have to ferret out from unpublished writings, class notes, syllabi, and infrequent footnotes—Niebuhr is not given to much footnoting in later years, apparently because he did not want to obstruct communication by scholarly notations. We will look for connections of conscious interest and unnoticed similarities. It is affinities, not influences, we seek.

We will first show the critical nature of four theological contemporaries and then consider three contemporary postcritical philosophers: Michael Polanyi, whom he knew well and quoted in his writings; Ludwig Wittgenstein, whom he was becoming interested in and discussed in his last seminar; and Maurice Merleau-Ponty, whom he knew through the writings of other phenomenologists and by directing a dissertation on him, even though he nowhere refers to him. Finally, we will investigate explorers in "symbolic forms," beginning with Ernst Cassirer, who first articulated the phrase. While these many thinkers in diverse disciplines in no sense constitute a group—many would not accept Cassirer's rubric—they are of common interest to Niebuhr because they are working towards postcritical conceptions of the nature of symbols.

Critical Theology: Niebuhr's Contemporaries

There are major theological differences, of course, between Karl Barth, Rudolf Bultmann, Paul Tillich, and Reinhold Niebuhr, but each is similar in employing a critical view of religious language, and is, therefore, set over against Niebuhr's emergent postcritical point of view.

The affirmation of divine sovereignty is characteristic of these four great theologians. In their hands, whether they recognize it or not, this fundamental theological tenet is an implicitly linguistic concept: it locates the meaning of religious language and defines its power. In their efforts to safeguard divine sovereignty in terms of God's independence from self and world, they locate the meaning of religious language, not in words in use and in the agency of human speakers, but in the reality of God—whether in the Word of God for Barth, the acts of God encountering us through proclamation for Bultmann, Being itself for Tillich, or the ideal of divine love for Reinhold Niebuhr. Each in his own way employs a referential view of language, making God the divine object to which religious language points or refers. The divine meaning to which the words point lies beyond or behind language; meaning and word are therefore separable. The power of religious language is merely referential; the power of its meaning resides in God. Our use of words and our agency as speakers are not essential to meaning. There is even a move in Barth to appropriate the referential function of words to God himself so that they do not refer truly to God except as God makes them refer.

Separated from meaning by pointing to it in the independent divine reality, words are in no way constitutive. They shape neither the reality of which they speak nor the reality of the speaker. Meanings are independent realities rather than forms of life enacted by human language-users in relation to God, self, and world. The nerve that connects personal commitment to articulate meaning has been cut so that commitment has no bearing on religious meaning—the creation of religious meaning is entirely the prerogative of God. While different in many important ways, these are all critical theologies in their referential perspective on religious language. Seeking independence for religious meaning from human agency, they locate it in an independent referent, God, rather than in its use by a self, and thus divorce it intentionally from the language-using self, from the personal involvement characteristic of a postcritical perspective.

Barth makes this critical perspective evident at the beginning of his CHURCH DOGMATICS. Human religious language "points towards a fact, an object,"[1] which is the Word of God. While our words point to the Word of

---

[1] Karl Barth, CHURCH DOGMATICS, vol. I, THE DOCTRINE OF THE WORD OF GOD, Part 2, trans. by G. T. Thomson and Harold Knight (Edinburgh: T. & T. Clark, 1956), p. 464; see p. 466. See Karl Barth, CHURCH DOGMATICS, vol. I, THE DOCTRINE OF

God, they never reach it; they never correspond to it: the self's word "only points to that. What God said was always quite different." But God makes human words correspond, point truly, to himself by making the Word of God present time and again in human speech about God and making it speak itself about God.[2]

He is thus separating divine content from human form and making the human form incapable of even referring aright to divine meaning. In this critical separation of word and meaning, human and divine, he believes he has guaranteed the sovereign independence and grace of God. God's Word, because it is indirect (and yet not even "indirect") communication, is both powerful, because it makes a permanent impression on us, and mysterious, because its "unveiling" in revelation is always also a "veiling." Human words are neither. In religious language, God is the agent and selves are but powerless, passive recipients: the incarnation of religious meaning in our words is in no way a function of our words but is done by the divine prerogative.[3]

The critical lineaments of Bultmann's theology are more obvious in his concern to "demythologize" the New Testament in face of the modern world understood in Kantian terms as a closed, objective system of cause and effect. This task is to show that myth does not essentially refer to the objective world but to the subjective realm of existential being.[4]

Language is referential: myth refers to the existential realm; existential language refers simultaneously to God and self; and revelatory encounter refers to the original revelatory act of God in Christ. As in Barth, the divine

---

THE WORD OF GOD, Part 1, trans. by G. T. Thomson (Edinburgh: T. & T. Clark, 1936), p. 57. On the general referential character of language as such see pp. 127, 136, 149, & 159. Cf. Dallas M. High's incisive discussion of Barth's view of language in relation to this and closely related passages, in LANGUAGE, PERSONS, AND BELIEF: STUDIES IN WITTGEN-STEIN'S *PHILOSOPHICAL INVESTIGATIONS* AND RELIGIOUS USES OF LANGUAGE (New York: Oxford University Press, 1967), pp. 188–193.

[2] Barth, CHURCH DOGMATICS, I/1, pp. 160 & 106; see p. 149, and I/2, p. 469.

[3] On Barth's view of "veiling" and "unveiling" see I/1, pp. 188ff & 198–205; on the impotence of human speech see I/1, pp. 154 & 160; on the inherently direct communication of human speech see I/1, p. 189. On the permanent impression made only by the Word see Dallas High's discussion of the Humean (in our terms, "critical") character of Barth's linguistic point of view—the Word makes an impression upon us as a *tabula rasa*—in LANGUAGE, PERSONS, AND BELIEF, pp. 189–190.

[4] For the Kantian framework of Bultmann's thought see his "New Testament and Mythology," pp. 3–4 & 37, "A Reply to the Theses of J. Schniewind," p. 117, and "Bultmann Replies to his Critics," pp. 197–199, in Rudolf Bultmann, KERYGMA AND MYTH: A THEOLOGICAL DEBATE, ed. by Hans Werner Bartsch, Harper Torchbooks (New York: Harper & Brothers, 1961). There are ambiguities in the way in which Bultmann talks about myth in different places: whether myth in fact refers, although mistakenly, to the objective realm or whether it only appears to as a result of our misunderstanding (see pp. 10 & 36); whether transcendence as existentially interpreted is non-mythological or mythological in a different and acceptable sense (see pp. 11, 22, 43, & 102–103).

referent, God, makes the human words meaningful by becoming present in them; it "re-presents" the act of God in Christ without which human words, as in Barth, fail to reach the Word.[5]

Concerned to preserve the sovereignty of God, Bultmann similarly denies power to human language and linguistic agency to selves. Religious meaning does not issue through use by language-users but inheres in mythic words themselves as they refer. Separating mythological form from existential content and conceiving the existential language as referential, he denies that words are forms of life enacted by selves.

While Tillich seeks, more than the others, to overcome the critical perspective of modernity, in his view of language he embraces it. "Symbols and myths" are referential; they "point to the depth of reason and its mystery";[6] they refer to the ground of being—thereby separating word and meaning. Pointed at, the meaning is not in enacting the word but exists outside or behind it, as an independent "structure."

Ironically, Tillich stresses the indispensability of religious language to human existence in ways Barth and Bultmann do not, and yet it is they who define the nature of language as speech—the Word *speaks* within the triune Godhead and is repeated to the self, for Barth, and the Word is re-presented as it *addresses* the self, for Bultmann. Tillich conceives it, rather, as logos, a structure or order, but not an act of speaking. While myth and symbol are taken much more seriously by Tillich, nevertheless they can eventually be dispensed with in the face of ultimate reality which is non-mythic and non-symbolic. Myth is necessary to the fallen state of finite existence but not to the realm of essence in the "end" time; all symbols are founded upon the "non-symbolic" affirmation that God is Being itself.[7] Divine content is separable from human form.

As in Barth and Bultmann, the divine referent makes religious language meaningful by becoming present in it. For Tillich words become "transparent" to depth, to the ground shining through them. But language is impotent and the self passive where language is referential or transparent; God determines religious meaning. Words do not shape reality; they simply become transparent to an already existent structure, the divine logos. While Tillich insists that symbols do participate in the reality to which they point,

---

[5] See Bultmann, "Bultmann Replies to his Critics," p. 196; for Bultmann on the re-presentational character of religious proclamation see p. 204.

[6] Paul Tillich, SYSTEMATIC THEOLOGY, vol. 1 (Chicago: The University of Chicago Press, 1951), p. 110.

[7] For Tillich's identification of God as ground of being with structure see Tillich, SYSTEMATIC THEOLOGY, vol. 1, p. 238; for the delineation of this structure as logos rather than speech see p. 157; on the transparency of religious language see p. 124; on the indispensability of language to the human condition see pp. 124 & 222, but on the expendability of myth in the realm of essence see p. 80; on the non-symbolic affirmation of God as Being itself see pp. 238–239.

nevertheless, the self is passive at the moment of this pointing or transparence. This is the moment of faith, but faith is conceived as a "state of being grasped"—a passive state, rather than a human act, in which the self is the recipient of the work of the Spirit. Like Barth, true knowledge of God is had by God knowing himself through the self and its language.[8] Like both Barth and Bultmann, Tillich is seeking to maintain the sovereignty of God in the sense of independence. Meaning and agency are attributed to God, not to the self; religious words are but pointers to divine structure, not life forms we enact.

For Reinhold Niebuhr religious language is similarly referential. Christian symbols and myths of creation, fall, and redemption manifest a "dimension of depth" by pointing. The symbols and myths of Christianity have "the intention and the power to illumine the facts of life and the course of history by pointing to sources of meaning which lie beyond the facts we see and the history we experience." While they are indispensable to the expression of transcendence, the meaning exists behind the language as a reality external to word and self.[9]

Like the other three theologians, he preserves divine sovereignty by placing the meaning of religious language beyond the borders of human existence. Meaning and word are separated: words are devoid of power, as their meaning exists beyond them, and selves, even though conceived of as "self-transcending," are passive, as words do their pointing apart from being used by language-users. Yet unlike them, he rejects their more "mystical" conception, in which religious language is made meaningful by the divine referent's momentary residence in our language. The ideal of love, functioning as a Kantian regulative idea, can never become present in this world except paradoxically in Christ crucified. Nevertheless, in separating word and meaning by making the word point beyond itself to a transcendent meaning, he, like these others, represents a critical perspective on religious language within contemporary theology.

Postcritical Philosophers: Polanyi, Merleau-Ponty, Wittgenstein

While there are great differences in philosophical style and interests between Polanyi, focused on epistemology, whose paradigm is scientific

---

[8] On Tillich's view of the passivity of faith see Tillich, SYSTEMATIC THEOLOGY, vol. 1, pp. 108–114; Paul Tillich, SYSTEMATIC THEOLOGY, vol. 2 (Chicago: The University of Chicago Press, 1957), p. 178, and Paul Tillich, SYSTEMATIC THEOLOGY, vol. 3 (Chicago: The University of Chicago Press, 1963), p. 130; on God knowing himself through the self see vol. 1, p. 172. See also High, LANGUAGE, PERSONS, AND BELIEF, pp. 195–197, for an incisive discussion of Tillich's view of the passivity of faith.

[9] Reinhold Niebuhr, "The Truth in Myths," in THE NATURE OF RELIGIOUS EXPERIENCE: ESSAYS IN HONOR OF DOUGLAS CLYDE MACINTOSH, ed. J. S. Bixler, R. L. Calhoun, H. R. Niebuhr (New York: Harper & Brothers, 1937), p. 131; see pp. 129 & 135.

knowing; Merleau-Ponty, attentive to our bodily being in the world, whose paradigm is perceiving a figure against a background; and Wittgenstein, concerned with the nature of words, whose paradigm is persons speaking ordinary language; nevertheless, they share a postcritical commonality, affirming tacit commitment as fundamentally and inseparably underlying knowing, bodily being, and speaking.

Polanyi descries a "critical tradition," initiated by Descartes, epitomized by Kant, and characterizing much of our thought today, that objectifies meaning through methodological doubt, divorcing it from all non-rational, non-explicit factors, such as commitments, beliefs, trust, desire, sensation, feeling, and the context of words and acts. Descartes, forging the temper of an age, used doubt in the belief that the dissolution of belief under the probing of critical reason would leave an unassailed residue of certain knowledge. The result was, however, to drive apart mind and body, subject and object, leaving the self in irreconcilable disunity, constantly threatened by scepticism and solipsism. In contrast, Polanyi develops "postcritical" thinking that recognizes all explicit consciousness is grounded, not in rational, explicit knowledge, but in nonrational, "tacit," "a-critical," "fiduciary," "subsidiary," personal acts and beliefs.[10]

This "tacit dimension" or "fiduciary" framework is present in learning and using skills, ordinary perceiving, using literary and mythological symbols, and scientific knowing. At each of these levels the structure of knowing is the same: to know something explicitly we rely upon tacit commitments to elements of which we are unaware explicitly.

While nowhere employing Polanyi's distinction between critical and postcritical thought,[11] Niebuhr is strikingly similar. He agrees with Polanyi that modernity is "self-ignoring" and rooted in Cartesian doubt: "it is the way both of Descartes and of radical empiricism. It begins with radical doubt, undertaking to question every received notion and to form in the present moment new patterns for interpreting events." While Cartesian doubt has been of help to science in freeing itself from earlier anthropomorphic patterns of interpretation, its application to selves "has been successful only to the extent to which we have been able to reduce selves to objects, to unknowing knowns, noninterpreting reactors."[12]

In a literary fragment, acknowledging his conscious connection with Polanyi, Niebuhr agrees that Cartesian doubt opposes trust as a starting point:

[10] Polanyi, PERSONAL KNOWLEDGE, pp. 265–266 & 269.

[11] Though Niebuhr does not use the distinction itself, he does use the Kantian word "critical" in distinguishing "critical idealism" and "critical realism" in their bearing on history (see MR pp. 20 & 65–66).

[12] RS pp. 115, 101, & 102.

1. Trust—the web that runs through social life. Santayana—animal faith. Clockwork of instinct, organic action.
Basic trust in the infant.—Not organic or instinctive. Something to be learned. The trust that makes it possible for us to
use a million bits of knowledge not our own. The fact that
Descartes overlooked when he tried to begin with doubt.
What Polyani is questioning—doubt as a way of beginning.[13]

While employing critical categories earlier—inner and outer history, fact
and value—Niebuhr later recognizes their fragmenting character in his
search for a fiduciary framework for knowing and being. Speaking of Polanyi
in 1959, Niebuhr quotes Polanyi's own declaration of such an enterprise:

> Michael Polanyi in his effort to understand the personal
> element that enters into all scientific knowledge has struggled
> to understand the meaning of this scientific commitment. He
> writes, "'I believe, that in spite of the hazards involved, I am
> called upon to search for the truth and state my findings.' This
> sentence, summarizing my [fiduciary] programme, conveys an
> ultimate belief, which I find myself holding."[14]

Niebuhr pursues his fiduciary program in each of his heuristic metaphors: history as a confessional theological method; valuing as present in
being; faith as the basis for all knowing when understood as trust in, and
personal commitment to, the reality and intelligibility of the world, and the
community of knowers; and feeling as that which undergirds community and
knowing and provides non-conceptual ways of knowing reality.[15] This last is
clearly being developed as he explores with interest Polanyi's conception of
different passions:

> In part such an author writes and publishes what he is able
> to articulate of his views or vision because he is animated by
> the "persuasive passion." Professor Michael Polanyi in his
> book on PERSONAL KNOWLEDGE calls attention to the

[13] H. Richard Niebuhr, "Questions about Faith in Many Contexts" (unpublished fragment in
Niebuhr Folder III-AP-2, titled by Richard R. Niebuhr "Faith—Miscellanies," among untitled
batch beginning "Intro.—Questions about faith in many contexts. . . ," from 1958 or later
(dating because of previous reference to Polanyi's PERSONAL KNOWLEDGE), p. 2.

[14] Niebuhr, "Science in Conflict with Morality?," in RMWC pp. 132–133; quotation is from
Polanyi, PERSONAL KNOWLEDGE, p. 299. Bracketed word was accidentally omitted in the
printing of Niebuhr's quotation.

[15] On Niebuhr's confessional method see MR pp. 38–42; on value see "The Center of Value";
on faith see MR pp. 20 & 79, and RMWC pp. 78–83; and on feeling see "Toward the Recovery of
Feeling," pp. 24–29.

way this passion operates among scientists alongside their
heuristic passion.[16]

Even though Niebuhr never employs Polanyi's way of speaking of the
tacit structure of knowing, "responding" exhibits a fiduciary program as tacit
"balancing" according to "the fitting," that is, according to a wholeness
transcending explicit organization, inclusive of the self's "timeful" and "triadic" situation. As we respond to a certain time and space, our response
must be nonexplicitly sensitive to other realms not focused on, whether past,
present, future, or nature, society, self. Even though Polanyi never employs
Niebuhr's way of speaking of the structure of responsibility, he uses the word
frequently to describe knowledge based on tacit awareness: all knowing is a
"responsible act."[17]

The closest Niebuhr comes to speaking in Polanyi's terms is in his earlier
history-shaped distinction between "looking with" and "looking at," which
resembles Polanyi's looking *from* what we know tacitly *to* what we know
explicitly. Niebuhr says: "One must look *with* them and not *at* them to verify
their visions, participate in their history rather than regard it if one would
apprehend what they apprehended."[18] And he comes close to Polanyi's
terms when he speaks of adjustments—"inconspicuous shiftings," he calls
them—a bicycle rider makes, as he talks of the unconscious "balancing" we
analogously do in thinking and living:

> Movement in theology as well as in other theoretical
> enterprises may be compared to the kind of balanced physical
> movement which we can observe in the case of a bicycle rider
> and which has its analogies in all other physical movements
> from walking to sailing ships and riding in airplanes. If you
> want a scientific account of how a man rides a bicycle read
> Michael Polanyi's PERSONAL KNOWLEDGE: he knows
> something about a bicycle rider the bicycle rider himself
> doesn't know. The bicycle rider does not proceed in a straight
> line nor remain in a perfectly vertical position. His progress is
> marked by an almost infinite number of variations of the
> wheels to right and left and by a constant balancing of his body
> through small inconspicuous shiftings of weight. If the varia-
> tions of the wheel or of his balance become extreme in one
> direction they must be compensated for by extreme variations

---

[16] Niebuhr, 2. "The Place of the Author in the Structure of faith," "Adumbrations," p. 1.

[17] For a discussion of the "fitting act" in Niebuhr see RS pp. 108–109, and of "response" in a
"timeful" and "triadic" situation see RS chapters 2 & 3. For reference to knowing as a
"responsible act" in Polanyi see PERSONAL KNOWLEDGE, p. vii; cf. pp. 27, 64–65, 268,
299, 303, 309, 311–313, 320–321, 323, 334, 339, 343, 363, 368, 377, 379, 380, & 402.

[18] MR p. 73; my italics. On the "from-to" structure of tacit knowing see Michael Polanyi, THE
TACIT DIMENSION, Anchor Books (New York: Doubleday & Company, 1967), p. 10ff.

in the other direction, and when the corrections become over-
corrections there is catastrophe. So it is with the life and
thought of men.[19]

There are, of course, significant differences in content, between an
epistemology extrapolated from scientific knowing and theological explorations into religious ways of being, knowing, and speaking. And in style: while
both exhibit notable clarity, Niebuhr's writing has a denseness of multiple
levels—metaphoric, grammatical, dialogical, mythic—absent from Polanyi's.
Nevertheless, even if Polanyi does not use a comparative grammatical
method, there is a marked resemblance in their grammatical theories of
meaning. Their fiduciary programs have a fundamental linguistic thrust.
They similarly insist on the inseparability of meaning and word, word and
self, language and reality, the acritical and the articulate. Words for both are
"forms of existence," constitutive of selves existing in the world and dependent upon the self's tacit relations to indeterminate realities.[20]
    In an unpublished fragment of the late 1950's Niebuhr explicitly defines
his own theological method as "phenomenological":

> Under the circumstances it seems desirable to the theolo-
> gian and the moral theologian to turn to his own task. Engage
> in phenomenological inquiry. And that is what I propose to do.
> Phenomenological inquiry into one of the phenomena, or sets
> of ph[enomena] sometimes called faith, without worrying too
> much whether other folk will think that this is its proper
> name.[21]

Nowhere in his published writings does he identify with a phenomenological method, but it is clear from unpublished fragments and
lecture notes that the late 1950's and early 1960's were a time of consciously
rethinking theological method. Early in rethinking he sees continental phenomenology and Anglo-American linguistic analysis in opposition and feels
obliged to choose between them:

> The time seems to be ripe to many of us, perhaps in
> theology and others [i.e. in reflections other than theological]
> particularly for turning from historical, semantic and logical to
> *phenomenological* analysis. Instead of dealing with words and
> sentences, their meaning and their logic, it seems desirable

---

[19] Niebuhr, "Toward the Future," pp. 6–7.
[20] For Polanyi's discussion of the nature of language within his postcritical perspective see
PERSONAL KNOWLEDGE, pp. 250–255, as well as pp. 103–105 on the self-transformative
process of speaking, and p. 208 on his use of the phrase "forms of existence."
[21] Niebuhr, "Questions about Faith in Many Contexts," p. 1.

that we undertake to examine some of the phenomena in human life to which such words refer ambiguously or ambivalently without undertaking to engage in dispute about the greater or lesser importance of the one set of phenomena or another. So I propose that we try to examine tonight one of the phenomena which goes under the head of faith.[22]

While hesitantly embracing a phenomenological method here, he later speaks unhesitatingly of his ethical reflections as a "phenomenology of the Moral Act."[23] This method is, in fact, a newer name for reflections on the actuality, rather than ideality, of being that he has been engaged upon ever since his conversion to, what he at the time called, "theological realism." As we have seen, he has similarly been developing a linguistic method long before he consciously embraces it.[24] By 1961 the opposition between the phenomenological and linguistic methods has disappeared, as he has learned more about each and has come to see that "phenomena in human life" are shaped by and accessible through language. While he immersed himself during these years in reading many phenomenological thinkers, the phenomenologist his work most resembles is Merleau-Ponty.[25]

In opposition to the subject/object split of critical thought, Merleau-Ponty speaks of a "lived body" as "being in the world." Situated in a context of which it is not explicitly aware, my body tacitly sustains a background against which I see or know a figure.[26] My experience of the world is of figures I draw out against backgrounds I sustain at many levels. My experience of myself is of my unique embodied self known consciously through reflection and "pre-reflectively" through the unconscious act of being the self that I am in the body that is mine. Language-use, like perceiving, thinking, and so forth, understood within the figure-background metaphor, is creative of self and world. As complex "gesture," words are embodied "forms of

---

[22] H. Richard Niebuhr, "The Structure of Faith" (unpublished fragment in Niebuhr Folder III-AP-2, titled by Richard R. Niebuhr "Faith—Miscellanies," from 1958 or later), p. 2; his italics.

[23] Niebuhr, "Christian Ethics Lectures," February 15, 1961, p. 3.

[24] Niebuhr's at first reluctant acceptance of a linguistic method obviously comes after this rejection of a linguistic in favor of a phenomenological method.

[25] In courses Niebuhr referred to Husserl, Brentano, Heidegger, Marcel, Scheler, Unamuno, Spiegelberg, O. Bollnow, W. A. Luijpen, A. Dondeyne, R. C. Kwant (in H. Richard Niebuhr, "The Religious Emotions" [student seminar notes, handwritten by R. Melvin Keiser, taught at Yale Divinity School, spring semester, 1962]), and J. Wild (in H. Richard Niebuhr, "Christian Theory of Sin" [student seminar notes, handwritten by R. Melvin Keiser, taught at Yale Divinity School, fall semester, 1961]); in print he refers to Heidegger and Marcel (RS pp. 112 & 116). He was also acquainted with Merleau-Ponty through the writings of Luijpen, Dondeyne, and Kwant, and directed a dissertation on him in the 1960's.

[26] See Maurice Merleau-Ponty, PHENOMENOLOGY OF PERCEPTION, trans. by Colin Smith (London: Routledge & Kegan Paul, 1962), pp. 259, 363, & 385.

behavior" that are figures drawn out from the background of linguistic and prelinguistic significance.[27]

Even though Niebuhr does not base his theology upon bodily perception, he speaks in strikingly similar ways of "me in my body" and says "man must be understood in terms of embodied, concretized projects." An embodied self is a unique self: "But none of these interpretations of biological events touches the fact that it is *I* who am in or with this body, that *I* have this body, that this is *my* body."[28] Similar to the lived body, inner history is a "lived history" which exercises an "animal faith" rooted in bodily reliance upon our environment without which we could not exist, and dwells within a non-objective durational time. Within triadic response-relations there is a spatial as well as temporal background.[29]

Niebuhr nowhere uses the phrase "figure-background," but rather speaks for the most part of an "ethos" or "total context."[30] Yet he does speak, in unpublished remarks about faith, of "foreground" and "background": "We live by faith, but never by faith alone. Faith is the background of all our relations. But there is always something in the foreground."[31] He speaks elsewhere of God's promise of glory as a "background of existence":

> The "promises of God" to us do not designate certain statements which are said to have been made to Abraham and to his children. They designate that sense of meaningfulness and splendor with which personal being awakes to existence. There is in the *background of existence*, whether as memory of childhood, or as Platonic recollection of something heard in another existence, or as the echo of an inner voice, the sense of something glorious, splendid, clean and joyous for which this being and all being is intended. . . . The promise of life is the promise of glory and splendor, not for me, but for existence and for me as part of this world of being.[32]

And in what probably comes from direct awareness of Merleau-Ponty, he links background with "being in the world": "symbolic patterns . . . represent their sense of 'being in the world,' which are the background and the

---

[27] Ibid., pp. 184, 192, & 236.

[28] RS p. 109; his italics. Cf. MR pp. 91–92.

[29] For Niebuhr on "lived history" see MR pp. 59–73; on his use of Santayana's phrase "animal faith" see MR p. 79; on time see MR p. 69 and RS chapter 3; on lived space see RS pp. 79–80 & 106.

[30] See RS pp. 79, 98, & 107.

[31] H. Richard Niebuhr, "The Reconstruction of Faith," in "Memphis Lectures" (Niebuhr's lecture notes, handwritten, in Niebuhr Folder III-AP-2, titled by Richard R. Niebuhr "Faith— Miscellanies," n.d.), p. 1.

[32] Niebuhr, chapter 5, "Broken Faith," in "Faith on Earth," p. 20; my italics; cf. p. 2.

ultimate assumptions (though unanalyzed) of their reasonings and apprehensions."[33]

In spite of such resemblances, there are evident differences. Merleau-Ponty works against empiricist and idealist theories of perception, showing the indispensable presence of the lived body here and on other levels—such as motor skills, sexuality, freedom—while Niebuhr explores religious forms of life within the ultimate background, the "circumambiency" that is "the mystery behind the mystery of human existence."[34] While Merleau-Ponty articulates a similar theory of meaning (affirming the inseparability of word, meaning, and self, and the constitutive nature of language), uses a comparative method, and defines the embodied self as essentially linguistic, he does not write with Niebuhr's metaphoric, mythological, and dialogical richness. Rather he writes with an involutedness and ponderousness. Following Merleau-Ponty through the intertwinings of his long, complex sentences, we are forced to rely more on somatic than conceptual awareness, grasping the emotional content or gestural significance, rather than merely explicit ideas. We find ourselves no longer beholding objects in two dimensions but plunged into three—in fact, four, given the time it often takes to read through a paragraph. We are drawn into dwelling among phenomena that disclose their four-dimensionality as we move with the curvatures of his language in and around, up and down. As our perspective is constantly shifting, we begin to get a sense of the lived-world in which things are at hand in a background to be drawn forth and grouped into figures of perception or thought. While Niebuhr's evocative style takes us to an integrative depth beneath critical fragmentation, Merleau-Ponty's heaviness obstructs and dissolves it.

In the following remarks at the end of his last seminar, on "The Religious Emotions," Niebuhr displays an incisive understanding of some important aspects of Wittgenstein's thought they held in common. Speaking of him in relation to logical positivism, Niebuhr said: "Logical positivism is the present-day form of what has been with us for three hundred years. It says a thing is what it is and nothing else; it deals with the external relations of things, as dependent on sense experience." After remarking that this is "so out of touch with modern science," he referred to Wittgenstein's use of two symbols, "picture" and "game." In explaining what these mean, he observed: "We do not just have a picture of a state of affairs out there but we are involved in them." In the next and last class meeting of the semester, he spoke of the difference between existentialism and positivism in their view of emotions. The former affirms that "emotions are revelatory of being," while

[33] H. Richard Niebuhr, "On the Nature of Faith," in RELIGIOUS EXPERIENCE AND TRUTH: A SYMPOSIUM, ed. by Sidney Hook (New York: New York University Press, 1961; delivered at the New York University Institute of Philosophy, held at Washington Square, New York, October 21–22, 1960), p. 101.

[34] On the "circumambient" see RS p. 153, and on "the Mystery Behind the mystery of human existence" see PCM p. 36.

the latter believes that "emotions are ancillary to being." He then remarked: "There is bound to be dialogue between these continental and Anglo-American philosophical movements, and Wittgenstein in his later years may be the median point."[35]

Through investigating ordinary language in its actual use Wittgenstein attacks the critical "picture theory" of language and belief in transcendent essences. Language does not picture another reality, a realm of essences, to which it refers, but functions like a game, involving us, having its meaning in being played or used. Meaning for both Wittgenstein and Niebuhr is contextual, performative, and personal—existing as used by a speaker in a context founded upon tacit commitments, "an ungrounded way of acting." Language is indispensable to our humanity, an ineradicable part of our "natural history," and is creative, shaping the self through words as "forms of life," and the world through words embodying an "inherited background" or "mythology" that informs us what sort of world we inhabit. The richness of meaning requires a comparative method that places words in use alongside each other describing what is actually there rather than speculating on what lies as essences behind them.[36]

In addition to grammatical theory and method they are similar in their interest in the dialogical, even confessional, mode of thinking. Wittgenstein's investigations are an ongoing dialogue with himself and reader-listener about the nature of language. Like a conversation he returns to a theme time and again from different perspectives, looking not for conceptual classifications but "family resemblances," arriving at conclusions that are always open-ended. He confesses succumbing to temptation and being taken captive by a picture of words as copies of some other reality. His confession leads to a therapeutic concern to redeem us from the consequent "deep disquietudes" whose "roots are as deep in us as the forms of our language," to transform us in those depths so as to gain "a new way of looking at things."[37]

The grammatical theory and method are, of course, much more exten-

---

[35] Niebuhr, "The Religious Emotions," May 1 & 8.

[36] On Wittgenstein's picture theory of meaning see pars. #1 & 115; on "picture" and "game" see #23; on meaning as "use" within a context see #20 & 43; on criticism of the ideal in favor of the actual see #98 & 130–135; on "natural history" see #25 & 415; on language telling us what things are see #373; on "form of life" see #19; on comparative method see #130–135; on descriptive method see #109—in Ludwig Wittgenstein, PHILOSOPHICAL INVESTIGATIONS, trans. by G. E. M. Anscombe (New York: Macmillan Company, 1953). On founding language upon "an ungrounded way of acting" and embodying an "inherited background" or "mythology" see par. #110, in Ludwig Wittgenstein, ON CERTAINTY, ed. by G. E. M. Anscombe (New York and Evanston: J. & J. Harper Editions, 1969).

[37] On the multi-perspectival nature of Wittgenstein's method see p. ixe; on criticism of a goal of conceptual completeness see p. 206e; on confessional mode see initial quotation from Augustine's CONFESSIONS, #1; on "family resemblance" see #65–78; on captivity see #115; on therapeutic concern see # 133 & 255; on deep roots see #111; on a new way of looking see #401—in Wittgenstein, PHILOSOPHICAL INVESTIGATIONS. On "family resemblance" in Niebuhr see CC pp. 40 & 44.

sive in Wittgenstein, and even with this therapeutic impulse, he does not reflect much on religious language. He attends to the "fine shades of behaviour"[38] of our ordinary talk, whereas Niebuhr explores heuristic metaphors that express total ways of being. Where Niebuhr's style is evocative through metaphor and myth, Wittgenstein's is ironic; much like Kierkegaard's use of Socratic irony, Wittgenstein throws his readers back on their own resources as they are puzzled, at least initially, by what the author really thinks in the midst of the barrage of questions and shifting answers.

Postcritical Explorers of Symbolic Forms

In his Earl Lectures Niebuhr expresses his programmatic intention to explore "the nature and the role of symbolic forms."[39] Ernst Cassirer is the pathbreaking thinker who first used this phrase in his PHILOSOPHY OF SYMBOLIC FORMS. A profound and comprehensive attempt, it argues that symbols are not copies of an already existent reality but are instruments for forming self and world through shaping cultural forms of language, myth, and scientific knowledge.[40] Yet Cassirer does not succeed, as Niebuhr does, in transcending his Kantian origins. Although he believes he has transcended the critical dualism of idealism and empiricism, in what he calls a "critical phenomenology," he admits this is "a general system of philosophical idealism."[41]

The effect of this is evident in his theory of meaning. While he wants to say a symbol is a "life form,"[42] it does not have its meaning through being lived or used. Language only comes into being when meaning and existence, significance and sound, intelligible and sensuous, are separated to enable word to point to meaning.[43] This disembodiment of meaning through Kantian disjunction means the uprooting of any connection between the fiduciary and articulate, since language begins where sensation and feeling cease; and it means the self is an "ideal unity" who is a maker "moulding this self." The result is that the highest reality we know is our own spirituality.[44]

---

[38] Wittgenstein, PHILOSOPHICAL INVESTIGATIONS, pp. 203e, 204e, & 207e.

[39] RS p. 151.

[40] Ernst Cassirer, THE PHILOSOPHY OF SYMBOLIC FORMS, vol. 2, MYTHICAL THOUGHT, trans. by Ralph Manheim (New Haven and London: Yale University Press, 1955), p. 156; cf. Ernst Cassirer, THE PHILOSOPHY OF SYMBOLIC FORMS, vol. 1, LANGUAGE, trans. by Ralph Manheim (New Haven and London: Yale University Press, 1953), pp. 107 & 269.

[41] Cassirer, THE PHILOSOPHY OF SYMBOLIC FORMS, vol. 1, p. 72. For Cassirer's use of "critical phenomenology" see vol. 2, p. 13.

[42] Ibid., vol. 2, p. 153; cf. pp. 6 & 99, and also in vol. 1, pp. 81, 285, & 287.

[43] Ibid., vol. 2, p. 239; cf. p. 237 and in vol. 1, p. 106; see also use of "refer," vol. 2, p. 237.

[44] On language's beginning point see ibid., vol. 1, pp. 111 & 189; on the self as ideal unity see vol. 2, p. 166; on the self molding itself see p. 172 and vol. 1, p. 106; and on our spiritual form as the known see vol. 1, p. 111.

Cassirer comes closer to Niebuhr's postcritical perspective in his discussion of myth, for myth does not point at but bears actuality, and the self is not a transcendental "I" but a social self inextricably interrelated with community.[45] But poetry is finally seen as "a world of illusion and fantasy," and myth is superseded by the "conceptual sign" of science.[46]

While Cassirer is a central stimulus, Niebuhr is interested in many others, earlier and later, who have worked with symbolic forms in various fields, who have succeeded better than Cassirer in wrestling free from a critical mind-set. Although he does not mention many names, we can reconstruct his dialogical companions from the writing and teaching of his last years.

He speaks first of

> psychologists who have called attention to the manner in which both in dreams and in other more or less unconscious production we express deep-rooted desires, fears, and conflicts in pictures and dramas that disguise as well as reveal the sources of their inspiration. In this case we are dealing with images and stories that need to be interpreted.[47]

He may well have in mind Freud and Jung concerned with dream-images and desires, both of whom see myth as the indispensable language of maturity; Erik Erikson interested in faith as a form of early life;[48] the Gestalt-psychology of Koffka and Köhler; and the psychology of perception.[49]

In the history of art Niebuhr mentions E. H. Gombrich who, in his ART AND ILLUSION, says we grasp art as a global whole or gestalt within time, shaped by past artistic forms and techniques, and anticipating future answers to questions addressed to what is being seen.[50] In literary criticism he mentions Erich Auerbach, who distinguishes two forms of life: the "fore-

---

[45] On myth see ibid., vol. 2, pp. 38–41 & 237–238; on the self see ibid., vol. 2, p. 175.

[46] Ernst Cassirer, LANGUAGE AND MYTH, trans. by Susanne K. Langer (New York: Harper & Brothers, 1946), pp. 97–99.

[47] See RS p. 151 for mention of others as well as Cassirer.

[48] For evidence of Niebuhr's involvement with Freud, see "Christian Theory of Sin"; with Jung see CC p. x; and with Erikson see H. Richard Niebuhr, "Faith as Virtue" (student seminar notes, handwritten by R. Melvin Keiser, taught at Yale Divinity School, fall semester, 1960), January 11, 1961, and RS p. 118.

[49] See RS p. 151; for Niebuhr's use of "gestalt" see RS pp. 154 & 175. A number of psychologists of perception are referred to in E. H. Gombrich, ART AND ILLUSION: A STUDY IN THE PSYCHOLOGY OF PICTORIAL REPRESENTATION (London: Phaidon Press, 1960), pp. viii–x, whom Niebuhr mentions under art history.

[50] For Niebuhr's reference to Gombrich see RS pp. 152–153. For Gombrich on the interpretative act in art see his ART AND ILLUSION, pp. 246, 255, 275, & 276; on the integrative and global character of interpretation see pp. 254 & 262; and on the temporal shaping of perception see pp. 254, 256, & 271.

ground" world of Homer's Odysseus and the life "fraught with background" of the Hebraic Abraham. In the latter God speaks to Abraham within the "dialogue" of everyday life, who responds with "a constant interpretative change," seeking to fit all that is past and emerging into universal history, which shapes his unique individuality.[51] While he mentions only Auerbach, he is interested in the Coleridgean tradition, such as I. A. Richards, Philip Wheelwright, William Empson, Cleanth Brooks, W. K. Wimsatt, and T. S. Eliot, who conceive metaphor as a form of life enacted by the poet which shapes both self and world.[52]

In the history of religions, he is probably thinking of Weber, Durkheim, Lévy-Brühl, Malinowski, and Wach, who deal with the shaping of life by myth and "interpretation of the holy."[53] Within the scientific community, besides Polanyi, he is in dialogue with Alfred North Whitehead and Blaise Pascal.[54]

Finally we come to "those great artists, the metaphysical philosophers" who have given us "the root-metaphors of generating substance, of the republic, of the organism, of the machine, of the event, and of the mathematical system." Acknowledging the source of "root-metaphor" in Stephen Pepper,[55] Niebuhr has in mind the three philosophers we have already considered, but also what we might call the philosophies of self. One part of this conversation is with those social and dialogical philosophers who affirm the social nature of the self—such as George Herbert Mead, George Horton Cooley, Harry Stack Sullivan, Josiah Royce, John Macmurray, and Martin Buber—who in various ways present the self as born and growing into maturity within the social matrix, knowing the world and itself only through its relations to other selves.[56] A second part is with those existentialist philosophers such as Kierkegaard, Marcel, and Jaspers, who conceive our being as "elusive selves."[57]

[51] For Niebuhr's reference to Auerbach see RS p. 153, n. 3. For Auerbach's discussion of "foreground" and "background" see Erich Auerbach, "Odysseus' Scar," chapter 1, MIMESIS: THE REPRESENTATION OF REALITY IN WESTERN LITERATURE, trans. by Willard Trask, Anchor Books (New York: Doubleday and Company, 1957), especially pp. 4–9; for his mention of "dialogue" see "Fortunata," chapter 2, p. 39–40; for "a constant interpretative change" see chapter 1, p. 13; and for the formation of personality see chapter 1, pp. 14–15.

[52] Niebuhr deals with Coleridge in "The Religious Emotions"; Wheelwright in "Toward New Symbols," pp. 10–11; Richards, Empson, Brooks, Wimsatt in "Language and Theology"; and Eliot in "Christian Ethics" (R. M. Keiser, 1961).

[53] RS. 153. Niebuhr mentions Weber and Durkheim in RMWC pp. 35, 88, 128, & 131; Lévy-Brühl in KGA pp. 6 & 199; Malinowski in CC pp. 31 & 33; and Wach in a book review, H. Richard Niebuhr, "Wach, SOCIOLOGY OF RELIGION," in Theology Today, II, No. 3, (1945), pp. 409–411.

[54] For Niebuhr's use of these see MR chapter 3, especially pp. 91–99,

[55] Both quotation from Niebuhr and reference to Stephen Pepper occur in RS p. 153.

[56] For Niebuhr's mention of Mead, Cooley, Sullivan, and Buber see RS pp. 71–73; of Royce see RS p. 83; and of Macmurray see "Christian Ethics" (R. M. Keiser, 1961).

[57] For Niebuhr's use of "elusive selves" see MR p. 64; for his discussion of Kierkegaard see

The final part focuses on the grammatical self. John Macmurray sees the "form of the personal" and the search for the "functional unity" of thought, emotions, and body as the chief problem of our day. The personal is constituted in language. While from the theoretical point of view, "I's" and "You's" are indistinguishable, from that of the agency of the self, the form of being is different in the grammar of the "I" or "You."[58]

Conclusion

In Part One we have been exploring Niebuhr's five different perspectives on language—metaphoric, grammatical comparisons and meaning, dialogical, and mythic—and inquiring into the context of their convergence. While he is in dialogue with his critical theological contemporaries, the ambience of his final reflections is the postcritical philosophy of Polanyi, Merleau-Ponty, and Wittgenstein and the interdisciplinary exploration of symbolic forms. Amidst these he seeks for ways to affirm multiplicity in the world, fullness of the self, and the inherent interrelatedness between them. Beyond dualisms which deny or denigrate parts of self and world, he conceives of the self as committed and articulate, indwelling the spatial-temporal world, and responding as a whole to the total environment. Through meaning incarnate in and expressed through the religious language of metaphor, myth, and dialogue, he is able to achieve in those responses an integrity of being. Grasping the linguistic nature of Niebuhr's postcritical thought, we now turn to an investigation of the nature of the committed self as it uses heuristic metaphors in the theological quest for integrity.

H. Richard Niebuhr, "Sören Kierkegaard," in Carl Michalson, ed., CHRISTIANITY AND THE EXISTENTIALISTS (New York: Scribner, 1956), pp. 32–33; for Niebuhr's mention of Marcel and Jaspers see RS p. 112.

[58] On the "form of the personal" as the central problem see John Macmurray, THE FORM OF THE PERSONAL, vol. 1, SELF AS AGENT (London: Faber and Faber Limited, 1957), p. 17; on the "functional unit" of the self see John Macmurray, THE FORM OF THE PERSONAL, vol. 2, PERSONS IN RELATION (London: Faber and Faber Limited, 1961), p. 12; on the personal as constituted in language see vol. 2, p. 12; and on the grammatical distinction between "I" and "You" see vol. 2, pp. 19 & 22–23.

PART TWO:

The Committed Self's Theopoetical Quest for Integrity

CHAPTER FOUR
HEURISTIC METAPHORS: HISTORY AND VALUE

While the linguistic, postcritical nature of Niebuhr's theological method is most fully developed within the metaphor of responsibility, we can see its presence, explicit some of the time, latent always, in the other heuristic metaphors—history, value, faith, and feeling.

The problem he addresses at the roots of our modern critical age is the loss of integrity. What he is groping towards through these metaphors, and recognizes fully only at the end, is that this is essentially a linguistic problem requiring a linguistic solution. Integrity is achieved by a committed self using certain linguistic forms of life grounded in and expressive of commitment, that bring the disparate parts of self and being together within the context of a real and shared world. As we move from earlier to later metaphors, we will find a deepening understanding that a fiduciary foundation sustains a real and shared world and is expressed through personal, symbolic language.

History as Threat to Language and Integrity

In taking up the metaphor of history in the modern world, what we encounter immediately is the phenomenon of historical relativism: "the realization that the point of view which a man occupies in regarding religious as well as any other sort of reality is of profound importance." Theology has had to acknowledge that it could only view "God in human experience," not as he is in himself. Its knowledge is not universal because our "concepts are something less than the categories of a universal reason," and because they are inseparable from words, and every language is particular, not universal.[1]

The impact upon our lives has been the shattering of confidence in language and commitment. Dismayed by the loss of universality in language and reason, we have fallen into scepticism, proclaiming "the unreliability of all thought" to grasp reality, and into solipsism, taking "Arbitrariness and isolated subjectivity . . . as the characteristic features of the world of

[1] See MR pp. 6–9 & 13–14.

selves."[2] Once language floats free from its fiduciary moorings in reality and community, we withdraw into the privacy of our sceptical and solipsistic minds, into the "utter solitude" of "evil imaginations" that prevent true knowledge of the "Thou," "great areas of life," and our own past, and thus obstruct our achieving integrity in the present.[3]

Faced with this confusion and impoverishment of the self, many are tempted "to understand ourselves and others as beings without selves— things that are to be understood in a context of things." The linguistic crisis of historical relativism is the religious crisis of self-integrity. It is to come at the last turning to the despairing belief "that persons do not belong to the real structure of things in this world."[4]

Living inescapably nevertheless as selves, we have fled in terror before the facts of an inviolable fate and irrevocable death, believing them to be but the workings of a cosmic system of objective determinants fundamentally alien to personal existence. For refuge we have all the more insistently exercised our critical doubt, most particularly upon ourselves and commitments in the hope that some place of certainty and security might be found. The more rigorously we have applied critical reason, the more the real and shared world has receded from our view, leaving us withdrawn into solipsism and scepticism, and the more our selves have appeared meaningless and illusory, leaving us existing as things. When driven back upon ourselves to answer why we hold a particular view, and why we make those assumptions upon which our view is based, we answer not in terms of personal commitment, but of conditioning factors that have played upon us in our society and history. Doubting our fiduciary foundation, we doubt the capacity of language as bearer of a real and shared world and as agent of self-integration.

Inner and Outer History

In face of the threat of historical relativism, Niebuhr explores the nature of history itself to see if what has been dissolved by history can be recovered through history. He begins by asking, if history means relativism, how can it mean revelation? He answers with his well-known distinction between two types of history: relativism with its objective conditioning factors belongs to "external history," while revelation with its personal commitments belongs to "internal history." The former is the history of spectators, or a "succession of events . . . seen from the outside," "occurrences in a stranger's life"; the latter is the history of participants, "our own history," "the path of one's own destiny."[5]

[2] MR pp. 16–17 & 100.
[3] MR pp. 99–102 & 117.
[4] MR pp. 102–103 & 150.
[5] MR p. 59.

Consider two examples from medical and social history. We all would recognize the difference between a scientific case history and an auto-biographical account of a particular event, say the healing of blindness. The report of the former would describe the state of the eye, the medical treatment administered, and the stages of recovery of sight, while the tale of the latter would "tell what happened to a self that had lived in darkness and now saw again trees and the sunrise, children's faces and eyes of a friend."[6] In operating, the surgeon is oblivious of the purposes of the patient, of his or her hopes and fears; during convalescence, the doctor observes the process of the healing of tissue rather than the experience the patient has as sight returns, the joy and the new sensibility in the visual experience of again seeing colors and shapes.

Or consider the story of the founding of the United States as told from within by Lincoln in his "Gettysburg Address" and as told from without by the *Cambridge Modern History*. Lincoln speaks of what "our fathers brought forth" while the British textbook says, "On July 4, 1776, Congress passed the resolution." In one case the story tells of the events which have been formative of the speaker's identity, to which he is committed, in which he discerns something of his own purposes, his own destiny. In the other the events are held at arm's length, located in calendar rather than personal time, and described as the effects of institutions (the Congress) rather than the efforts of persons—not just anyone, but our ideological, if not physical, progenitors. Here is history "as lived" and "as seen,"[7] our own inner history and an outer succession of events.

Participant and spectator history involve a distinctive kind of relationship between knower and known, between "being a relationship between dif-ferent terms" and "being directed toward different aspects of reality." In inner history, the knower is a participant and the known is a self; in outer history, the knower is a spectator and the known a thing. Events for surgeon and British textbook are occurrences in outer history because the knowers are not participants in the medical and American experience as are the patient and Lincoln, and because the knowns, the tissue and the institution, are things—not the commitments, purposes, and destiny characteristic of personal existence.[8]

To call both tissue and institution a "thing" suggests Niebuhr is grouping everything less than what is fully personal under this one rubric. Thus biological organisms as well as physical entities are things, and even persons are things if they are seen only as impersonal parts, as complexes of ideas or of psychological or economic drives. External history is reductionistic; both

[6] MR p. 60.
[7] MR p. 60. See section heading "History as Lived and as Seen," MR p. 59.
[8] MR p. 144. For this two-fold distinction see MR pp. 63 & 65.

the human and the living seen externally are understandable strictly as inanimate, as physical and chemical processes. When approached objectively the self as well as all other things are reduced to "atomic individuals related to each other by external bonds." Existing within an objective causal sequence, things are not totally devoid of value, but their value is "valency," the "effect" quantitatively measurable of one atom upon another. Change is irrevocable: "past events are gone and future happenings are not yet."[9]

The self as the known of inner history, on the other hand, is a living organization of parts into a transcendent whole, not reducible to the sum of its parts, but internally related to other selves and to its own past and future. "Here we do not only live among other selves but they live in us and we in them. Relations here are not external but internal so that we are our relations and cannot be selves save as we are members of each other." This is an organic relationship, where an effect upon any part of the whole affects the entirety. For oneself to be hurt is for all to feel the pain; for one to rejoice is for all to enter into that joy. Time and value are similarly organic: "time is our duration. What is past is not gone; it abides in us as our memory; what is future is not non-existent but present in us as our potentiality. Value is qualitative worth for selves, that which resounds within the basic tonalities of our lives and which bespeaks the tragedies and triumphs of our days, the destiny of our years.[10]

Relating to different knowns, the knower is correspondingly different. Using the language of Martin Buber, the knower in an "I-It" and "I-Thou" relation is different. Where the known is a thing of outer history, the knower is the sole agent. We manipulate the object, "a passive and dead thing," by the questions we put to it, by the concepts we apply to it, by the standards with which we measure it, and by the experiments we put it through. Yet when the known is impersonal, the knower is correspondingly impersonal. "He cannot really say of himself, 'I think, therefore I am,' but must rather say, 'Thinking goes on in me but that same thinking may and must go on in any other brain so related to such objects.'"[11]

When the known is a fully personal self, the knower cannot be the sole agent: "To know a knower is to begin with the activity of the other who knows us or reveals himself to us by his knowing activity." Known and knower are active alike; rather than manipulating an inert thing to procure answers from it, the knower responds to the already unveiled intentionality of the known as another knower. "Selves are known in act or not at all. . . . One cannot know a lover by any activity of one's own love."[12]

There is, however, a known which is a self and yet belongs to outer

[9] MR pp. 67, 69, & 70; see pp. 64 & 144.
[10] MR pp. 68–70.
[11] MR pp. 67 & 144–145.
[12] MR pp. 145–146.

history. A stranger's life, while no inert thing, belongs to outer history because the self's commitments are changed into objective factors, things, when known spectatively. A self is only truly known participatively, as self-in-act, enacting its commitments by "step[ping] into direct relation to it,"[13] engaging it personally in its commitments. The knower, as participant or spectator, is therefore determinative of the known, as self or thing. Relativism's threat is answered as Niebuhr finds history to mean not only external conditionedness but internal commitment.

Recovering a Shared World: Revelation and Pattern

Within this historical realm of inner commitment Niebuhr recovers a shared world. The self-in-act exists in organic relations with other selves—"we are our relations and cannot be selves save as we are members of each other"—committed to a community, participating in a "common memory and common hope no less than in a common world of nature." The community is a common world; self and world are one as we are committed to a god or center of value. But more often than not we find our communities and selves lack integrity because we are committed to more than one god.[14]

In the face of the fragmentation of our world through commitment to many gods, Niebuhr shows inner history, the realm of commitment, to be the realm of revelation and pattern: as revelation it is the sphere which elicits our commitment to God, as pattern it is the presence in our world of an underlying structure to which we are committed in our personal being. Through these meanings of history a way is found towards the recovery of a shared world.

From the perspective of inner history, revelation is the manifestation within the life of selves-in-act of ultimate reality as the divine self-in-act "unveiling of his hiddenness" and "giving of himself in communion." Through "divine self-disclosure" we come to trust in the one God, creator of one world, who "forces us to trust him wholly."[15]

As we come to trust in the Lord of one world, we come to see the unity and commonality of this world; revelation illumines within our inner history the presence of a pattern of meaning which makes intelligible everything as part of one shared world and holds together past, present, and future as a coherent whole:

> By revelation in our history, then, we mean that special
> occasion which provides us with an image by means of which
> all the occasions of personal and common life become intelligi-

---

[13] MR pp. 145–146.
[14] MR pp. 70 & 71; see pp. 77 & 78.
[15] MR pp. 152 & 155.

ble. . . . Through it a pattern of dramatic unity becomes apparent with the aid of which the heart can understand what has happened, is happening and will happen to selves in their community. [16]

Through revelation we recognize our past to be part of one common world, to be the past history of the world. The revelatory moment "makes our past intelligible. Through it we understand what we remember, remember what we have forgotten and appropriate as our own past much that seemed alien to us." For the individual, revelation is the event that makes "significant and intelligible the apparently haphazard course of his earlier existence" so that "all that has happened to him may then assume continuity and pattern as it is related to the moment for which he knows himself to have been born." Under the impact of revelation a group such as the Christian church understands what it remembers. Within its memory there lives the Hebrew and Gentile, prophecy and philosophy, the martyrdom of Jeremiah and of Socrates, the loyalty of a chosen people and the light of learning. All this now becomes a unity interpreted through revelation. Not only Greek and Hebrew, but through the trust elicited and illumination given in revelation, the entire history of humankind now takes on an intelligibility for the church which before had seemed alien, inconsequential, and incoherent: "the whole past is potentially a single epic." [17]

Not only do we understand what we remember; we remember what we had forgotten. We seek to repress our follies and transgressions deep in the unconscious, to forget all that seems trivial or will not fit. Nevertheless, this history is within us, "indestructible . . . written deep into our lives"; our forgetting is our refusal to acknowledge it as our own. Not only do we remember what we have forgotten, acknowledging it as our own, we appropriate the history of all people as our own. [18]

This is true as well of our present. Where we had not understood what we do as nations, as parents, as friends, we now begin to understand "what is going on" and how we can fit in. Using the revelatory image of Christ, we now see the deeds and sufferings, the tragedy, of contemporary life in "a total picture of significant action." Where before much had seemed confusion, viewing it from a framework in which our self was center, we see through the "parable" of Christ "evidence of a pattern in which, by great travail of men and God, a work of redemption goes on which is like the work of Christ." [19]

Not only is there pattern present in our past and present; what is implicit in the present becomes explicit in the future. Through revelation we "dis-

[16] MR pp. 109–110.
[17] MR pp. 110 & 112–113.
[18] MR pp. 113, 114, & 116.
[19] MR pp. 123–125.

cover what is implicit in our lives and will become explicit." What we discover implicit within us, which will become explicit, is our own death. Revelation illumines that fact and shows us another possibility, though not implicit in us, but in the Lord of life and death: "the possibility of the resurrection of a new and other self, of a new community, a reborn remnant."[20]

Through revelation in inner history we come to trust the world sufficiently to look at what the revelatory image illumines. What to our solipsistic minds had seemed alien and illusory—meaningless—we now discover to be a world we inhabit with all of mankind, and thus a shared world. And through revelation we come to see a pattern of meaning inherent in our own history, which is present in the entire world as the foundation of its unity. Recognizing the one common world we in fact are dwelling within, we begin to recover self-integrity. To remember, understand, appropriate this past, is to move towards integrity, for "Our past is what we are," and now the parts are beginning to fit into a coherent whole.

> To remember all that is in our past and so in our present is to achieve unity of self. To remember the human past as our own past is to achieve community with mankind. Such conversion of the memory is an important, indispensable part of the soul's conversion. Without the integration of the personal and social past there can be no present integrity of the self nor anything like brotherhood.[21]

And so it is with our present and future, as we embrace all that is within our present context and all that will emerge in the future in the light of the revelatory image, the parts of the world and of the self are being integrated into a whole.

The reason this pattern integrates world and self is because it is a divine pattern, a pattern in which self and God interact—"a pattern . . . [of the] great travail of men and God."[22] The world and self are one, or are becoming one, because the pattern revealed throughout history is that of the divine initiative: God meets the self in every event. Through revelation we can see and respond to God active in every event. To do so is to find no part of self or world alien or meaningless, but ingredient in a whole, filled with God. God meets us in every event, natural as well as social, as "the reality and power of the world . . . , the life-giving and death-dealing power," demanding "our integrity."[23]

---

[20] MR pp. 130 & 131.
[21] MR p. 117.
[22] MR p. 125.
[23] MR pp. 184–185 & 186–187.

We recover a shared world through inner history because in this realm of commitment we can acknowledge organic relations with other selves, in which we participate in order to be a self-in-act, and can know ourselves to be committed to some God or center of value, that can unify self and community, but most fundamentally because we encounter there revelation illumining through an image an inherent pattern of meaning, which is the presence of the divine self-in-act, interacting with human selves-in-act, through which both self and world are being integrated.

Recovering a Real World:
Animal faith the Ground of Knowing

While the objective conditionedness of relativism belongs to external history, relativism does make inroads into internal history insofar as inner historical knowing is always from a limited point of view. Is it possible, then, to know that the universal pattern of meaning and the divine self-disclosure are real? While relativism rises as a threat, Niebuhr greets it as an opportunity. We can know the real, but only through a particular standpoint. The limited perspective, so far from preventing true knowing, is what makes it possible.* While it is true our concepts are not universal, what we know through our historically conditioned language is universal. We grasp the real through, and only through, the particular; but it is the universal, and not merely the particular, we grasp.[24]

The idea of humans' natural equality is a case in point. While the idea arose in the eighteenth century, its truth is not restricted to that century. The fact we must reacquire the standpoint of the early democrats in order to see its truth does not make it untrue for us. To occupy a standpoint not only brings us into touch with limitations, but with reality. Even though human equality is not visible from certain other perspectives, such as the ancient Greek's or the modern racist's, nevertheless, "what we see from the democratic point of view is really there, even though all men do not see it and even though our way of expressing it is not a universal way."[25]

There are three criteria of verification that function within common social history: social corroboration, consistency, and fruitfulness. These must operate in close touch with individual experience. When we interpret the world, from our limited perspective, we engage in an ongoing dialectic between reason and experience: "we move back and forth from reason to experience and from experience back to reason. And in that dialectic of the mind our concepts are enriched, clarified and corrected no less than our experience is illuminated and directed."[26]

[24] MR pp. 18–19.
[25] MR p. 19.
[26] MR p. 136; see pp. 20–21 & 141.

Even though historical reason is in constant touch with experience, and is measured against the three criteria of verification, what is to keep the entire community from being deluded, from constructing an illusory world corroborated by companions, consistent and fruitful only from the communal perspective? Niebuhr's answer is that we are in touch with reality in an act of faith which provides fundamental assurance of the objectivity and intelligibility of reality.

> The acceptance of the reality of what we see in psychological and historically conditioned experience is always something of an act of faith. . . . A critical idealism is always accompanied, openly or disguisedly, by a critical realism which accepts on faith the independent reality of what is mediated through sense, though it discriminates between uninterpreted and unintelligible impressions and verifiable, constant, intelligible content.

In the depths of our relation to our everyday living lies a belief in the reality of the external world. Employing Santayana's phrase, Niebuhr calls this "animal faith":

> The relation is something like that of animal faith in the existence of an external world and the data of experience. . . . we believe in the reality of the trees we see, the ground we walk upon, the tables, chairs and houses we touch and use, the food and drink we taste. We count upon enduring realities and are not usually put to shame. No matter how refined our scepticism grows, how far into infinity we pursue the constituent elements of our objects, how ethereal to the mind's eye the natural world becomes, we rely upon the enduring stuff of our environment and we continue to be nourished and to be borne up. . . . if we were true sceptics we would be errant fools to eat food made up of sense-data only, to breathe an unsubstantial air with unreal lungs, to walk with unreal feet upon a nonexistent earth toward imaginary goals.[27]

In the unconscious dimension of our living from day to day, in what Polanyi would call the "tacit dimension" and Merleau-Ponty the "body," we can become aware of commitment to the objectivity of the world, a "rely[ing] upon the enduring stuff of our environment." This trusting is "an unconquerable compulsion, given with life itself." Apart from this primordial relation of bodily or tacit reliance upon the world we would not exist: "Without this animal faith in a dependable external world we literally would not live as

[27] MR pp. 19–20 & 79.

bodies." It may be "prior to all experience" but it is activated *in* experience
of the world, for "concrete faith in any particular element in our world as
dependable does not exist save as it is made possible by sense-experience."[28]

Concomitant with this unconscious faith in the objectivity of the word is
trust in its intelligibility. This is especially evident in natural science "which
cannot abandon its faith in the intelligibility and unity of nature without
destroying itself." The postcritical perspective underlying the heuristic
metaphor of history is most fully evident here. In making faith the ground for
knowing, Niebuhr is founding truth upon an "acritical" basis: all knowing is
dependent upon "convictions which are not subject to criticism, since they
are the bases of all possible criticism."[29] Unconscious commitment within
our somatic existence to a real world provides the ground for our assurance
that what we know consciously is really there.

While this animal faith in the objectivity and intelligibility of the world
underlies all that we know both within external and internal history, it does
not provide assurance of the reality of God experienced in revelation. What
makes us sure that what we know of God is real is the nature of the
experience itself. The divine self-disclosure so "incontestably touches and
seizes us that we wholly yield ourselves to him" and "forces us to trust him
wholly."[30] In this experience of God our lives are so altered by the trust
elicited and the illumination shed that we do not doubt the presence of the
divine reality. In distinguishing inner from outer history Niebuhr has developed an answer to history through history.

Critical Ingredients in the Heuristic Metaphor of History

Nevertheless, Niebuhr is not entirely satisfied with the heuristic metaphor of history. At the beginning of his discussion of the relations between
inner and outer history, he says this "two-aspect theory of history, like the
two-aspect theory of body and mind . . . does not solve the problem of unity
in duality and duality in unity," and thus resigns himself to acknowledging
this duality as essential to Christianity. He recognizes that this is part of the
critical legacy of Kant, now historicized. Like external history, theoretical
reason is concerned "to abstract from all that is merely secondary, from
subjective and partisan accounts of what happened," and seeks "to set forth
the primary characteristics of each event." Like inner history, practical
reason is concerned with "'tertiary qualities,' with values."[31]

By historicizing Kant, Niebuhr has moved towards overcoming the basic
critical opposition between objective knowledge and personal belief, and

[28] MR pp. 79–80.
[29] MR p. 140.
[30] MR p. 152.
[31] MR pp. 65–66 & 81–83.

thus towards a postcritical world. No knowledge is completely objective and certain; commitment is necessary even in external history as we rely on the credibility of eye-witnesses and documents, and on the communal point of view we occupy, and as we find ourselves believing through animal faith in the objectivity and intelligibility of the world.

Historical reason, both outer and inner, is contextual rather than pure. Operating always in relation to imagination, it interprets experience and language through sensitivity to the context of meaning, which it in part supplies. The spectator of external history, while defined as detached, is in fact a participant. Values operate in external history even though they are "valency," the quantitatively measurable effect an event or factor has upon another event or factor, rather than having qualitative worth for selves. While historicizing theoretical reason qualifies its objectivism, historicizing practical reason avoids subjectivism. Though practical reason is concerned with values rather than the objective characteristics of events, these values are, nevertheless, "not private and evanescent" but "common and verifiable" socially.[32] In exploring the nature of commitment essential to being a self-in-act, and most especially in affirming an acritical foundation for all knowing, external as well as internal, he affirms that all knowing is dependent upon convictions which are not subject to criticism because they are the basis of all criticism.

No matter how much he has modified his critical terms, however, he still ends in dualism:

> It is enough to point out that the distinctions which appear in all critical philosophy as between knowledge of the external world and knowledge of the internal, which drive even the most dogmatic positivists to assert that ethics and religion belong to some other realm than that with which objective knowledge is concerned, must also be made in our understanding of history. There is a descriptive and there is a normative knowledge of history and neither type is reducible to the terms of the other.

Using critical terms to achieve a postcritical perspective retains dualism and issues in multiple inconsistencies evident in his handling of the metaphor of history. For example, the known for scientific knowing (outer history) is an inert thing; nevertheless, he speaks of the way scientists actually relate to it as valuable and revelatory of novel aspects, making discovery possible.[33]

A second inconsistency: the interpretative image of revelation discloses a pattern of meaning inherent in the world; yet Niebuhr also speaks at times as

[32] MR p. 66.
[33] MR pp. 66–67; see p. 173.

if interpretative images bestow order on what would otherwise be chaos.[34]
This typically Kantian view of image imposing form on formless sensation
exists in unresolvable tension with image expressing a pattern of meaning
inherent in our living. In the first case, an image is an abstraction; in the
second, a form of life. With the abstracted image, there is no way of
confirming its bearing on reality; fabrications of our minds alone, the real and
shared world dissolve, dropping us into the void of scepticism and solipsism.
With image as life form, however, we know that it bears on reality since it is
an expression emerging from our unconscious participation in the actuality of
living—though we have no explicit and independent access to this lived
reality by which to adjudicate it apart from this and other expressions.

In light of this second inconsistency, what is the relation between animal
faith and the faith elicited in revelation? Does the revelatory image impose
intelligibility upon the world or bring the intelligibility of the world and
animal faith in it to expression? Niebuhr embraces the irreducibility of
normative and descriptive knowledge; yet if there is prelingual pattern in our
world, is not description normative? To make articulate such a pattern is to
affect our norms and selves; to understand what is given is persuasive,
especially if we are already tacitly committed to it by relying on it. If there is
no pattern but only formlessness, description is not normative; norms and
self are not affected by describing what we ourselves have already imposed
upon a formless given. The methodological implication of the latter is to
think about abstract ideas. This stands in tension, however, with Niebuhr's
phenomenological description of "what is going on"[35] in the metaphor of
history and much more importantly later in the ethics of responsibility.

Through exploration of the heuristic metaphor of history Niebuhr has
sought to resolve the problem of modernity. Remaining dissatisfied with the
capacity of the two-aspect theory to provide adequately for the recovery of
self-integrity, Niebuhr nevertheless felt satisfied enough with his answer to
the epistemological dimension of the problem of modernity not to raise it
again as a problem to be solved. In the acritical foundation of faith he has
located an adequate basis for knowing, answering historical relativism with
historical commitment. Even though he has not worked out fully the relation
of commitment to knowing, he turns to exploring further the nature of
commitment, working towards recovery of self-integrity within a shared and
admittedly real world.

Commitment in History and Beyond

While he no longer speaks of history as inner and outer after THE
MEANING OF REVELATION, he continues to explore commitment in

---

[34] MR pp. 96–97.
[35] MR p. 123.

history. In his next book, CHRIST AND CULTURE, while historical relativism is briefly discussed, he turns to the act of decision, rather than knowing, as a way to recover a shared world. What some had taken as the mark of the lone individual, Niebuhr sees as the sign of a shared world: self-examination and decision-making go on within dialogue with, and therefore commitment to, companions. Nature, relegated previously to the inert reality of external history, is now drawn by way of trinitarian thought into the sharedness of the social world. External nature is no longer a sphere alien to selves in act; it, along with culture, is the realm of God and God in Christ's creative and revelatory presence in the Now, working towards transformation of all things.[36]

Later in RADICAL MONOTHEISM, however, he goes beyond history as the explicit context within which to do theology. This change does not mean the rejection of history, for it continues of major importance both in RADICAL MONOTHEISM and THE RESPONSIBLE SELF. Instead Niebuhr's investigation of commitment leads him to search for a method and context peculiarly fitting to theology and distinguishable from a historical method.[37]

The Heuristic Metaphor of Value

Interwoven with his use of the historical metaphor, yet important later as well, the heuristic metaphor of value becomes a means for Niebuhr to deepen his analysis of commitment, extending his search for a shared world, in response to the critical problems of modernity. Criticizing the fact/value, object/subject dichotomies, based on the Kantian distinction between theoretical and practical reason, he seeks to make a postcritical affirmation of the inseparability of value and being. By shifting the correlative term with value from "fact" to "being," from the explicit and verifiable to the more ambiguous, dynamic, and experiential aspect of reality—we prove facts but relate to beings—he uncovers the relational dimension of our living, within which he will be able to locate commitments that underlie, and therefore belie, these dichotomies. As we will see, this shift still retains some critical elements. Niebuhr's dissatisfaction with the value metaphor is implicit in his turning later to other metaphors and becomes explicit in THE RESPONSIBLE SELF when he speaks of fact and value, dealt with in the context of being, as nevertheless dissolving the unity of the self.[38]

In a major though brief exploration of the metaphor of value, Niebuhr presents modern thought as caught within the extreme disjunction between

---

[36] On relativism see CC pp. 234–236 & 239; on decision pp. 244–245; on nature pp. 192 & 195; and on trinity pp. 80ff, 108, 114, 131, 188, & 192ff.

[37] RMWC p. 15.

[38] See RS pp. 82–83.

value and being, believing itself forced to choose in its conception of the good between value as a subjective phenomenon of desire and feeling or as an objective fact, an object independent of existence, such as an idea or spiritual entity. Subjectivism "results in the irrationality of separating value judgments from fact judgments," whereas objectivism succumbs to "prejudice . . . for the goodness of the spiritual as opposed to the material, and for the goodness of the nonexistent as opposed to the existent."[39] The outcome in either case is the fragmenting of our lives: by accepting one side of the dichotomy and rejecting the other, an aspect of our existence is denied.

Niebuhr seeks a way beyond this disjunction by deepening his exploration of the nature of commitment. Looking beneath what the subjectivist and the objectivist value theorists say about the good, he employs what in reality is phenomenological description of their actual handling of concrete ethical problems. Beneath their theories he discovers both have an implicit "relational theory of value" that affirms, however covertly, the interrelation of value and being.[40]

Thus objectivists, such as Nikolai Hartmann and G. E. Moore, after defining the meaning of value abstractly, when they turn to concrete ethical questions use value, respectively, as "good for free man" and good for "a being with consciousness and sociality." Similarly, subjectivists, such as David Hume and A. J. Ayer, after defining value as feeling, approach concrete particular ethical problems in terms of what is "useful to society" and "good for man."[41] To describe what value theorists actually do with concrete cases is to discover unacknowledged commitments to a relational value theory in general and to specific goods depended upon for ethical judgments.

Niebuhr's phenomenological approach undercuts other expressions of the Kantian dichotomy as well. Often "ought" and "is" are taken as manifestations of subjective value and objective fact. For Niebuhr, however, an "ought" always occurs in the midst of relations between beings. It is never definable "in the abstract but only by reference to the nature and the relations of beings in interaction." "Ought" emerges within what is because that "is" is always a situation of a self necessarily committed within complex relations to other beings. This is true, for example, of the "oughtness" of truth; as something we owe to each other, the truth occurs within commitments between selves in communication.[42]

This has implications as well, although not drawn out by Niebuhr, for the descriptive/normative opposition. As there are commitments underlying

[39] Niebuhr, "The Center of Value," pp. 106–107.

[40] Ibid., p. 100.

[41] Ibid., pp. 100–102. Since Ayer rejects all values as nothing but emotional outbursts, it is the scientific method he values as "good for man."

[42] Ibid., pp. 108–109.

facts and what is, so there are commitments present in description both as subject matter described and as act of describing. To describe selves in their "isness" is to portray commitments because to exist as a self is to exist in relations of commitments to various beings. But all commitments are normative inasmuch as they recommend themselves as worthy of holding. One may need to distinguish between describing and advocating commitments, but this distinction should not deny the normative quality of all commitments as such. The act of describing also involves commitments. A factual descriptive judgment is always selective in what it attends to, what it finds significant.[43] In fact, only those things which are significant enough to be noticed and important as verifiable are called facts. In more general ways the describer relies upon commitments: in the form of animal faith they provide a natural environment for our being and they underlie our acquiring and maintaining a language and a body of knowledge and skills we use in describing.

Relational Value: The Realm of Tacit Commitments

Niebuhr's view of commitment is evident in his definition of the nature of value. His relational value theory's "fundamental observation is this: that value is present wherever one existent being with capacities and potentialities confronts another existence that limits or completes or complements it." Value is not a mode, nor a function, of being in isolation; it is a function of being in relation. Not that it *is* a relation; rather it occurs *in* relation. It appears wherever beings with capacities and potentialities confront one another either in reciprocity or in becoming. Insofar as it does not exist in itself, it cannot be intuited by itself nor defined by itself. Value is the "*good-for-ness* of being for being."[44]

Value is present in the relations between being and being in two ways: in their reciprocity and in their becoming. In their reciprocity, good and evil are present as the "fittingness or the unfittingness of being to being." In their becoming, good and evil are present in achieving or not achieving "their own internal possibilities of becoming good for others, or of supplying to others in the community of being what they 'owe' them." Within such becoming, Niebuhr distinguishes two kinds of values within the commitments between beings: the realizing of potential and the state of realization. One being is good for another in assisting it in realizing its potential; and a being is good for other beings just as the being it is, to the degree it is realized as a being.[45]

This distinction within becoming is traditionally, but misleadingly, called

---

[43] Ibid., p. 107.
[44] Ibid., pp. 103 & 107; his italics.
[45] Ibid., pp. 103–104.

the difference between "means" and "ends," between instrumental and intrinsic goods—misleading because within a relational context "every good is an end and every good a means."[46] That which contributes to one's own self-realization, traditionally called the instrumental or complementary good, may be sought for itself, the achieving of which only consequently contributes to one's self-realization. In fact the self is often realized precisely in the achievement of ends other than those focused on itself. Truth about nature and history, for instance, is sought as an end in itself but contributes, nevertheless, to the realization of the self. When the excellences of the self are attended to within a relational context, they are seen to be good primarily for others and only secondarily for the self exhibiting them. The self then does not become by focusing on its own becoming; and what it has become is of primary value to others.

This refusal to sort out means from ends in a clear and final way suggests that, as selves, we inhabit a world through multiple commitments, most of which are not explicit. Beneath the level of consciousness, beneath a "conscious finalism"[47] which rationally orders our priorities, we are committed to many beings in many ways. As Niebuhr asserts in KINGDOM OF GOD, the "will is always committed to something. . . . Life never begins in a vacuum of freedom, but awakes to its tacit commitments."[48] Beneath the level of explicit consciousness there is a complex pattern of meaning in which the self relates to the goods in these relations sometimes as means, sometimes as ends, sometimes as both simultaneously.

Value for Niebuhr, therefore, falls neither into the objectivist nor subjectivist categories of critical thought. It is not "objective" in the sense of being a reality independent of such interrelations, nor is it "subjective" in the sense of being dependent on desire or feeling. It is relational: the self lives in tacit commitment to many beings—it inhabits a world. Inasmuch as the beings to which the self is committed are similarly existing in commitment to the self and other beings, the self through its commitments lives within a shared world.

History and Value in Comparison

In developing this relational theory of value, as in working with the theme of history, Niebuhr affirms the existence of patterns of meaning inherent in living. When revelation illumines the pattern of meaning in past, present, and future, it discloses our commitments to a multiplicity of beings, that is, our value relations. It also discloses the presence of divine action encountering us in every event, uniting all events into one world. In value

46 Ibid., p. 105.
47 Ibid., p. 104.
48 KGA p. 103.

the equivalent way of speaking of this divine cohering of the world is in terms of the One as center of value. Monotheistic faith begins with "the transcendent One for whom alone there is an ultimate good and for whom, as the source and end of all things, whatever is, is good."[49] Whatever is, is good because the One, source of all value and being, is the center of value who values all that exists. Or, in the language of history, it is good because the divine self, creator and redeemer, is active in all that happens.

In "Value Theory and Theology" Niebuhr calls this similarity between revelation in history and intrinsic worth in value a "remote analogy": "there is at least a remote analogy to the unique fact of revelation in the 'giveness' of all beings having intrinsic value." God is present in this pattern of meaning inherent in our living in the world either as act in or valuing of every creaturely reality. Inasmuch as we are tacitly committed to this pattern in our living, even if not in our reflecting, we are tacitly committed in some way to God. Continuing the passage above, Niebuhr says:

> the content of revelation is not the self-disclosure of an unknown being, but the unveiling of the value of a known being. What is revealed in revelation is not a being as such, but rather its deity-value, not that it is, but that it "loves us," "judges us," that it makes life worth living.[50]

We are already committed, negatively or positively, to this "known being"—to what he elsewhere says many call "fate" or "chance."[51] Throughout our tacit commitments to manifold beings we are tacitly committed to this fate or chance as it bears upon these commitments. To recognize the One to be our center of value or the divine self to be active in all occasions is to become aware of the "deity-value" of that known being, of the meaning of the inherent pattern. Both value theory and historical theology affirm the presence of a pattern of meaning inherent in our living together in the world in which the divine is present.

Through exploration of the nature of commitment Niebuhr has shown us to be participating tacitly and sometimes explicitly in an entire world of beings: a world that is one because God values all of it, and shared because we are tacitly committed to multiple beings who are committed to us and to other beings. By grounding our ethical living in an acritical foundation he is reaching beyond the fact/value, object/subject dichotomies, and their bifurcations of self and world, toward a unified self within a postcritical world.

---

[49] Niebuhr, "The Center of Value," p. 112.

[50] H. Richard Niebuhr, "Value Theory and Theology," in THE NATURE OF RELIGIOUS EXPERIENCE: ESSAYS IN HONOR OF DOUGLAS CLYDE MACINTOSH, ed. by J. S. Bixler, R. L. Calhoun, H. R. Niebuhr (New York: Harper & Brothers, 1937), p. 116.

[51] See CC p. 254.

Residual Kantianism in the Metaphor of Value

While this exploration of commitment as value relations has gone far towards resolving the modern problem, there are obstacles within it of which Niebuhr is not wholly aware. While it is Niebuhr's intention to make value relations internal to the beings who exist in them, there is a degree of externality in speaking of being *and* value. The fact that their inseparability has to be argued suggests the problem. The externality comes from the abstractness inherent in discourse about value. Rather than speaking of selves committed, he is speaking of beings valuing. Speaking of a self committed, it is easier to show that commitment is an act of the whole self than to show that a being, existing in multiple value relations to other beings, is present fully in each of its relations. While Niebuhr intends for these relations to be dynamic, the valuation metaphor does not allow, as the historical does, for speaking of the dynamic aspects of a self. Within the language of history we can talk of act, event, and decision, and of the transition the self undergoes through revelation in moving to the One as center of value.[52]

The problem of knowing within this valuation context involves externality as well. Niebuhr speaks in "The Center of Value" of being and value as if they involve three types of knowing: knowledge of beings themselves; of the values within which they exist; and of how those values are good-for-me.

> There is no rational knowledge of value without rational
> empirical knowledge of the beings for which others and states
> of itself are valuable; but the rational knowledge of value is

---

[52] See the illuminating analysis of the relation of value theory and existentialism in Niebuhr by Hans Frei, "The Theology of H. Richard Niebuhr," in FAITH AND ETHICS: THE THEOLOGY OF H. RICHARD NIEBUHR, ed. by Paul Ramsey, Harper Torchbooks (New York: Harper & Row, 1965), pp. 78–81, in which he speaks of the abstractness of Niebuhr's value relations in comparison to the concreteness of his selves-in-act. He sees, moreover, a shift from valuation theology to existentialism which he believes is evident in moving from THE MEANING OF REVELATION to CHRIST AND CULTURE (see ibid., p. 78, n. 29–31). The publication of a major statement on value, "The Center of Value," comes, however, after both of these, so that he has not yet left value theory behind. There is a movement in Niebuhr's thought, I would agree, toward an understanding of the self in its concreteness, but it is not evident between these two books; the contrast should be drawn, rather, between his first two books and these two, and then between these and his last two books, which were unavailable at the time of Frei's writing. While the historical metaphor is more concrete than the valuational, they are developed at the same time, with value being worked on, in fact, later than history. It would be more accurate, I believe, to see history and value as used simultaneously to move towards concreteness, having eventful or relational virtues the other lacks, both of which are taken up into and transmuted, resulting in greater concreteness, in the metaphor of faith in RADICAL MONOTHEISM and once again in the metaphor of responsibility in THE RESPONSIBLE SELF. If one sees the underlying problem of modernity as attacked in both history and value, moreover, it is easier to understand the relation between them and why Niebuhr is developing them concomitantly.

inadequate to move a being toward its own goods. Beliefs about the good-for-me may be true; they do not become effective until the good-for-me becomes the object of desire.

While his point is to affirm that knowledge of value always occurs with knowledge of beings, it sounds as if one might have the latter apart from any knowledge of value, a conclusion which runs contrary to his affirmation that commitment underlies all knowing and that all knowing is valuational. To distinguish the "true" from the "effective," the "known" from the "desirable," is to suggest, contrary to his basic intentions, that the true is not effective and the known is not desirable. This dichotomy easily leads Niebuhr into the Kantian separation between knowledge and desire:

> The "blooming and buzzing confusion" of sensation unorganized by rational pattern is no greater than the vagueness, confusion, and indeterminacy of desire reaching out for it knows not what. A version of the Kantian observation seems applicable in connection with the knowledge of value: "Desire without reason is blind; reason without desire is impotent."[53]

But is desire blind? Does it, apart from reason, reach out for it knows not what? Central to value theory for Niebuhr, as we have seen, are tacit commitments that one being has in relation to other beings. While not rational, that is explicit, they are not confused. They may be relatively indeterminate but they do "know," even though we may not know explicitly what they are committed to, what they are reaching out for.

Finally, to distinguish between a knowledge of what is valuable and of what is valuable for me—between "the rational knowledge of value" and the knowledge of "the good-for-me"—is to distinguish objective from valuational knowing. But Niebuhr has rejected any objective knowing of values; they are known not by spectators but by participants. As I participate in knowing values, are they not, in some way, values for me, inasmuch as they are attractive, recommending themselves to me as held by another? There is a difference between simply being committed to these values in knowing them and embracing them so they become central for our own living. The difference is, however, in the degree of commitment and its place within the sphere of other commitments, not between what is "true" and what is "effective." Every truth is to some degree effective inasmuch as it is held by someone who, in his or her holding of it, recommends it.

Conclusion

Through the heuristic metaphors of history and value Niebuhr has sought a postcritical resolution for the critical problems of modernity that

---

[53] Niebuhr, "The Center of Value," p. 108.

assail us—scepticism and solipsism on the one hand, and dichotomizing of self and world (in terms of fact/value, object/subject, descriptive/normative, is/ought, reason/desire), on the other. Within history Niebuhr has established knowing upon a fiduciary foundation, answering the problem of scepticism to his satisfaction, and has explored a common world in the midst of historical conditioning as a realm of acritical commitment to reality, community, revelation and inherent pattern of meaning. He remains dissatisfied, however, with the fragmenting character of the critical categories underlying his inner/outer history distinction. Taking up value simultaneously, he finds beneath modernity's critical dichotomies a fiduciary foundation of a shared world as a realm of tacit commitment underlying the actual doing of ethicists as they confront real ethical problems.

There are, nevertheless, critical ingredients in this emerging postcritical perspective. While there is a sense of the linguistic nature of the problems and the need for linguistic solutions—explicitly in history as we have seen earlier in our discussion of religious meaning, and implicitly in value, as he focuses on the acritical foundation and pattern of value relations, organized by a center of value, which later he will see as that which is becoming articulate in religious language—neither has become sufficiently conscious of language to deal adequately with these problems. Sensing these inadequacies Niebuhr turns to two further heuristic metaphors: faith and feeling.

CHAPTER FIVE
HEURISTIC METAPHORS: FAITH AND FEELING

Through the heuristic metaphors of faith and feeling Niebuhr carries further his theological quest for integrity. Each metaphor is intertwined with history and value but receives major attention later—faith extensively in the 1950's culminating in RADICAL MONOTHEISM and "On the Nature of Faith" of 1960, and feeling succinctly but significantly in the early 1960's culminating in "Toward a Recovery of Feeling," Lecture III of "Next Steps in Theology," and his final seminar, "The Religious Emotions." Through these further metaphors Niebuhr continues to wrestle with the deep foundations of our critical age by deepening his postcritical understanding of the fiduciary foundation of our being in the world.

As he does so he begins to glimpse the linguistic center of a postcritical perspective in the emergent relation between acritical background and explicit articulation, and the necessity for religion to show this in personal language. Our search in these metaphors for the fit habitation of integrity, a real and shared world, will take us further, consequently, into consideration of the language-using self as it indwells this context as well as into the context it inhabits, and thus moves us closer to dealing with the self as it enacts the linguistic life form of responsibility.

The Heuristic Metaphor of Faith

Recognizing the heart of the modern problem to lie in the nature of commitment, he focuses more directly on the fiduciary foundation of our being by bringing his extensive work with faith to culminating expression in 1960.[1] While going beyond history and value, he nevertheless carries with him the concerns of each as he brings together something of these two modes of discourse in the heuristic metaphor of faith. Within faith he intends to

---

[1] Complementing Niebuhr's published work there is among his unpublished papers considerable reflection on the nature of faith. During the 1950's he wrote the lengthy book manuscript "Faith on Earth." For discussion of it see James W. Fowler, TO SEE THE KINGDOM: THE THEOLOGICAL VISION OF H. RICHARD NIEBUHR (Nashville: Abingdon Press, 1974), pp. 201–147 & 283.

combine the dynamism of history with the relational character of value, as suggested in his speaking of faith as both "attitude and action."[2] The result of combining these two metaphor-engendered languages in a third is to transcend them by bringing to expression more of the self in the personal concreteness of its integrated being. Through faith the self is being integrated: "radically monotheistic faith," as Niebuhr calls it, is faith in the One—who is both the divine self of historical revelation and the principle of being and value of value theory—in relation to whom the self becomes one. Integration through faith in the One opens upon the necessity of using personal language that gives symbolic expression to our sense of being in the world.

Five Types of Faith

Faith, interwoven, like history and value, throughout his religious reflections, emerges into central importance in RADICAL MONOTHEISM. Both the problem of contemporary culture and the task of the theologian are now defined in terms of faith.[3] Modernity practices belief in finite gods, in no god, and in a supernatural god—all of which threaten belief in a shared world. Finite gods or value centers, such as family, capitalism, or the American Way of Life, exist in conflict, either as "henotheism," between a chief god and many others of lesser value, or "polytheism," between a multiplicity of gods (or goods) none of which are dominant. Both types of faith shatter the unity and commonality of the world, either by establishing a circumscribed hegemony to be defended against alien gods, as in henotheism, or by engaging in a war of all against all, as in polytheism.

A third type of faith, atheism, denies the very presence of faith in a center of value. In the actual living of our lives, we are, nevertheless, whether we recognize it or not, persons of faith. While there are atheists in the sense of persons who deny the existence of a supernatural god, there are no atheists in the sense of selves who live without faith in some god or center of value. To be a self, as we have already seen, is not only to trust with animal faith in the reality of the world but is to value some good or goods that make life worth living—without which we could not exist. Atheism in Niebuhr's thinking is like scepticism and solipsism, the result of critical doubt dissolving the acritical foundations of life, and is to be rejected because life in actuality is grounded in commitment.[4]

Attaining in RADICAL MONOTHEISM an explicitness and developing a sustained critique not before realized, Niebuhr attacks not only atheism and the theisms of the finite god(s); he seeks to counteract supernaturalism as

[2] See RMWC p. 16.
[3] RMWC p. 11.
[4] RMWC pp. 24–25.

well—and for the same reason, that it is an expression of the problem of modernity. Supernaturalism, a fourth type, is the belief in a divine being who is separate from, though occasionally intervening in, the world. This is the being to whom one prays to defend oneself from some aspect of being and before whom one tries to prove one's own worth.[5]

Faith in such a supernatural being issues in the denial of a shared world, for this god is always set apart from the totality of being and defined in terms of relations to only part of the self's being, such as its spirituality or morality. Often this supernatural entity is defined as "person" but is understood to relate to only that part of the self which is valued. Perhaps this is why Niebuhr moves away from using the term "Self" for God, as in THE MEANING OF REVELATION, to the predominant, though not exclusive, use of "One" in RADICAL MONOTHEISM. God is still spoken of as personal but now as a modification of One, qualified by "person-like." As a fifth type, radically monotheistic faith is in

> the One—the principle of being which is also the princi-
> ple of value. . . . It is not a relation to any finite, natural or
> supernatural, value-center that confers value on self and some
> of its companions in being, but it is value relation to the One to
> whom all being is related.

A supernatural self is not God; Being is:

> When the confidence is so put into words the resultant
> assertion is not that there is a God but that Being is God, or,
> better, that the principle of being, the source of all things and
> the power by which they exist, is good, as good for them and
> good to them. It is relied upon to give and conserve worth to
> all that issues from it. What otherwise, in distrust and suspi-
> cion, is regarded as fate or destiny or blind will or chance is
> now trusted. It is God.[6]

The divine self of supernaturalism denies this equation of divinity with Being. God is not, however, other than fate, destiny, blind will, or chance; divinity is this reality, but seen in a different light—seen in radically mono-theistic faith.

By equating Being with God Niebuhr does not mean to deny to God his essential transcendence. God is not to be equated with any finite entity or their sum, just as fate and chance are not to be so equated. To insist on this transcendence, he indicates in a footnote that he uses "principle of being and

[5] RMWC pp. 29 & 53.
[6] RMWC pp. 32 & 38; see p. 47.

value" as synonym for the One in order to suggest that God is beyond both being and value.[7] While his rejection here of Being, when he embraced it earlier, may seem contradictory, it is not; he is distinguishing what we have been calling the pattern of divine meaning from the mere sum of beings. God is Being as the pattern of divine meaning active in all events in the world, but not as a particular being, not even the highest, nor as the sum of beings.

It is perhaps for these reasons that Sydney Ahlstrom ruminates that RADICAL MONOTHEISM "is more radical than is often supposed,"[8] and later goes on to declare:

> From beyond the grave Dietrich Bonhoeffer's demand for a "secular interpretation" of biblical language was answered by a deluge of serious efforts to meet the needs of a "world come of age." In America it was H. Richard Niebuhr who, at the age of sixty-six, delivered the crucial inaugural address to the sixties with his great essay RADICAL MONOTHEISM (1960).[9]

It is with some justice, and indeed characteristic insight, that Ahlstrom sees in RADICAL MONOTHEISM the inauguration of the "secular" theologies of the sixties. What has been a constant theme from his conversion at the end of 1929 comes to full flower here in 1960.[10] Niebuhr is attempting to articulate his conviction that God is in the *saeculum*, in the world, and not apart from it, while at the same time affirming divine transcendence as "the Mystery behind the mystery of human existence." Niebuhr will have no truck with "the prevalence of self-pity among some modern men because 'God is dead,'"[11] inasmuch as his god is neither the finite god of capitalism or some other cultural sphere, which has proven destructive, nor a supernatural being outside the world, which has proven illusory, but the One, principle of being and value.

---

[7] RMWC p. 33, n. 7.

[8] Sydney E. Ahlstrom, ed., THEOLOGY IN AMERICA: THE MAJOR PROTESTANT VOICES FROM PURITANISM TO NEO-ORTHODOXY (New York: The Bobbs-Merrill Company, 1967), p. 589.

[9] Sydney E. Ahlstrom, A RELIGIOUS HISTORY OF THE AMERICAN PEOPLE (New Haven: Yale University Press, 1972), p. 1082.

[10] From "Moral Relativism and the Christian Ethic" on, Niebuhr has spoken of God as the "pattern of existence" and the "pattern of ultimate goodness" (Niebuhr, "Moral Relativism and the Christian Ethic," p. 10), the "structure in things" and "the structure of the universe" (H. Richard Niebuhr, "A Communication: The only Way into the Kingdom of God" [THE CHRISTIAN CENTURY READER, ed. by Harold E. Fey and Margaret Frakes (New York: Association Press, 1962), originally published in *Christian Century*, XLIX (April 6, 1932)], p. 229), "the reality and power of the world" (MR p. 186), and "that faithfulness [which] is the moral reason in all things" (CC p. 255).

[11] PCM p. 36 & RMWC p. 31.

The faiths of supernaturalism as well as finite theism (henotheism and polytheism) and atheism are manifestations of the modern problem, threatening the dissolution of a real and shared world—the first two by narrowing the sphere of God's concern to something less than the totality of being, and the third, atheism, by rejecting our way of being in touch with and inhabiting a world through commitment.

Faith and the Theological Task

Having now identified the problem of modernity as that of faith, the task of the theologian is appropriately redefined. Beginning necessarily from faith in God, since God and faith are inseparable, theology, first, reasons in faith: "reason permeates the activity of faith: it organizes, compares, reflects, criticizes, and develops hypotheses in the midst of believing"; it "intuits the intention of the divine artist in the wholeness of his masterpieces"; it raises questions about the nature of the self, the meaning of creation, and the destructive elements within it; and it doubts—it doubts the value of the self and beliefs about God.[12]

Theology, secondly, is to criticize faith to "illuminate and seek to bring order into the life of faith."[13] Niebuhr's interest is now directed more towards faith than faith's object, a shift consonant with his own understanding of his later years, which he saw as turning against the "theology of crisis, of the dominant movement of the 1930's," and "resuming contact with the earlier modes of theological thought."[14] While he is resuming contact with earlier theologians, most especially Schleiermacher, he continues to reject the nineteenth century's effort "to drop the objective side of theological inquiry in favor of a psychology of faith or a psychology of religion which considers only the subjective element."[15] In attending to faith he sees himself as merely shifting his focus within the fundamental correlation of God and faith.

Value within the Metaphor of Faith

Concerns present in value are continued within faith as Niebuhr defines faith in relation to value, but now distinguished in its twofold nature of trust and loyalty, confidence and fidelity, and related to the principle of value and beings as One. Faith now has both a passive and active side; it trusts "in that which gives value to the self" and it is loyal "to what the self values."[16] The

---

[12] RMWC p. 12; see pp. 13–14.
[13] RMWC p. 15.
[14] Niebuhr, "Reformation: Continuing Imperative," p. 71.
[15] RMWC p. 12.
[16] RMWC p. 16; see p. 17.

nationalist, for instance, relies on the nation as one's source of value. One trusts it as that which gives meaning to one's life. At the same time one is loyal to it as that which defines what is valuable and right, apart from the fact it bestows value upon oneself.

In contrast to the embodiment of faith as trust and loyalty in the polytheisms and henotheisms of our day, radically monotheistic faith is life lived in trust in and loyalty to the One, which is beyond, yet source and context of, the many. The One is principle both of being and value, indeed, "the principle of being is identified with the principle of value and the principle of value with the principle of being."[17] To separate them is to deny that all of being is valuable, is to locate only a certain limited sphere within being as having worth. In traditional language this is to separate creator from redeemer. To separate them is also to acknowledge the possibility of developing an ontology prior to theology, in order to establish the coherence of being before speaking of what value it has, to lay claim to knowledge of God apart from faith. Being for Niebuhr, however, not only lacks precedence over value in the order of knowing, but in the order of being as well.[18]

The One is both principle of being and of value, and not one before the other. Faith in the One is trust in the principle of its being and of all being as valuing it and all being, and is loyalty to the principle of being as its cause and to that principle's cause, the entire realm of being. The One bestows value and is the valuable cause; concomitantly the One has a cause, to which we are called to be loyal as well as to the One itself, the cause of the universal community of being—including the inorganic as well as non-human life, the ideal and the dead.[19]

Historical Revelation within the Metaphor of Faith

Concerns from history are also drawn into his exploration of faith, but in moving from one metaphor to the other, there is a shift in meaning of revelation. Where Niebuhr had earlier defined revelation rationally as sense-making, as making intelligible our personal and communal life, past, pre-

---

[17] RMWC p. 33; see pp. 24–32.

[18] RMWC p. 32. Niebuhr is probably clarifying his own view of the inseparability of being and value in both orders of knowing and being in the light of Hans Frei's comments in the *festschrift:* "Niebuhr said that being, structure of process takes precedence over value in the order of being, since value 'arises in the relations of being to being'" (Frei, "The Theology of H. Richard Niebuhr," p. 71; quotation of Niebuhr is from "The Center of Value," as first published in Anshen, ed., MORAL PRINCIPLES OF ACTION: MAN'S ETHICAL IMPERATIVE, p. 169). That value *arises* in the relations of being to being does not mean the precedence of being over value in the order of being insofar as value is present wherever beings with capacities and potentialities exist, for to exist is to be in value relations. Value and being arise together both in being and our knowing, as Niebuhr is here trying to make clear.

[19] See RMWC pp. 33 & 37.

sent, and future, now he defines it more existentially as evocative of trust and loyalty; revelation "elicits" faith in the One.[20]

Revelation within the metaphor of history does, of course, involve faith—"God reveals himself in that he forces us to trust him wholly"—and revelation within the metaphor of faith still does involve understanding— response to the disclosure of the One "is in part an affair of reasoning faith."[21] This is a subtle shift in emphasis. In faith Niebuhr no longer speaks of understanding the whole world through revelation but rather of trusting the One in every situation and thus discovering unfathomable mystery and one intention present throughout the world. The self is concomitantly less one who knows order and more one who trusts in and responds to divine mystery and intention.

This shift is evident in Niebuhr's delineation of "the three notes of faith" ingredient in the experience of revelation:

> that the valuing, saving power in the world is the principle
> of being itself; that the ultimate principle of being gives and
> maintains and re-establishes worth; that they have been called
> upon to make the cause of that God their cause.[22]

Put succinctly: God is being, being is God, and the recipient of revelation is challenged to choose God's cause as one's own.[23] The movement in the metaphor of faith is towards the concreteness of personal existence as it develops further the context of self-integrity. Revelation elicits our faith in being: through trust we are assured we live in a real world, and through loyalty to the realm of being we are assured we dwell in a shared world.

Integration and the Personlike Integrity of the One

The One that meets us in revelation confronts us with the unity of a self, a "personlike integrity." Under this impact we become confident in the unity and universality of a shared world we are called to take up as our cause, and we respond by becoming integrated ourselves.[24]

Integration is characterized, on the one hand, by reasoning in faith. Whereas depersonalized reason looks for recurrent patterns and laws in various events, "reasoning faith looks for the presence of one faithful person in the multiplicity of the events that happen to the self," one self-consistent

---

[20] MR pp. 109–110; see RMWC p. 42.
[21] MR p. 152 & RMWC p. 47.
[22] RMWC p. 43.
[23] See RMWC p. 43.
[24] RMWC p. 47.

intention in all that occurs, whether apparently good or evil from our point of view.[25]

While this is *reasoning* faith, it is primarily a matter of practical reasoning, for it calls for decision as to how to respond to action upon us. Where THE MEANING OF REVELATION mentions decision only as the way of shifting from outer to inner history, and CHRIST AND CULTURE offers extensive consideration of decision-making, specifically in relation to reasoning faith, Niebuhr speaks now of reasoning faith as discerning One intention and deciding how to respond to it in the given situation—out of loyalty either to the inclusive cause or to some partial object of loyalty.[26] Self-integration issues from reasoning in faith inasmuch as seeing One intention in all that acts upon different parts of ourself, we can decide upon a fitting response to the One present in each system of action, so that each part of ourself, drawn forth by a particular action in the world, is embraced as part of our one self consistently responding to the One.

On the other hand, integration is characterized by responses of confidence and loyalty. In moving from one sphere of the world to another, the self is always confronted by the One. Through faith it comes to find a consistency within itself. Its loves are no longer scattered, drawn forth in different ways by different spheres of the world, but are drawn together into unity.[27]

While history and value as attempted resolutions of the modern problem were reaching for ways of articulating the integrity of the self in the midst of their move to recover a real and shared world, it is their coalescence in the mode of discourse of faith that carries us further into an understanding of the manner of the unification of the self in its world. Through radically monotheistic faith, response to One action in all events, the world is integrated beyond the fragmenting thrust of atheism, finite theism, and supernaturalism, and the self is integrated beyond the fragmenting impact of multiple actions. Drawing together and transfiguring history and value, the metaphor of faith deepens our understanding of commitment and integrity, and thereby carries us further toward overcoming the oppositions between theoretical and practical, fact and value, object and subject, science and religion.

Beyond Critical Dichotomies to Personal Speech

Without indicating implicit criticism of the inner/outer distinction present here, Niebuhr is working through the metaphor of faith toward a

---

[25] RMWC pp. 47–48.
[26] See MR p. 83, CC p. 251, & RMWC pp. 47–48.
[27] RMWC p. 48.

personal method of reflection that transcends the theoretical and practical alternative of critical thinking. Here our inquiry into Niebuhr's use of the metaphor of faith converges on our earlier discussion of myth. We have already seen that RADICAL MONOTHEISM presents a major shift in his understanding of myth that carries him toward the personal. Once Niebuhr identified practical reason with the personal. Now reason, either theoretical or practical, is set over against personal speech because both kinds of reason employ impersonal categories. In contrast to the critical dichotomy of practical and theoretical (or, for Niebuhr, of inner and outer, value and fact), he proposes "mythological" or "prelogical" speech that "use[s] personal pronouns as ultimate terms of reference."[28]

This postcritical distinction between the mythological or prelogical personal talk and the dichotomous language of theoretical and practical is made in order to bring a certain dimension of human existence to expression, which can only be done through the use of personal categories. Earlier in inner history this personal dimension was the "subjectivity" of the self. Now it is interpersonal interaction, most especially interpersonal truth. While in THE MEANING OF REVELATION he had spoken of the organic relations within which selves live, so that "they live in us and we in them," this was then interpreted to mean that members of the community shared the pains and joys of other members, and each shared the common memory of the whole.[29] Now he sees that where they are members one of another through the sharing of a common memory and thus through commitment to the same community, they are committed not only to a memory and a community but to each other. All our thinking and experiencing have ingredient within them, and are dependent upon, faith between selves, or what Niebuhr calls truth in "the interpersonal situation." He distinguishes two kinds of truth: "the truth that is the opposite of error or ignorance and the truth that is antithesis to lie or deception."[30]

Interpersonal truth is neither objective nor subjective. Over against objective/subjective truth we come upon a third category, "personal truth": "The problems we face in this region are not those of the difference between objective and subjective truth or between what is universally true and what is true for me. They are rather those of impersonal and personal truth." While personal truth is distinguishable from objective truth, they are inseparable: "in any situation in which objective truth is considered interpersonal truth is also involved." What this means—contrary to the theoretical/practical, universal/individual, outer/inner, fact/value, science/religion oppositions—is that all knowing is personal. The self in its personal dimension of

[28] RMWC p. 45.
[29] MR p. 70; see pp. 64–65 & 71, & RMWC pp. 45–46.
[30] RMWC p. 46.

faithfulness underlies it, whether scientific or ethical, and comes to expression in it:

> No scientific inquiry or treatise, no logical analysis, as well as no poem or political address, but what brings before us a self who in addition to being a thought-ful being dealing with objects is a faith-ful being to be trusted or distrusted as truthful or untruthful toward other selves.[31]

Whereas the external knowing of science was understood earlier as devoid of the personal, even though he affirmed the presence of animal faith in its knowing of objectivity and intelligibility of reality, it now becomes one realm among many through which personal commitment is evident. Science now exemplifies persons living a shared world, for scientific thinking requires a community of selves knit together in interpersonal trust and loyalty. It exhibits a commitment to a certain style of life of "constant self-criticism," to "the openness to newness, the nondefensiveness, the desire for *metanoia*, of change of mind." It is committed to the belief that everything in the world is "potentially meaningful" and "that whatever is, is worthy of attention." It is committed to a cause, to the cause of "universal truth" sought with "universal intent." And it is committed to society as a whole within which it carries on its enterprise; scientists have sought to keep faith with their fellow citizens.[32]

Through the exploration of the nature of commitment in the mode of faith Niebuhr has discovered that scientific thinking is grounded upon commitment—commitment to fellow scientists and fellow citizens, to the life style of self-criticism, to the meaningfulness of all being, to the cause of universal truth approached with universal intent. Having used Polanyi's phrase "universal intent," Niebuhr quotes the passage, which we have already considered, about a fiduciary program that lies at the heart of Polanyi's concern to develop a postcritical philosophy, and then goes on to comment:

> And so he struggles to unravel all the implications contained in this unscientific fact in the life of a scientist. To the moralist there is nothing strange or wonderful—though there is something not yet wholly intelligible—in the presence of this fact, namely, that science does not explain itself but rests on a commitment, on a loyalty which is personal; that no matter how impersonal all the objects and ends of science, the

---

[31] RMWC p. 46.
[32] See RMWC pp. 86–88 & Niebuhr, "Science in Conflict with Morality?," pp. 134 & 137.

scientist himself remains even in science a person of whom the moral act of devotion to a cause is required. [33]

Reflecting on his own scientific activity, Polanyi discovers it to be grounded upon commitment. The scientific world that had seemed to exclude the self because there was no place for it among inert things viewed externally by spectators has now been found to be a personal world. Rather than having to carve out another, inner, world along side of the external, Niebuhr now finds within our knowing of that external world the presence of the self: science as well as poetry "brings before us a self." [34] The scientific knower as well as the knower of other selves is a participant. As a participant committed to the world, he or she finds no part of it alien. As a participant committed to a community of fellow knowers, he or she finds that world to be a shared world.

Noetic Faith: A Residual Dichotomy

Niebuhr explores the nature of the scientific community with the declared purpose of overcoming the fact/value dichotomy [35] and goes far towards achieving his aim. Nevertheless, a residual dichotomy remains, since the metaphor of faith speaks of a duality of "objective" and "interpersonal" truth. The two are inseparable, but they are different. They are different because, for Niebuhr, personal commitment is to fellow knowers and their common cause (and as animal faith to the context); but it is not to the known itself. For Polanyi, on the other hand, the known is as well the "object" of commitment, without which it would not be known. The known is a gestalt that emerges from tacit commitments to, and tacit integration of, particulars unconsciously known.

While Niebuhr has not taken Polanyi's further step to found the known as well as knowers on an acritical basis, nevertheless, he goes on to recognize, in an essay written after completing RADICAL MONOTHEISM, the need to explore the relations between these two kinds of faith, interpersonal and what he now calls "noetic," in the hope of moving wholly beyond the fact/value dualism:

---

[33] Niebuhr, "Science in Conflict with Morality?", p. 133. For the passage on Polanyi's fiduciary program see ibid., pp. 132–133. Polanyi may have influenced Niebuhr in distinguishing "personal" from "objective" and "subjective" inasmuch as this distinction is central to his philosophy: "This distinction establishes the conception of the *personal*, which is neither subjective nor objective. In so far as the personal submits to requirements acknowledged by itself as independent of itself, it is not subjective; but in so far as it is an action guided by individual passions, it is not objective" (Polanyi, PERSONAL KNOWLEDGE, p. 300; his italics).

[34] See RMWC p. 46.

[35] RMWC p. 78.

> An inquiry into the relations of interpersonal "faith" to
> noetic "faith." . . . It might, for instance, be rewarding for our
> understanding were we to construct model types of "faith" in
> which we did justice to the polarity in our existence of inter-
> personal trust-loyalty with theoretic orientation. This would
> shift, at the same time, the focus from the old intellection-will
> (or fact-value) dualism in which the problem has usually been
> set, and also move away from the effort to establish one nor-
> mative form of faith.[36]

To explore the relation between interpersonal and noetic faith means
that within the faith metaphor, Niebuhr is reaching for, even though not yet
attaining, an affirmation of the noetic dimension of non-rational commitment. Discerning this direction clarifies what has perplexed critics regarding
his affirmation of true knowledge based on faith in the face of historical
relativism. In THE MEANING OF REVELATION Niebuhr has not yet
asserted the reality-bearing capacity of the non-rational. He seems to be
grounding knowing upon faith and asserting that what is known is therefore
real. Thus Paul Ramsey says that if knowing is based only on an act of faith,
then Niebuhr has not escaped "skeptical relativism."[37] While it is understandable that Ramsey reaches this conclusion, he does so because he has not
taken with sufficient seriousness Niebuhr's talk of animal faith. It is not
primarily our intellectualizing that is grounded upon faith but our living.
Niebuhr is doing a phenomenological analysis of selves-in-act. In describing
selves in their actual living, he discerns a dimension of commitment indispensable to that living. Whatever we *think* as selves, to *live* as a self is to be
committed to the real, to the beings we live among everyday. This is not an
arbitrary and dogmatic assertion that all knowing is grounded upon some
belief; it is rather a description of what actually is going on in our living.

Ramsey's perplexity would be resolved if Niebuhr had been able to show
that what we know rationally emerges from our tacit grasp of being. This he
did not at the time do, though he was moving towards it. While it is
understandable that Ramsey takes Niebuhr's talk of commitment as "only an
act of faith," it is less so that he puts forward an alien rationalism as the means
to understand what Niebuhr is saying:

> But in interpreting Niebuhr one can lean just as far in the
> other direction, in the direction of objectivism. It is important

---

[36] Niebuhr, "On the Nature of Faith," p. 101. This essay was delivered in the fall of 1960 when
RMWC was in press, and was presumably written that fall while teaching his seminar, "Faith as
Virtue."

[37] Paul Ramsey, "The Transformation of Ethics," in FAITH AND ETHICS: THE THEO-
LOGY OF H. RICHARD NIEBUHR, ed. by Paul Ramsey, Harper Torchbooks (New York:
Harper & Row, 1965), p. 155.

to say whether the human mind or only an act of animal faith breaks through the charmed circle of the categories of historical reasoning and lays hold on reality. David Hume, even when at table with his friends, never believed *that the mind* could know anything; he *only believed*, with the animal faith requisite for backgammon, in the reality of friends, table, cards. The faith Niebuhr mentions is by contrast the faith that, in its views of the universal, the *mind* knows the real world. The belief of his "belief-ful realism" is actually the belief of a "critical realist." Amid relative historical perspectives, something of the universal is really grasped by reason.[38]

There is, to be sure, an "objectivism" in Niebuhr's relativistic knowledge; Niebuhr is a critical realist who believes that what he knows is real and universal. But he is more realist than Ramsey's rationalism, for his faith is not in the capacities of reason but in the reality of being. His faith is not fundamentally a "belief *that*" the mind knows the real but a "belief *in*"—and not in the *mind* but in *reality*. Moreover, it is not really a *belief*, in the sense of cognitive assent, but a tacit *trust* in the real. Reason does grasp the universal; it grasps it because the self has faith—not, however, in reason, but in reality, on the basis of which it knows the real and is assured by living this trust that what it knows is real.

In short, sensing the fruitfulness of personal commitment for the resolution of the critical problems of modernity, Niebuhr has deepened his investigation of the tacit dimension through his exploration of the metaphor of faith. Drawing upon his discovery of a fiduciary framework underlying both knowing in the metaphor of history and valuing inseparably related to being beneath various forms of theoretical/practical dichotomy in the metaphor of value, he defines faith as trust and loyalty in the principle of value and being as the One, shows how faith underlies science as well as other types of cognitive knowing, and explores the process of integration of a committed self existing through interpersonal faithfulness within a shared world as it responds to the One.

Symbolic Expression of Being in the World

In the midst of developing the metaphor of faith we have caught the suggestion of a noetic dimension of the non-rational, which merits further inquiry. In the same essay, though in another connection, Niebuhr also suggests that the dimension of commitment has not only a noetic but an explicitly linguistic dimension. We have already seen that he affirms the presence of an integrating faithfulness in all areas of life, the "fact world" of science as well as the "value world" of religion, and discerns the need for a

[38] Ibid.; his italics.

mythological or prelogical language that uses personal pronouns to express, not only the subjectivity of the self, but the self in its interpersonal faithfulness. Now he suggests that personal language brings to expression our entire "sense of 'being in the world' ":

> A second task is the dispassionate attempt to elucidate the sources and the meanings of these large symbolic patterns in human minds which represent their sense of "being in the world," which are the background and the ultimate assumptions (though unanalyzed) of their reasonings and apprehensions. We deal here with the "faith" or the "myth," not of religious believers only, but of all men and all times. Further, we need careful analysis, especially in theology, of the relation of these large patterns of interpretation to our explicit postulates or dogmas.[39]

Using the phenomenological phrases, "being in the world" and "background," he now suggests that the fiduciary foundation of the entirety of our existence comes to expression in the large patterns of symbolic meaning, or what we have been calling heuristic metaphors. He now employs faith and myth interchangeably. Faith is the symbolic expression of our being in the world which exists as the background for all our knowing, and Niebuhr points us towards inquiry into its relation to explicit forms of conceptualization. Where he once saw faith as commitment to the objectivity and intelligibility of the world and, through revelation, as a making sense of it, faith is now thought of as having a linguistic dimension in which our basic sense of being is expressed. Here is an intimation of what will become central in THE RESPONSIBLE SELF: our fundamental form of life, our sense of being in the world, becomes articulate in the language of faith or myth.

The Heuristic Metaphor of Feeling

Only in the last three years of his life does Niebuhr begin to work explicitly with a fourth heuristic metaphor, that of feeling. First investigated as a distinct subject for inquiry in the fall of 1960,[40] it is explored further in "Toward the Recovery of Feeling," in April 1961, and in the last course he taught, a seminar on "The Religious Emotions," in the spring of 1962. Consequently it is not developed at the length of other heuristic metaphors. Nevertheless it provides another mode for continuing exploration into what he has proposed for further inquiry in "On the Nature of Faith"—the noetic dimension of the non-rational and the relation of language to our being in the world.

---

[39] Niebuhr, "On the Nature of Faith," p. 101.
[40] See Niebuhr, "Introduction to Theological Study."

Feeling in a Critical Age

There is in our time a deep suspicion of feeling which relegates it to insignificance and impotence:

> The emotions are deeply suspect in our time, and not least suspect are the religious emotions. That we are emotional creatures is all too evident to us. But that our feelings put us into touch with what is real, objective, powerful, abiding, this we greatly misdoubt. That we can rely upon them in any way so as to guide us in our reactions to the environing powers as to bring forth good, this we scarcely dare to believe. The climate of opinion, that is the accepted presuppositions of our era, predispose us to value most highly our observing, our spectator reason and our technical intelligence.

Since Descartes, we live in an age which sets reason and feeling in opposition. While we have confidence in disinterested, unemotional observation, we indict feeling in a threefold manner: emotions are subjective, private, and projective. Emotions have no bearing on "objective" being; they are in no way in touch with reality; they are noetically impotent. Feeling is evidence of the subjectivism of our inner life; it is in no way an opening into reality whether through our being or our knowing, nor is it "elicited, we believe, by objects."[41] Ironically, the assertion of the subjectivism of the emotions in our modern day involves a "passion for objectivity": "'to be objective' is an emotional word today."[42]

Secondly, emotions are private: while "ideas can be held in public,"[43] feeling is merely the expression of the attitude of the individual having it: "The emotional statements that something is good or bad, that there is loveliness, ugliness, fearsomeness, holiness around us are personal individual statements expressing the attitudes of those who make them." This attitude is locked up within the privacy of the individual's subjectivity and thus is not accessible to social verification nor expression of human commonality: emotions are not "statements on the whole of a common spirit subject to corroboration by others who deal with the same objects."

Finally, they are projective. They are not elicited by objects nor do they "discover value in what is present to them and what excites them," but rather they "project unreal objects before us," and "attribute value to what has nothing of value in itself." Because they are imposed on a valueless, non-

---

[41] Niebuhr, "Toward a Recovery of Feeling," in "Next Steps in Theology," pp. 2 & 5.
[42] Niebuhr, "The Religious Emotions," January 30, 1962.
[43] Ibid.

emotionally laden world, they cannot be relied upon for guidance in our existence or for bringing forth good. [44]

If feeling is subjective, private, and projective, we live neither in a real nor shared world and are fragmented selves. The reality our emotions convey to us we are forever having to discount as illusory. Emotions are the products of our own devising imposed inappropriately upon reality, a reality which neither elicits nor fits emotional apprehension but is known only, if we can ever achieve it, through Cartesian clarity. If there be any commonality, we look for it in shared clear and distinct ideas, even though we in fact find ideas more often than not divisive. As feeling does not open us to knowing reality, so it does not extend us into the sharedness of human experiences. In denying an essential part of our being we split ourselves into productive reason and meaningless feeling—a life enervated by the loss of emotional energy from our daylight world and threatened by eruptions from their repressions in an irrational underground. As we have seen in the other three, so with feeling, Niebuhr uses heuristic metaphors as ways of illuminating the critical problems of modernity and working towards their resolution—by recovering the context of integrity and the wholeness of the self.

Religion—an Affair of Emotion

When we consider the nature of true religion, however, we find that it is "primarily an affair of emotion."[45] The Bible "is written largely in the language of emotions. It is a book of images, eliciting and expressing emotions" about a reality that "cannot be known without feeling." God is "objective but objective to man as emotional being," not the object of intellect but of the heart, not an idea thought but a glory manifest. For this reason the devotional use of the Bible in the church has never been replaced by the conceptual schemes of theology. The life of wholeness is not reason's suppression of emotions but a life of rightly ordered emotions.

Jonathan Edwards on Feeling and Emotional Wildness

While devout persons have been deeply affected by the biblical language of emotion, theologians for the most part have been as suspicious of feeling as the philosophers. Nevertheless, there have been a few pioneers who have ventured forth, even though not very far, into this largely unknown territory:

[44] For Niebuhr's discussion of modernity's threefold indictment of feeling, see Niebuhr, "Toward the Recovery of Feeling," pp. 5-6.

[45] For discussion of the emotional character of religion in this section see Niebuhr, "Toward the Recovery of Feeling," pp. 14–17.

Schleiermacher's theory of the feeling of absolute dependence does remind men fleetingly and abstractly of relations to
their God and to their Christ that lie at a deeper, more
personal level than their explicit believings can express. But
Schleiermacher did not venture far into the region of man's
emotional apprehension of reality; the feeling of absolute
dependence is really not an emotion.

Kierkegaard is another, although "he presents the picture of a man who was
himself somewhat emotionally impoverished."[46] Other explorers important
to Niebuhr include Augustine, Luther, Pascal, and Wesley.

In America the most significant and comprehensive theological consideration of the emotions is in the work of Jonathan Edwards. Differentiating
theologies in terms of the physical senses, for Niebuhr, if Luther's is an
"auditory" theology and Thomas Aquinas' "visual," then Edwards' is "gust-
atory."[47] Finding the emotional life of the self awakened and invigorated in
the Great Awakening, he defines religion as consisting in great part in the
affections. The problem for him was how to nurture, not rationally suppress,
the good affections of true religion while coping with the emotional "wildness" let loose.[48]

In order to discern the presence of true emotion, Edwards conceived
several tests which Niebuhr distinguishes as essentially three.[49] The first test
is that true emotion be "proportionate." There should be a commen-
surability—or in the language of responsibility, a fittingness—both between
emotion and its object and between emotion and the situation. The second
test of true emotion is "steadiness." Niebuhr clarifies this by drawing upon
the work of the contemporary German existentialist phenomenologist, Otto
Bollnow, a follower of Heidegger and Scheler, who distinguishes between
emotions, the "tonalities" or "moods" of life, and feelings, addressed to
particular things. "The religious emotions are," then, not the momentary
outpouring of emotion as such but exist on the level of the deep-lying, steady
tonalities of existence as "states of being of the whole self."

The third test is that "Emotion must be objective"; it must be elicited
by, and have a bearing on, reality. True emotion is not when you "want more
of the affection, but want more of the object." "When you want more love of
God, not more of God, more love of the neighbor, not more neighbors," you
are not exercising a true affection.

---

[46] Ibid., p. 19.

[47] Niebuhr, "The Religious Emotions," February 13, 1962.

[48] See Niebuhr, "Toward the Recovery of Feeling," pp. 22–23.

[49] For Niebuhr's consideration of Edwards' tests of true emotion in this section see Niebuhr,
"The Religious Emotions," February 13 & 20, 1962; on Bollnow see May 1, 1962.

Divine Election and the Objectivity of Emotion

There is a danger in this last test of seeking the result: that "emotion becomes its own object," and thus we get "heat without light."[50] It is like the aesthete who "takes pride in the fact he takes pleasure in pictures; he sees the pictures for pleasure, instead of seeing the beautiful pictures." "Edwards' problem is a useful God rather than a good God"—using God for our own ends rather than experiencing God's objective reality. The old Protestant conundrum, whether you are willing to be damned for the glory of God, exhibits this: "It is a contradiction to ask if Edwards was willing to be damned for the glory of God because salvation is rejoicing in the glory of God." To be willing to be damned for it is to be thinking about your own being rather than divine reality. If you are rejoicing in it, how can you be damned, for rejoicing in God's glory is itself salvation. Experiencing the beauty of sovereign glory issues in delight, but it ought to be sought, not for the sake of the delight, but for the nature of the objective reality. We are then to

> love God for what he is, not for what he is for me. Most people doubt God's goodness because God is not good to others, not that he is not good to me. For the Christian, God is good to me but Jesus is killed. For the Hebrew, the nation suffers though the individual Hebrew knows God's goodness. When we see God as good we see him as good to all creation and not just to me.

This raises the puzzle of divine election: "If I am elected and I am the worst of sinners then all can be elected." Here is a "chance for optimism but also a problem: that I am elected and this other isn't, so he must be predestined to eternal death." There is a logic that works itself out here; I move from what I know by experience, that is my own election, to what I think is the case about others who do not appear to have the same experience. This can be supported with an "aesthetic consideration: to have great music you must have some disharmony." But Niebuhr emphatically rejects this predestinary logic: "Barth's refutation of double predestination is irrefutable. Our God isn't one who says Yes and No; this isn't the scriptural God." The doctrine of double predestination, that not only are specific people elected for heaven but others are actually singled out for hell, assumes an "understanding of men as atomic beings, individuals, that one can be taken and another left." We share in the commonality of human and creaturely existence so that it is impossible to pluck someone out of this organic matrix and shunt him or her off to heaven or hell.

[50] For ensuing discussion on divine election see Niebuhr, "The Religious Emotions," February 13, 1962.

Parabolic Understanding and Emotional Truth

Talk of election leads Niebuhr into some suggestive remarks about parables: "Almost all doctrines of hell are based on parables; a family is separated in hell and heaven and those in heaven are happy because they see God. But in Jesus Christ we see our relation to God and to God in man, that is our brothers."[51] While various parables set up a separation between heaven and hell, the biblical image of Jesus shows our inextricable relation to our fellow humans inasmuch as we see in him not only our relation to God but God's relation to all mankind.

This involves a distinction between doctrine and parable. For Edwards, Niebuhr remarks, "Knowledge begins with the concrete and then moves to the more abstract; Edwards begins with images and from them makes abstractions, which always retain some elements of images." All too often, however, this concrete origin of conceptions in images is not recognized by thinkers; concepts, it is thought, can adequately comprehend the truth of our being. But, says Niebuhr, "We don't grasp the reality in which we exist by analysis. To understand America you must tell the story of America. You must deal with Jesus Christ, not Christology, to understand." Parables arouse a felt knowledge, a feeling apprehension, not of another world but of our present context. The emotions elicited are objective; they bear on a reality, that in which we live, move, and have our being. When we liken spring to resurrection, for example, we are not contrasting two different worlds. There is a coherence between the two but also a leap to another level of the present reality in which we exist:

> Is spring a simile; is it like resurrection or is resurrection in spring? What is the meaning of becoming and passing away? The meaning of Jesus Christ is made in part understandable in spring. Resurrection is on another level but is not discontinuous. There's a coherence and a leap between Old and New Testament. Theology of nature is needed to understand theology of revelation but there is a leap.[52]

By telling our story we gain an emotional grasp of divine election—that we live within a context chosen by God. What is ingredient in this context? Niebuhr mentions the infamous Enfield sermon of Edwards, where he speaks of God holding sinners like spiders over the flames of hell, and suggests this may be more a parable of destruction than of punishment. Telling the parable of our election can be a way of our awakening to the reality in which we exist, that is to one in which we are elected and

---

[51] Ibid.
[52] Ibid., February 20 & 13, 1962.

experience God's goodness to all of creation, but also to one in which we encounter much destruction, some of which flows as consequences from our own actions.

There is an emotional truth that parabolic understanding makes possible which conceptual cognition cannot comprehend. For this reason Edwards attends to the use of language:

> Any use of language, of symbolism and of imagery which did not have in view among other things the stimulation and the redirection of the affections, which was not emotionally true as well as conceptually true, was an inadequate use of language. Edwards worked at his sermons that their symbolism might be right, imagery which expressed and elicited the emotions.[53]

Discussion of the objectivity of emotions as illustrated by divine election opens out into a consideration of parabolic understanding and the question of religious language. In a manner only they can do, as they put us in touch with what is real, objective, powerful, and abiding, our emotions awakened by parabolic story-telling grasp the nature of this reality as we dwell within it. This affirmation issues in a concern for the fitting language that can elicit, express, and redirect emotions so as to realize the truth that can only come through an emotional grasp of the reality within which we exist.

Our Task: An Affectional Awakening

While Edwards is an important medium for exploration of the religious affections, Niebuhr sees our task, however, as different.

> Theology is not going about its tasks in a church that has been invigorated and also confused by strong reassertions of man's religious emotions. Our task may rather be to prepare for such an awakening than to deal with its purification and its defenses.[54]

Contributing to such an awakening in his day, tentative explorations into the emotions are being carried on by the pastoral counsellor, liturgical theologian, artist, and existentialist phenomenologist. In the midst of this Niebuhr

---

[53] Niebuhr, "Toward the Recovery of Feeling," pp. 22–23; reading "a symbolism and" for "and a symbolism had a symbolism imagery."

[54] For ensuing discussion on "our task" see Niebuhr, "Toward the Recovery of Feeling," pp. 22–30.

senses a need for "some unified, systematic inquiry, so that all the various approaches which theologians in different fields are making may be related to each other more effectively," and comes to reflect in a moving way on his own career and on his desire to explore further this newly emergent heuristic metaphor of feeling:

> For myself, who am at the end rather than at the begin-
> ning of my work in theology, I can only say that were I at the
> beginning . . . I should want to follow in Edwards' footsteps
> more, and undertake an exploration of the land of the emotions
> with a certain hypothesis almost amounting to conviction to be
> proved or disproved, refined or extended. The hypothesis that
> contrary to prevalent opinion about emotions—they put us
> into touch with what is reliable, firm, real, enduring in ways
> that are inaccessible to the conceptual and spectator reason.

Niebuhr finds this metaphor fraught with as yet unrealized potentiality in the postcritical quest for an objectively real world. While much of his admittedly brief consideration of feeling is focused on its noetic dimension, nevertheless, we have already seen that the recovery of a real world is also the rehabilitation of a shared world—we dwell in a real world through multiple emotional relations, beneath conceiving, to human community and all our fellow creatures:

> The objectivity of emotional experience seems indubita-
> ble, though much discrimination is necessary in judging which
> objects are transitory and which are enduring, steadfast. Fur-
> ther, I believe that emotional relations to otherness, to objec-
> tive being, are prior in meaningfulness to intellectual
> relations. Trust in parents or distrust of them is prior in time
> and probably personally prior to all identification of parents.
> So also it may be that love of God or enmity to God, hate of
> God, is prior to all articulation of our idea of who God is. And
> so with all relations to his creatures.

Within a world of reality and community we live our lives in large part in our emotions. While Niebuhr has not gone far in exploring the nature of the self maturing in integrity, nevertheless, he is concerned with the overcoming of the reason/feeling dichotomy of critical rationalism and in the redirecting and ordering of the feelings. Perhaps, he muses, we will discover that the emotions are educable, just as we have learned the senses are, and that it is the task of religion to educate them. While he does not flesh out the nature of this education, he does speak of that by which we are becoming integrated selves beyond understanding within the fellowship of being—our task is the love of God and neighbor:

Whatever be the way of future progress, by practical and theoretical theology into the realm of the religious affections and human emotions in general, we have the warrant of scriptures as well as our own feeling to testify to us that the love of God and of our neighbor in him is more important than the understanding of all mysteries and all knowledge. Following these guides we shall not likely go astray, if we think of theology as primarily bound to serve in its own way that increase of that love, always remembering that true religion in great part and true life in great part consists in the affections.[55]

Feeling—the Symbolic Layer

Whether explicit non-rational consciousness or tacit awareness, feeling is commitment—to reality and community. Niebuhr does not make such a distinction between explicit and tacit feeling, but the kinds of feelings he talks about involve both: the steady tonalities of our being, while becoming explicit at various times, are largely tacit; the feelings elicited by liturgy and art are usually explicit, though prior to conception and shading off into tacitly experienced emotions. Whichever, Niebuhr in the metaphor of feeling is exploring the fiduciary foundation of our existing in order to overcome the critical distortion of our being from opposing reason to the non-rational—whether as feeling, faith, valuing, or historical imagination—to reestablish a living union and vital commerce between our roots of being and region of mind.

Emergent within this quest for integrity is the recognition of a linguistic dimension of the emotions. As we have seen, affirmation of a noetic dimension of feeling awakens to the need for a parabolic and symbolic language that can grasp and express the reality within which we exist through the eliciting and redirecting, the educating, of our emotions. Moreover, he identifies feeling and language:

> I have tried . . . to penetrate to that layer of our consciousness as selves lying beneath our conscious thoughts and our explicit intentions whence both thought and action flow. Schleiermacher—the realm of feeling: I will call it the symbolic layer where we are related to totalities, to ultimate contexts, to the circumambient, which modifies all our thinking and doing—which may not influence what we do so much as how we do it.[56]

---

[55] Ibid., p. 30. This is reminiscent of Niebuhr's eloquent "definition of the goal of the Church as the *increase among men of the love of God and neighbor*" and his subsequent exploration of the nature of love (see PCM pp. 31 & 34–36; his italics).

[56] Niebuhr, "Christian Ethics Lectures," March 15, 1961, p. 1.

Existing as the source of explicit thought and intentional act, the realm of feeling is a "symbolic layer." This is to affirm: the relational character of feelings—they are relations to objective reality; their background quality—the relations are not only to individual beings but to totalities and contexts; and their ultimacy—the totality beyond all others we relate to is the background of all being, the circumambient, or God, which modifies all thinking and doing by transfiguring the very form (the how) of our being.

But he also means to identify the realm of feeling with the symbolic level of consciousness, just as he has identified faith with the symbolic patterns expressive of our being in the world. Suggestive of insight into the nature of feeling and symbol as heuristic metaphors is his realization that both situate us within the encompassing ultimate background of our being. Implied by this identification is that feeling, like symbol, grasps and shapes circumambient reality, that feeling is a relatively determinate form emergent from tacit commitments, though not as determinate as the articulate form of word and symbol. And it implies that symbols are pregnant with feeling. But beyond these it suggests that feeling can take tongue and speak—the forms of emotional life can be taken up into forms of speech. There is not only a noetic but a linguistic dimension of emotion. Just as feeling is not separate from reason, so feeling is not separate from word but similarly underlies it and is emergent within it. Commitment, as we have seen in the other metaphors, emerges into articulate form, modifying our life.

It is more than coincidental that, at the end of his seminar exploration into the religious emotions, Niebuhr should speak so tellingly of Wittgenstein. As we have already remarked, Niebuhr was only beginning to come to terms with him but, nevertheless, his talk of the metaphors of "game" and "picture" shows his awareness of how much they share in their affirmation of the personal involvement of the speaker in his or her speech—what becomes focused powerfully for both in the apprehension of language as life forms. Between the linguistic concerns of Anglo-American philosophy and the existentialists' belief that "emotions are revelatory of being," Niebuhr saw, we will remember, the possibility of Wittgenstein becoming the "median point" of this increasing dialogue. Here Niebuhr shows himself to be moving towards the realization that the emotions in their noetic grasp become articulate in the forms of our speech which are forms of life.

Conclusion

Within his profound wrestle with our critical era, Niebuhr moves from one heuristic metaphor to another in search for an adequate resolution to the problem of integrity. In each he gropes toward overcoming critical dichotomies through exploration of the fiduciary foundation of our being in order to recover the context of integrity. We have discovered critical ingredients in his metaphors that have obstructed the full recovery, but less and less as we move from history through value to faith, and none in the admittedly briefer treatment of emotion. As the critical elements have lessened, we have found a deepening sense of the self engaged in the process of integration and a growing awareness of the linguistic dimension of our basic commitments.

We have now seen him explore this foundation as faith. He has sought to recover the commonality of the world, the context of the integrity of the self. Over against the fragmenting views, on the one hand, of supernaturalism, finite theism, and atheism, and on the other hand, of fact/value, theoretical/ practical, scientific/religious dichotomies, he has presented a view of the world as personally inhabited through commitment. Dwelling within these commitments to a real and meaningful world and to fellow knowers, the self can come to have faith in the One who in personlike integrity elicits in the self the response of integrity. Trusting in the One, present in every event, and loyal to the entire realm of being, the cause of the One, the self becomes one self in the midst of all that it does and is, and expresses itself in its unity in all its complex relations to the world.

We have also seen Niebuhr explore the fiduciary foundation as feeling. Here he gains yet another purchase on critical dichotomies by overcoming the traditional Cartesian split between reason and feeling through affirming feeling's noetic grasp of objective reality, its manner of emotional relating to our fellow creatures, and the establishment of self-integrity through the eliciting and reordering of emotions by God.

In all four metaphors there is an underlying linguistic orientation as each is founded upon commitment to that which comes to expression through religious language, to inherent pattern: as divine meaning inherent in intelligible pattern in our past, present, and future; as center of value ordering our complex value relations to being; as One action and intention present in the midst of every action in the world; and as the ultimate totality, the circumambient, which elicits and reorders our emotions. But there are varying degrees of length and clarity of discussion about language in them. While history presents a more extensive discussion of language among these four metaphors, it, nevertheless, does not go as far toward a fully postcritical perspective on language as do these last two in their suggestiveness. While through history Niebuhr glimpses something of the linguistic nature of the critical problems of modernity and responds with a call for a grammatical theology and development of a theory of meaning, he is so encumbered, as he himself recognizes, with Kantian dualism as to need to attend to ways of overcoming these self-disintegrating dichotomies before the linguistic perspective can emerge in its fullness. And thus in his work with the metaphor of value we find his attention drawn toward resolving critical oppositions. The linguistic thrust is largely latent as he works with what will later be seen to be what comes to expression in religious language—the dimension of commitment and the pattern of value relations.

Succeeding better in dissolving critical dualism through the metaphor of value, Niebuhr takes the next two metaphors in such a way that, as he explores further the fiduciary foundation of our being, we begin to get intimations of the relation of the articulate to the acritical. In faith he speaks of the need for a personal language, transcending objective and subjective talk, through which our sense of being in the world can come to expression. In feeling he suggests the importance of a parabolic and symbolic language that can elicit and redirect the emotions through which we grasp the reality within which we exist. Fraught with intimations of what we will find in fullness in his fifth and final metaphor—explicit use of what we have called heuristic metaphors and the recognition of the emergent relation between acritical commitment and linguistic articulation—he identifies both faith and feeling with the symbolic: faith with "large symbolic patterns" or "myth" and feeling with the "symbolic layer."

Having developed the richness latent in the incipiently linguistic metaphors of history, value, faith, and feeling, Niebuhr comes to realize the wholly linguistic nature of both problem and solution within the last magnificent heuristic metaphor of responsibility. Through this metaphor the linguistic method, latent in each, emerging into explicitness at various points within his theological quest for integrity, comes to its fullest flower. In THE RESPONSIBLE SELF a word-using self finds a grammatical resolution to our critical era's linguistic obstruction of integrity.

PART THREE:

Responsibility as Linguistic Life Form

CHAPTER SIX
SPEAKING OF AN ELUSIVE SELF

Within the religious reflection of H. Richard Niebuhr we have discerned, in Part One, a richly complex linguistic theology of five convergent perspectives—metaphoric, grammatical comparison and meaning, mythic, and dialogical—dwelling within the postcritical ambience of the exploration of symbolic forms. In Part Two, through perspectives afforded by four heuristic metaphors—history, value, faith, and feeling—we have followed Niebuhr's deepening understanding that modernity's loss of self- and world-integrity can be overcome by recognizing the self is at bottom a committed self whose fiduciary foundation underlies a real and shared world and is expressed through personal symbolic language.

Having wrestled with the very foundations of modernity through the analysis and use of these metaphors, he comes at the end of his life to the culmination of his postcritical quest in his fifth and final heuristic metaphor of responsibility as he realizes that the problem of integrity is linguistic: the erosion of our confidence in and the potency of certain forms of personal speech. And its resolution is linguistic: recovery of certain linguistic forms as concrete forms of life. In Part Three we explore Niebuhr's most mature response to the malaise of modernity through the understanding and use of responsibility as just such a linguistic life form.

As he becomes more explicitly linguistic, he becomes more palpably phenomenological. While each of the previous heuristic metaphors has a universal intent, responsibility is more comprehensive, not only because historical knowing, valuing, having faith, and feeling are all kinds of responses, but because it develops the linguistic dimension and deepens the personal aspects of the self as irreducible and committed, tacit, elusive, and integrity-seeking. Responsibility is a linguistic phenomenology.

As we take up responsibility for our concluding investigation, we are confronted by two questions. How does Niebuhr's linguistic perspective illumine the way in which the sense of selfhood and Godhood has been lost and can be recovered? Secondly, reserved for the concluding chapter, how is religious language able to bring about self-integrity within the total context of our being? The first question carries us into an exploration of the nature of the elusive self and the space of God's appearing within the first person grammar of religious language; the second into the integrative function of this grammar.

As we have already seen, self and God belong together in religious language, and the responsible self is a multiply responsive agent, in primordial relation to selves, existing within a three dimensional time-consciousness. Within the previous four metaphors we have seen that he presents God as self-disclosing pattern of historical revelation, center of value, person-like integrating One of faith, and ultimate circumambience of feeling. We now reach for the roots of the metaphor of responsibility in order to comprehend the nature of self and God as they exist together as counterparts in religious language.

Once we have discerned Niebuhr's culminating expression of the relation of self and God in the first person grammar of religious language, we will be able to discover earlier indications of its emergence. We will especially be able to clarify difficulties in the metaphor of history by showing adumbrations in inner history and confessional method of what is realized in responsibility—affirmation of the speaking of an elusive self.

The Irreducible "I" and its First Person Grammar

We have already found Niebuhr perceiving a dimension of the self that can come to expression only through personal language. This is the dimension of "irreducible I's."[1] Having explored the subjectivity and interpersonal faithfulness of this irreducible "I"—transcending the subject/object and theoretical/practical dichotomies, coming to expression in scientific treatise as well as religious discourse—he probes more deeply in THE RESPONSIBLE SELF into the self's irreducibility: "I am, and I am I. That 'I am,' and 'I am I' here, now, bring to my awareness a radical deed which I cannot identify with any of the specific actions that have constituted the elements of my body."[2]

By speaking of the self in relation to a "radical deed," Niebuhr distinguishes the "I" from body, mind, and emotions. While intimately related to each of these, the "I" cannot be explained either in its origins or its being in terms of any one or all of these together. We can learn much, for instance, about forces acting upon the body and hence reasons for its stature, skin color, sex, and tendencies towards certain illnesses.

> But none of these interpretations of biological events touches the fact that it is *I* who am in or with this body, that *I* have this body, that this is *my* body. And none of the responses I make to the actions that constitute elements in my body are responses to the radical action by which *I am*.[3]

[1] RMWC p. 45.
[2] RS p. 109.
[3] RS p. 110; his italics.

Similarly, the mind and emotions each have their own history, explaining their present state but not the origin and being of the "I." While embodied, thinking, and feeling, the "I" transcends its own self-manifestations. It is not deducible from these processes: "Only if I posit the self can I refer this thinking, living, feeling, to myself."

What Niebuhr is doing is again distinguishing between the personal and the impersonal, between the committed and the conditioned self, as he did in his earlier inner/outer history distinction. Body, mind, and emotions are explained by reference to external causes; *my* body, *my* mind, and *my* emotions are, on the other hand, expressions of the self dwelling in, committed to, them. But the difference is now expressed in linguistic terms: between personal and impersonal statements, between language using the grammar of the first person and the objectifying grammar of the third person. The irreducible "I" or, as he calls it, the "central self," comes to expression only in language using first, not third, person pronouns. There is no way of moving from impersonal to personal statements, from "thinking is going on," "living is in process," and "feeling is occurring" to "the conclusion that therefore *I* am." The self must first be posited and this is done only by speaking in the first person.[4]

The Elusive Self—Irreducible and Committed

"I"-talk reveals an otherwise inexpressible dimension: the irreducibility and commitment of the self. While the self as irreducible is transcendent, it is as well immanent as committed. The two in fact work together. The "I" is transcendent by standing in relation with that to which it is committed. Drawing upon Niebuhr's earlier writings, we call this "I" an "elusive self," for it can never be caught fully in its expression; it forever eludes in its transcendence our effort to grasp it as it comes to expression. It forever stands behind while present in what it says, because to stand *in relation to* is different from being *identical with* what is said; it is not exhausted in its expression; it is never "known" as an object but only as "lived" mystery; there is more to the "I" than what, in the expression, meets the eye.[5]

---

[4]See RS pp. 110–111 & 115; his italics.

[5]While Niebuhr does not use the phrase "elusive self" in THE RESPONSIBLE SELF, he has employed it earlier. In THE MEANING OF REVELATION he writes: "Internal history, on the other hand, is not a story of things in juxtaposition or succession; it is personal in character. Here the final data are not elusive atoms of matter or thought but equally elusive selves" (p. 64). In "Søren Kirkegaard," while the phrase does not appear, the idea does: "the more we attend to the objective the more we leave out of consideration the presence of ourselves and our companions—these most real beings that can never become the *objects* of attention. . . . We have left out of reality what cannot be known because it is behind every knowing. The illusion is that reality is something that can be known, when indeed it is something lived" (Niebuhr, "Søren Kirkegaard," pp. 31–33; his italics). While affirming the elusive self, it is evident here in the mid-fifties that Niebuhr has not yet recognized the need to put this in a linguistic frame, to distinguish first from second person.

I and Thou: A Distinction

All this talk about the "I", its "intensely private experience of selfhood," should not be taken as "solipsistic." The "I" exists in dialogue with "Thou's" in the present and history. Ever since THE MEANING OF REVELATION Niebuhr has employed Buber's language of "I" and "Thou," but in his final work (evident in the preceding quotes focusing on the "I") he recognizes a crucial difference in grammar between first and second person statements.

Up through RADICAL MONOTHEISM he does not note any difference between the "I" and the "Thou," evident as he speaks in this book of both exhibiting the "scandal" of "personal concreteness."[6] This is as one should expect, for he is speaking here about interpersonal truth existing in relation between selves as they know and experience the world. But in the THE RESPONSIBLE SELF he has taken a further step toward clarity, discriminating the first from the non-first person grammar and locating the manifestation of irreducibility and commitment solely in the first person. The second person is dependent upon the first; as such, "Thou's" are also irreducible and committed, but only because they are other "I's."

Much of his earlier thought has been concerned to show the dependence of the "I" on the "Thou" as the community within which the individual comes into being and matures as human—as the compresent companion in dialogue. Now he has arrived at a complementary truth: the second person is logically dependent upon the first as an elusive self. I and Thou are interdependent, but the dependence is asymmetric: the "I" is dependent on the "Thou" for its existence and nurture, but the "Thou" is dependent on the "I" for its meaning as another elusive self possessing, though not manifesting, the agency of commitment and the transcendence of irreducibility. Without diminishing the significance of the second person, indispensable to affirmation of the dialogical nature of the self, Niebuhr discovers in THE RESPONSIBLE SELF another dimension of personal existence—the grammar of the first person. And this is principally singular rather than plural since the "we" cannot be committed and self-transcending unless the "I" is. All speech is therefore grounded in the grammar of the first person singular. When this foundation is denied, its ground is found in the impersonal third person, the language of "It." Along with the fullest development of his understanding of the dialogical nature of the self, he opens up in this book a grammatical-existential distinction between the persons involved in the I-Thou dialogue: a certain form of the self comes to expression through "I"-talk which is not manifest in "Thou"-talk—the form of the "I" in its commitment and irreducibility.[7]

---

[6] RMWC p. 45.

[7] W. H. Auden puts the case with characteristic succinctness: "Whenever we use the pronouns *You* and *I*, . . . uttering them is accompanied by a characteristic feeling-tone. The You-

Radical Action in the First Person

There is something else coming to expression in the use of the first person singular pronoun—the divine "Thou." To speak in the first person is to body forth the irreducible "I" transcending, and therefore not dependent upon, mind, body, and emotions for its origin or being; nevertheless, it is dependent—and absolutely—upon something for both its origin and present being: a "radical deed" or "radical action." This radical deed cannot be identified with the forces at play upon mind, body, or emotions, for they influence and cause these processes but not the irreducible "I". As the "I" transcends these forces, so does that upon which it is absolutely dependent transcend them. While the characteristics of my mind, body, and emotions are dependent upon these forces, the characteristics of the "I that I am" and the fact that "I am" are not. After the self has been exhaustively described in terms of the characteristics influenced by these impersonal forces, there remain two things undescribed: the origin and present being of my "I"—"the radical action by which I was cast into this particular historical religious process . . . and the action by which I am."

The irreducible "I" emerges out of and is sustained in "the mystery of being"[8]—or as he says elsewhere, by "the Mystery behind the mystery of human existence."[9] Rising out of and borne upon this mystery, there is a fatedness about the "I." That it is and who it is, it has no control over. Born as a human being into the world, born into a particular history, there is a mysterious givenness about the "I," which is part of its irreducibility. For a citizen of the Christian West "Jesus Christ is my fate . . . whether I accept or reject him."[10]

Not only are my origins beyond my or any self's control; I am held in being by the same ineluctable power that has flung me there, over which I have no control. While some have speculated or acted upon the belief that suicide is a rejection of that power and a taking control of one's own continuance in being, Niebuhr demurs on the possibility of suicide. "Biocide" is certainly a possibility, but whether a self, which has not elected itself nor been elected by other selves into being, can elect its "I" out of being in

---

feeling is a feeling of attributing-responsibility-to . . . , the I-feeling is one of accepting-responsibility-for. . . . Common to both the I- and the You-feeling is the feeling of being in the middle of a story with a personal past to remember and a personal future to make" (W. H. Auden, SECONDARY WORLDS [New York: Random House, 1968], pp. 124–125). See also William H. Poteat's illuminating discussion of the grammar of the first person in "God and the 'Private-I'" and "Birth, Suicide, and the Doctrine of Creation: An Exploration of Analogies," in NEW ESSAYS ON RELIGIOUS LANGUAGE, ed. by Dallas High (New York: Oxford University Press, 1969).

[8] RS pp. 111–112 & 115.
[9] PCM p. 36.
[10] RS p. 112.

destroying its body, we do not know.[11] Language of the first person singular brings to expression not only the commitment and irreducibility of the "I" but its fatedness of beginning and being, and the mystery, the creative and sustaining radical action, responsible for this fate.

The Space of God's Appearing

What Niebuhr has been wont to say throughout the bulk of his career, that God and faith belong together, is now transposed into a linguistic mode by affirming that the linguistic dimension in which commitment is expressed is similarly the place in which the divine reality manifests itself. Whereas earlier God disclosed himself through the human act of historical memory,[12] now first person speech is the space of God's appearing. Faith is evident in my commitment, as the "I that I am," to my body, mind, and emotions, in relying on them. So also in my commitment to the radical action which has flung me into existence and holds me there. This does not mean I like it, recognize it, or want to talk about it, but I do rely upon it in living my life. If, however, I do express such commitment, I also am speaking of God, whether I use the word or not, and I am doing that in the first person singular.

As the One comes to expression in the first person language of an "I," so the grammar of the speech of the personlike One is correlatively first personal. In RADICAL MONOTHEISM, noting Etienne Gilson's incisive commentary on God's encounter with Moses, Niebuhr suggests not only is God Being, but "the principle of Being is the First Person." Warning about the dangers of "anthropomorphism in our understanding of our ultimate environment," he goes on to affirm that "the one God who is Being is an 'I', or like an 'I', who is faithful as only selves are faithful."[13]

God speaks in the first person because the divine reality exhibits an "integrity that . . . is the oneness of the self" and a "faithfulness that keeps promises, is indefectibly loyal, is truthful in freedom," which can only be expressed in the language of the "I."

Being—the principle and power by which all things are—is neither impersonal chance nor fate but manifests the pattern of faithfulness and integrity of an "I." God speaks as the First Person in the first person because Being is committed, loyal, and trustworthy to the beings this "I" has brought into and sustains in being, and exhibits a "personlike integrity."[14]

Like a self, God has integrity because there is a continuity of response; God is present as one action and one intention in every event—the action

---

[11] See RS pp. 114–115.

[12] Niebuhr writes: "The revelation of God is not a possession but an event, which happens over and over again when we remember the illuminating center of our history" (MR p. 177).

[13] RMWC pp. 44–45. While he here acknowledges the first person character of the language of God, he has not yet recognized explicitly the distinction between first and second person.

[14] RMWC p. 47.

and intention of indefectible loyalty and irrepressible faithfulness. Everything that occurs is in some sense God's act, so that the divine "I" can and must speak in the first person of every event as "my doing." This is true no less of me than of any other reality, "so that it seems truer to say that I am being lived than that I live."[15] God, like a self, while present in every event as its manifestation, nevertheless transcends each of its expressions. God is an elusive self, committed to and coming to expression within all of being, yet transcendent beyond its parts and sum as an "I" in relation to that to which it is committed. Religious language has God speaking in the first person for the same reason that persons do: to express commitment and irreducibility—divine reality's transcendent mystery and inviolable nature.

The Space of Our Appearing: The Divine-Human Dialogue

Only within the first person speech do the commitment and irreducibility of the self come to expression. Only in the first person speech of religious language does our faith in the faithfulness of being come to expression. And only in expressing this life form of faith are we integrated. While we have not yet seen how faithfulness issues in integrity, we can see now that the committed and irreducible "I" exists through religious language in dialogue with the divine "I." God speaks in the first person in our first person speech of God. In religious language divine faithfulness encounters us in our expression of our own faith, effecting integration: "personlike integrity . . . elicits the confidence of selves in their ultimate environment."[16] As committed, irreducible, and integrated selves, the space of our appearing is in the dialogical language of first person religious expression, as we exist in dialogue with the world.

The Third Person Mood of Modernity

The mere utterance of religious words in the first person, the mere fact of speaking of God as speaking in the first person, does not, however, open up this divine-human encounter and integrate the self. As we have seen in chapter two, it is quite possible to speak of God but not express faith in being. We can use the word "God" and yet covertly manifest the life form of distrust in being, interpreted as indifferent or hostile. Similarly, we can use "I" and not express the committedness and irreducibility of our central self. This Niebuhr says is what in fact is occurring within the crisis of modernity. Within the modern world we continue to use the grammar of the first person in our everyday existence but enact through it, when reflectively serious, the life form of being in the impersonal third person.

[15] RS p. 114.
[16] RMWC p. 47.

The root of the modern problem we have seen lies in the denial of commitment. Now within an explicitly linguistic perspective, this problem is understood as rejection of all genuine first person speech. Denying the first person ground of second and personal third person speech, we are grounded in the third person grammar of the impersonal "It." The language of critical thought is never genuinely in the first person because it seeks an objective certainty through denial of all belief or commitment. Rejecting "I believe . . ." as the mere subjective expression of opinion, critical thought seeks to establish itself through "It is the case that . . . ." RADICAL MONOTHEISM shows Niebuhr groping toward a personal method, a mythological mode of speech, in contrast to the impersonal deliberation that is either theoretical or practical. Now it becomes evident, these are impersonal because they are not spoken of in the first person.

Modernity rejects first person being and expression because it searches for objectivity and certainty to be secure through control in an impersonal world. The "I" is a major obstacle to this. First person speech displays commitment, fatedness, and mystery beyond control. Modernity recoils and seeks as a result to forget the self. "Though the strange question of the I came to the self in youth," says Niebuhr, "though it encountered the alien power by which it existed—the mystery of being—it was soon distracted from attending to this daily, momentary, momentous action upon it" and was enticed away from the first personal to the impersonal, from the "I" to the "one." In shifting from the first person to the non-first person, "the self is lost among objects." Now "it responds in all its action not to the act by which it is a self but to the action by which the group of bodies or of minds or of emotions exists." This is to live in a "third-person mood":

> In this state we say "I think" but really mean "It seems"; we say "I believe" but really mean "It appears likely." Even contracts, promises, and commitments are made in a third-person mood as though our signature on the bond meant "Someone will see to it that this one or its heirs will meet this obligation." We may even make the commitment "I will love, honor, and keep thee" as though it meant "It seems likely something in me will continue to love, respect, and be good to you."[17]

Encapsulated within the third person language and living of modernity, the self comes to itself through the use of the first person grammar of religious language, and there finds coming to expression as well the pattern of faithfulness ingredient in being itself—"traces of the structure of faith in the whole realm of being"—which evokes in us faith in being—"confidence

[17] RS pp. 115–117.

in Being simply considered"[18]—issuing in integration of the entirety of our being. Lying at the root of modernity is the denial of the grammar of first person language and living. What he now recognizes that had concerned him for so long about the method of Linguistic Analysis was that it had not yet discerned the significance of first and second person grammar:

> The other question raised by logical and linguistic analysis.—The method is unable so far as it has been developed to deal with the logic and the meaning of moral language because moral language is first and second person language. And its method has no way of dealing with the meaning of the words "I" and "you."[19]

Lying at the heart of Niebuhr's life-long wrestle with modernity and now emerging into explicitness is a linguistic phenomenological method founded upon this insight: the pursuit of integrity is linguistic; its language religious; and its grammar first personal.

Divine Sovereignty in the First Person

While we have not yet seen how religious language contributes to the achievement of self-integrity, we have reached the heart of Niebuhr's linguistic theology. What we have traced, in his developing interest in religious language and in his multifaceted efforts at resolving the modern problem of integrity, all lead to and are embraced by the affirmation of the first person grammar of religious language. What is now emerging in linguistic terms has been affirmed earlier by Niebuhr in doctrinal terms of divine sovereignty. Aborning in the coming of the "conviction" of "the sovereignty of God," as he calls it in his autobiographical essay, is just this grammatical insight of the first person nature of religious language. Divine sovereignty for Niebuhr is an incipiently linguistic affirmation.

While divine sovereignty became an important category for most theologians of his generation, what is definitive of Niebuhr's use is the personal dimension of commitment to being. His turning to affirm sovereignty "was not a change of definition of God," but a change, he writes, "of *personal* relations to my world and the ground of the world, to the givenness of life, history, *myself*." It was not simply a commitment to a new idea of God, supreme, transcendent, initiating, but a recognition of his own absolute dependence upon and faith in the trustworthiness of being: "And now *I* came to understand that unless being itself . . . the ground of *my* being and of all being . . . was trustworthy . . . *I* had no God at all."[20]

---

[18] For this Edwardsian phrase see RS p. 120.
[19] Niebuhr, "Christian Ethics Lectures," February 22, 1961, p. 1.
[20] Niebuhr, "Reformation: Continuing Imperative," p. 72; my italics.

In the first four heuristic metaphors the conviction of divine sovereignty is present as commitment to pattern as an underlying integrating structure of the world which encounters us in every event as divine initiative. The self is integrated as it responds in commitment: as historical faith—to inner history as a pattern of meaning underlying the world disclosed through revelation by the divine self interacting with the self; as valuing—to the inextricable relation of value and being in a center of value which is the principle of being and value; as trust—to the personlike integrating One; and as feeling—to the total context of circumambience.[21]

In the heuristic metaphor of responsibility, conviction of the sovereignty of God emerges into linguistic explicitness. In this fifth metaphor we can see that commitment to pattern is an act performed in the first person, and the pattern to which we are committed comes to expression in religious language as life forms lived in first person speech. Living in commitment to pattern, we undergo transformation by pattern and commitment being brought to expression through dialogue between divine and human "I's," in the midst of dialogue with the world, in the first person grammar of religious language, moving us onward into integrity of self within a real and shared world. Niebuhr's theology has at its heart the affirmation of divine sovereignty in the first person.

An Emergent First Person Perspective

While the grammatical nature of this commitment to being does not become evident until the end of his career, explicitly in RADICAL MONO-THEISM, most fully in THE RESPONSIBLE SELF, it is emergent within each book following the conversion essay. In KINGDOM OF GOD it becomes briefly explicit in discussion of the "truth for me" in contrast to an "impersonal standard." What is here only briefly suggested is developed extensively in THE MEANING OF REVELATION, as the "truth for me" is placed within the context of Buber's I-Thou/I-It distinction. In his next work, CHRIST AND CULTURE, now under the influence of Kierkegaard, he presents an extensive discussion of the "irreducible self," who is "passionately concerned with what is true for him. Such subjective truth—truth for me—is found only in faith and in decision." And next in PURPOSE OF THE CHURCH he distinguishes God's addressing the "I" from study about this encounter: "In the moment of his study God and neighbor are not present to the theologian as *Thous* addressing or being addressed by this *I*. What is immediately present are forms, patterns, ideas ingredient in the *Thous*."[22]

---

[21] In the pivotal essay in which he first expresses the coming of this conviction of divine sovereignty and in which these four metaphors take their incipience, Niebuhr speaks of faith in and love of a "pattern in existence" and a "pattern of ultimate goodness" which are one (Niebuhr, "Moral Relativism and the Christian Ethic," p. 10).

[22] KGA p. 111; MR p. 65; CC pp. 241–242, see p. 243; & PCM p. 130; his italics.

Surfacing momentarily, even though not yet explicitly grammatical, this linguistic method undergirds each of these works. This is nowhere more readily discernible than in THE MEANING OF REVELATION, the book that uses the phrase "elusive self" and becomes conscious of the need for a linguistic theology. There is a tension, to be sure, between his manifest critical perspective, employing dichotomies of theoretical and practical, objective and subjective, and his emergent postcritical point of view. Nevertheless, we can see emerging at the heart of Niebuhr's wrestle with these critical terms, a postcritical distinction between first and non-first person grammar that will enable achievement of an integrated self in the world. While we usually read this book in a critical vein, to see its emerging first person orientation will resolve some difficulties in understanding his concepts of inner/outer history and confessional theology.

Inner and Outer History—A Grammatical Incipience

From a critical point of view outer history would seem to contain not only things but the inner histories of other persons who are strangers. The distinction between inner and outer history would thus appear confused. From a postcritical perspective, however, it is the incipient linguistic distinction between first and third person: the lives of strangers are grouped with things under external history because they are spoken of in something other than the first person.

Only in inner history do we speak in the first person. In outer history we speak in the second and third person of things and strangers' lives. In medical and social history an event occurs within inner history when it happens in *our* history: "Lincoln spoke of what had happened in *our* history, of what had made and formed us and to which we remain committed so long as we continue to exist as Americans."[23] Surgeon and British textbook can report the patient's recovery of sight and what commitments were at work in building America, but neither can speak of these events in the first person as *my* recovery of sight or of what happened in *our* history.

In this light the reasons Niebuhr locates revelation in inner history now become clear. "We can speak of revelation only in connection with our own history" because only there is it spoken of in the first person. To comprehend revelation in another community as revelation, we must abandon our present first person perspective and take up as our own the history of the other community. If revelation is only truly grasped in the first person, it cannot be "miraculous events as visible to an external observer" because viewing it in the third person would only disclose its external characteristics rather than internal reality. As events in personal history, they can be "sources of unconquerable certainty for us," and yet can "be analyzed in profane fashion by the observer"[24] in the third person.

[23] MR p. 62; his italics. See MR p. 60.
[24] MR p. 82.

The critical perspective misses the significance of the personal perspective and thus of the grammatical distinction between first and third person. From its perspective there is seemingly no difference between another's internal history and *mine*—they are both value-laden. What this misses is the postcritical recognition that internal history is not only value-charged but charged with *my* values.

The critical perspective is ahistorical. Not taking into account its own grounding in a particular history, it views all historical perspectives in the third person equally. Failing to grasp the difference between first and third person, it distinguishes participant and spectator, but takes a spectator's point of view on participants. While the participant is certainly involved, and spectator detached, it fails to see that the involvement is *my* involvement.

An event in inner history cannot be grasped from an external point of view because it is not visible from a third person viewpoint as an event in the first person. Niebuhr says: "One must look with them and not at them . . . , participate in their history rather than regard it if one would apprehend what they apprehended."[25] To *look at* selves is to regard them in the third person. To *participate in* their history is to *look with* them, to speak with them in the first person. To be a participant is to be a self in act, manifesting by enacting its own elusiveness. We can talk about the elusiveness of another, but awareness of this is different when I manifest my own through being and speaking in the first person. From a critical point of view perspectivism and involvement appear as the definitive marks of inner history, but from a postcritical perspective they are insufficient because they fail to acknowledge that both perspective and participation are *mine*.

In this light it is possible to understand Niebuhr's discussion of the ways in which inner and outer history are related. He offers a phenomenological analysis of "their functional relation for us." From a critical perspective these appear contradictory: if inner history is one perspective and outer history another, then to say an event in external history "becomes an event in inner history" is to speak of uniting mutually contradictory internal histories. From a postcritical perspective, however, it becomes clear that we internalize an external view, not by joining two mutually contradictory perspectives, but by embracing it as our own self-criticism in the first person. While "internal life does not exist without external embodiment," we do not embody one internal perspective within another. Rather whatever can be spoken of in the first person exists within a medium that can be spoken of in the third person, whether human memory embodied within the neural system or the church's memory within books and monuments. We cannot speak of my internal history contradicting another without denying its first person character. To be sure, my internal history can conflict with another's internal point of view,

---

[25] MR p. 73.

but from my perspective I cannot speak of their internal view in the first person and thus cannot call it internal history; their internal view is external history to me however much involved they are in it.[26]

Critical Categories and Postcritical Conclusions: A Tension

The confusions and contradictions a critical point of view sees in his discussion of inner and outer history Niebuhr has himself contributed to by using critical categories to reach postcritical conclusions. Critical and postcritical thinking exist in tension here inasmuch as his postcritical perspective is not yet fully explicit. This is evident in another way Niebuhr suggests of relating inner and outer history. There is a critical speculativeness in speaking of the church "see[ing] itself with the eyes of God." Elaborating what he means by this, he speaks of God's perspective on history as "simultaneous, unified knowledge from within and without." By this he means knowing, not as involved and detached, but as private and universal—the knowing of an event "from within as well as from without, in its isolation as well as in its community with all other events." What he wants to affirm at least is that the church should see itself with a universality approaching that characteristic of God. But he does this here by speaking of the union of inner and outer history which is a speculative leap for both critical perspectivism and postcritical grammar.

In fact he himself denies just such a leap: "There is no speculative escape from the dilemma." One term cannot be absorbed into another, nor can both be transcended. Only by a "decision of the self" can we move, he says, "from observation to participation." In critical thinking this move from thought to decision means a move from the objective, cognitive, universal to the subjective, non-cognitive, private, whereas in postcritical thinking it means a shift from third to first person.

There are other problems as well issuing from tension between critical and postcritical which we have already considered, such as defining dualistic thinking as essential to Christianity and yet recognizing its inherently fragmenting tendencies that do not resolve but rather restate the problem of the unity of the self.[27] Nevertheless, the problems inherent in a critical interpretation can be resolved by recognizing in Niebuhr's distinction between inner and outer history the emergent affirmation of the linguistic difference between first and third person grammar.

---

[26] MR pp. 83–84, 85, 87, 88, & 89. For a good representation of a critical approach to Niebuhr's distinction of inner and outer history see Van Austin Harvey, THE HISTORIAN AND THE BELIEVER: THE MORALITY OF HISTORICAL KNOWLEDGE AND CHRISTIAN BELIEF (New York: The Macmillan Company, 1966), pp, 234–242.

[27] MR pp. 88, 84, & 83; see pp. 81–82.

Confessional Theology: A First Person Method

Developed in conjunction with his historical reflections, Niebuhr conceives a confessional theological method grounded appropriately in inner
history, which similarly has emergent at its core the affirmation of first
person grammar. As reflection upon the inner history of our lives (and how
the inner relates to the outer)—or, as we have seen him say in THE
MEANING OF REVELATION, as stating, and thus elucidating, the grammar of a particular language—theology is centered in, though not restricted
to, the first person grammar of inner history. It is dialogical reflection—the
confession in ongoing first person conversation with other selves of what we
are experiencing and understanding in our inner histories of first person
dialogue with God.

In his own theologizing Niebuhr produced no system of thought, organized by a single principle, the product of disengaging himself from ongoing
first person discourse in order to carve out a clearly delineated objective,
third person position with explicit boundaries and organization, set over
against others. Irenic rather than polemical, Niebuhr's dialogical confessionalism is designed to reach behind rather than to set up defenses, and
to pursue inquiry with others wherever it might lead.

While not yet explicit, the first person, dialogical method is emergent
within the three reasons he gives, in THE MEANING OF REVELATION,
why theology, attentive to revelation within inner history, must be confessional. The primary reason is to guard against "self-defense and self-
justification, the turning away from the object of faith to the subject."
Turning from the object to subject of faith is to lose the dialogical nature of
theology. Secondly, losing the dialogical context, revelation is changed from
the act of God's elusive, committed manifestation to a religion or a "revelation idea" possessable by us, a thing spoken of in the third person—a truth
deposited in "a book, a creed, or a set of doctrines," dispensed by some
"custodian of revelation." To turn back upon ourselves is not only to lose the
act of divine revelation but the act of human faith directed towards the divine
act, both of which are manifest only so long as the dialogue continues. It is
also to lose the dialogue between selves. I become defensive. I become
polemical, attacking others' ideas of religion and revelation in the effort to
justify my own. I seek to verify these ideas as if they are realities like physical
objects for which I can provide indisputable evidence.

But why this defensiveness? Revelation "leaves man without defense
before God";[28] theology must be confessional, thirdly, to acknowledge sin.
We are defensive because we fear the vulnerability in the dialogical relationship with God, where we are beyond a place of security in which we can

---

[28] MR pp. 38 & 40–42.

control what will happen to us and what we will discover within us. We seek refuge from the uncertainties of events, from who we are, and from what we are committed to, and thus from facing our own sinfulness, in the sinner's posture of a defensive third person mood.

Method must fit subject matter. If the subject is revelation and faith, which occur only in dialogue, the method must make possible the continuance of the dialogue. Emergent within Niebuhr's articulation of a confessional theology is this fundamental postcritical orientation moving towards the explicit affirmation of the first person and dialogical nature, not only of religious language, but of theological method. "We acknowledge revelation by no third person proposition, such as that there is a God, but only in the direct confession of the heart, 'Thou art my God.'"[29]

Confessional Theology in Critical and Postcritical Perspectives

From within a critical point of view Niebuhr's confessionalism would not reveal its dialogical method nor grammatical sensitivity to first person speech but would rather appear as either subjectivism or objectivism. In the former case confessionalism would be taken as identical with relativism that denies objective criteria of truth, the possibility of error, and the critical employment of the law of non-contradiction. His theology would thus be taken as lacking a critical thrust that could have argued, for example, that God is either personal or impersonal, or that Christianity is either superior to other views or is not. For evidence of this loss of "either/or" thinking he or she would point to Niebuhr's own reluctance to criticize another position and say it is wrong.

From a postcritical perspective, however, we can see that the underlying principle of confessionalism is not relativism but avoiding self-defense, not historical conditionedness but the recognition that God and self can only be present in first person discourse. While confessionalism does begin in a situation historically conditioned, relativism does not simply mean historical conditionedness; it means commitment in the midst of these conditions— commitment to the history we participate in and commitment to a god or center of value.[30] Relativism for Niebuhr is not a determinism of a passive self issuing in subjectivism but a relatedness of a responsive self that transcends subjectivism. As he says later in his life, he should rather have called it "relationism" to avoid this confusion: "Some of my critics—and, alas, I myself—have called this position one of historical relativism, which for some people at once means subjectivism. Historical relationism is probably a better term, since it does not involve subjectivism."[31]

---

[29] MR pp. 153–154.
[30] See MR pp. 19, 23, & 37.
[31] Niebuhr, "Reformation: Continuing Imperative," p. 73.

Since relativism is not his basic principle, to speak confessionally does not, therefore, mean for Niebuhr the loss of a critical thrust. While his style of thought is irenic rather than polemical, he nevertheless does engage in criticism of other views and argues for the greater adequacy of his own. He argues in THE MEANING OF REVELATION that revelation occurs in inner rather than outer history; in RADICAL MONOTHEISM that radical monotheism is more adequate then henotheism or polytheism; and in THE RESPONSIBLE SELF that God is love rather than evil. He does not eschew criticism. As he says, theology "is not a queen but a servant, though its service may at times need to take the form of criticism and polemic."[32] What he does eschew is rationalistic argument in the third person.

In the third person we seek to prove we are right by providing evidence for irrefutable conclusions. In the first person we engage in dialogue, seeking a mutual sharing of experience. Persuasion in dialogical theology seeks first to avoid self-defense, which finds its own superiority and security in third person talk, and then to lure one's dialogists on to the level of first person utterance so as to speak of the real God. Persuasion here is not an adequately supported conclusion but the manifestation of faith in God, of commitment by the irreducible "I" to the mystery behind its own mystery. There is a suggestiveness and attractiveness in the disclosure of this dimension of commitment that can illume the other's present commitments and entice toward further commitment. To turn apologetic here, to judge my faith to be superior to yours, is to drive you from this evanescent realm of first person commitment into the third person stance of self-defense.

To speak confessionally of what is happening within our irreducible selves does not eliminate the possibility of error. We may have misunderstood our experience—as Niebuhr insists is the case when we interpret being as death-dealing rather than as life-giving. But we will not be persuaded by arguments that speak of God whom we have not experienced, of being apart from our value relations to it, nor by the assertions of the superiority of another's faith over ours. We are persuaded rather by hearing another tell his or her own story, illumining perhaps a new way of understanding our own, and by telling our own, where, in the telling, we may perhaps find our experience to be different from what we had thought. Within the confession of the heart there is no appeal to the divine being in itself nor a stance from which we can judge one faith to be superior to another. Niebuhr's confessional method is not subjectivistic; it is first personal, addressed to other persons.

Linguistically sensitive, confessionalism does reject the critical application of the law of non-contradiction to the being of God because the latter does not take into account the grammatical context in which the word "God"

[32] PCM. p. 110.

is being used. Either/or thinking is too abstract; to say "God is *either* X *or* not-X" is not sufficiently linguistically determinate to make sense. What we mean by "God" depends on whether we are speaking in the first or third person, for as we have seen, what we call "God" in the third person is different from what we experience as "God" in the first person—the difference between a static thing and personal act, between an object in (or outside) being and the faithfulness of being. To speak of God objectively in the third person is not to speak of what Niebuhr means by "God"—that personlike integrity and faithfulness that manifests itself in our first person speech of a first person God. Endless debates can ensue with no possibility of fruitful issue, if God is spoken of in the third person or if the grammar involved is not elucidated, because what is spoken of is not the real God but some phantasm or finite phenomenon. It is literally true there are no *objective* criteria in confessional method, for the criteria of truth in third person talk do not operate in first person talk. The law of non-contradiction is a case in point; appropriately applied in the third person, where objects and their attributes are dealt with, it does not fit first person language, where the mysterious elusiveness of the self, human and divine, comes to expression.[33] Nevertheless, this does not mean that what we know of God is not real. Rather we can only know the real God by speaking confessionally, in the first person.

Confessionalism is not subjectivism. It is possible, however, for a critical interpreter to argue that, while Niebuhr's confessionalism appears subjectivistic, it is really covertly and illegitimately an objectivism. Still assuming relativism as the underlying principle of confessionalism, the interpreter would see it as based on a non-confessional principle because the assertion of the truth of relativism must rest on something that is not itself relativistic—to claim that all is relative is a truth which itself cannot be relative. The assumption here is that relativism undermines itself; inasmuch as Niebuhr embraces relativism, his view must be grounded in non-relativistic or non-confessional principles. Otherwise he could not make universal claims either for his method or about the nature of God.

From within a postcritical point of view it is possible to see, however,

[33] While not dealing explicitly with the inappropriateness of the law of non-contradiction to much of religious talk, what William H. Poteat has to say in "Myths, Stories, History, Eschatology and Action: Some Polanyian Meditations," in INTELLECT AND HOPE: ESSAYS IN THE THOUGHT OF MICHAEL POLANYI, ed., with an Introduction, by Thomas A. Langford and William H. Poteat (Durham: Duke University Press, 1968), pp. 210–215, on the complexity of the personal backing we give our expressions; what Mircea Eliade has to say in PATTERNS IN COMPARATIVE RELIGION, Meridian books (Cleveland & New York: World Publishing Company, 1963), pp. 448–456, on the multi-dimensionality of meaning inherent in mythological language; and what Joseph Campbell has to say in THE MASKS OF GOD: PRIMITIVE MYTHOLOGY, pp. 21–29, on the ambiguity in mythic play—all have a fruitful bearing on this question.

that confesssionalism rests, not upon a non-confessional principle, but upon confessional affirmation. With some linguistic discrimination we can see that Niebuhr, in claiming the truth and necessity of the confessional method, is not making an absolutistic claim in the third person but a first person claim. To say that all theology must be confessional is to express my belief that all theology must speak in the first person. There is nothing inconsistent in espousing a first person method in the first person; my espousal is an expression of my first person commitment which the method calls for. Relativism does undermine itself when asserted objectively. If relativism means there is nothing I can be committed to as universally true, then the assertion of the truth of relativism does undercut itself as the manifestation of a commitment denied by it.

Universal claims are possible within confessionalism. Niebuhr certainly makes such universal claims—not that his concepts are universal, but that they are concepts of the universal.[34] But he is making these not objectively in the third person but personally in the first person. To speak in the first person does not rule out the possibility of speaking of the universally true, but it makes quite clear that what we are claiming to be true is what *we believe*. In fact, all truth claims, first or third person, are based on belief since they are accredited by persons on the basis of commitments; first person claims simply make this explicit. That is, the presumed detached objectivity of third person claims is mistaken; third person utterance is dependent upon first person commitments.

From a critical point of view there are only two options. Niebuhr's confessionalism must be either subjectivism or objectivism. Such a view is incapable, however, of discerning an emergent postcritical perspective in his confessional method, that is reaching beyond these critical dichotomies through sensitivity to language, whose theological task is to cherish that evanescent and mysterious logical realm of inner history where faith and revelation occur through divine-human interaction in the first person grammar of religious thought.[35]

Conclusion

Self and God belong together; to lose a sense of one is to lose a sense of the other. Through the erosion of certain forms of language we have lost an awareness of the depths of both humanity and divinity. Our critical age through its objectifying doubt has rejected as merely subjective that lan-

---

[34] See MR pp. 18–19.

[35] For a good representation of a critical approach to Niebuhr's confessionalism see John B. Cobb, Jr., LIVING OPTIONS IN PROTESTANT THEOLOGY: A SURVEY OF METHODS (Philadelphia: The Westminster Press, 1962), pp. 284–301.

guage of the first person in which the irreducibility and commitment—the elusiveness—of the self come to expression. In this search for the objective reality of the self and world we have withdrawn from this realm of human elusiveness and have consequently found our selves and world emptied of divine mystery. The space of God's appearing is the place of our being in the world as elusive selves. God is "the Mystery behind the mystery of human existence in the fatefulness of its selfhood, of being this man among these men, in this time and all time, in the thus and so-ness of the strange actual world."[36] As such Mystery, God is the background of our irreducible and committed being which confronts us in every event eliciting from our deep humanity the response of transcending and trusting being, opening toward our integration into "the strange actual world."

In becoming more aware through the heuristic metaphor of responsibility of the linguistic nature of our modern world's uprooting of humanity and divinity and simultaneously of the linguistic orientation emergent at the heart of his own thinking, Niebuhr explores the nature of religious language and discovers it to be, paradigmatically, speech in the first person—the dialogue of "I's" between the self and other selves, world, and God. Through elucidation by a confessional-dialogical theology fittingly grounded in the first person and the use of the first person grammar of religious language, he finds the possibility of recovering the elusiveness of the self and with it the mystery of the divine. Speaking religious language is enacting linguistic life forms in which this elusiveness and mystery become manifest, however indirectly.

Emergent throughout his mature thought from KINGDOM OF GOD on, this postcritical perspective underlies and, when understood, makes sense of Niebuhr's four prior heuristic metaphors. In this chapter we have looked particularly at the notions of inner history and confessional theology. While finding tension between residual critical commitments and a fundamental postcritical orientation, we have been able to dissolve seeming difficulties that appear when viewed simply from a critical perspective by seeing in inner history the incipient affirmation of the first person grammar of religious language and in confessional theology the emerging of the first person dialogical method of responsible theology. While emergent within the metaphors of history, value, faith, and feeling, it is only in the explicitly linguistic metaphor of responsibility that Niebuhr achieves a fullness in perception of the linguistic nature of the problem of integrity in the modern critical age and of its solution in a postcritical world—though even here his postcritical theology is not devoid of critical remnants.

Now we turn in our final chapter to a consideration of responsibility as the linguistic life form which opens on to a way for the speaking of elusive

[36]PCM p. 36.

selves and a space of God's appearing, and ask how this first person dialogical language issues in the integration of self in the world. We come then to our concluding remarks about Niebuhr's understanding of our being and speaking, and of their transformation through religious language—and thus to his understanding of the "logic of religious discourse."[37]

[37] RS p. 86.

CHAPTER SEVEN
SPEAKING AND BEING TRANSFORMED: THE LOGIC OF RELIGIOUS DISCOURSE

Through the heuristic metaphor of responsibility we discover our lives are shaped and expressed by language. Words are forms of life; through particular forms of religious discourse our lives achieve the concrete forms of religious maturity. We have come to see that these forms of life are spoken and lived paradigmatically in first person dialogue with the community of being and the circumambient One. By opening ourselves to this dialogue, we enter upon the way of ongoing self-transformation by the integrative potency of religious language. We come then in our exploration of the linguistically emergent postcritical theology of H. Richard Niebuhr to the final question of how the dialogical, first person grammar of religious language is able to achieve the integration of self in the total context of its being.

Language of Integrity and Divinity in Being

We have seen that we lack integrity because we doubt the capacities of language to bear on a real and shared world. Doubting the reality and commonality of the world, we withdraw into the narrow confines of a closed society. Encapsulated within a sphere of being, all that is excluded appears as threat. Threatened by hostile beings beyond the horizon of the seeming security of my limited world, I divide myself as well as my world into that which is safe and that which is alien. Existing in interrelations with all of being, my rejection of part of being is the repression of part of myself. In denying certain beings as alien, I deny those parts of myself existing in relation to them. To withdraw from a common world is to be divided within myself. Overarching the full expanse of being, existing as the end of my being in however narrowly circumscribed a sphere, death presents itself as the ultimate threat. Confronted by the multiple threats of alien beings and death, I seek to live and speak in the "self-ignoring existence" of a third person mood. Here I can forget the "I" who will die and who is grounded in uncontrollable mystery, and gain control over a narrowed world of objects I can fashion as a defense against hostility beyond.

Dismissing the "I" so as to find security in the third person, I lose the focus of my central self. Making myself as much as possible into an object dwelling among mere objects, I hope to escape the diverse threats to personhood; but I find as a result the shattering of my self-integrity, for I have rejected that dimension of self in which I can make consistent response to the many actions in being. Having repressed this capacity to grasp all actions from an inner center, to assimilate them and to make a coherent response to them from this center, I find one part of myself drawn forth by one system of action and another part by another without the possibility of responding to any of them as a whole self. In this seemingly hopeless situation, there is however within my being "a small seed of integrity"[1] that augurs a destiny other than fragmentation.

To speak in the first person is to bring to expression the dimension in the self of its own commitment and irreducibility. To use religious language is to speak in the first person, bringing to expression our faith in being as exhibiting faithfulness towards us. Within this experienced faithfulness of being towards us, we find support for our immanent commitments and transcendent irreducibility. Being is supportive of the existence of "I's." In the face of the threats of death and alien beings, religious language entices us forth into first person speech, providing a milieu of meaning supportive of persons. In being drawn out of a third person into a first person mood, I become aware of and no longer abjure my commitments. No longer wanting to dissolve my commitments through doubt to avoid what I took to be the subjectivism of personal belief, I come to myself; I begin to discover who I am, what I care about, what is of central importance to me. Concomitantly, I begin to discover, not only the nature of myself, but the reality of the world. No longer dissolving the commitments I find myself holding, I trust I am in touch with reality. I similarly become aware of the mysterious elusiveness of this irreducible "I" that I am. In the very act of commitment to a being I discover the capacity of self-transcendence, of standing elusively behind every relation I simultaneously stand within. No longer do I understand myself as borne down by events determining my mind, body, and emotions; rather I find within myself the resources to transcend every influence in the very act of embracing it. Paradoxically where I had sought control of my world in the third person mood, I found myself controlled by external determinants. Where I am not in control, in the mystery of my being founded on the mystery of being, I am not controlled but live in commitments I simultaneously transcend.

Not only does religious language recall me to myself by bodying forth the dimension of my personal being as a central self, it expands the sphere of my being from a closed society to the community of all being. In evoking the faithfulness of being towards me, I come to trust in being. Now the alien creatures earlier excluded are brought within my world by pushing the horizon of my being towards the furthest reaches of reality—from family, to

[1] RS p. 139.

nation, to humanity, to life, to the universal society of being. Not only the breadth of being but its direction becomes something I can face and embrace. Even though my life moves towards my death, the faithfulness of being makes present a faithfulness to me even in dying. I discover that being which is death-dealing is in its loyalty to me also life-giving; overarching my life in the full expanse of being, rather than the metahistory of death, as I thought, is the mythology of life, the ambience of resurrection. What is given here is not the cognitive certainty of the idea of immortality, but the living assurance of being's faithfulness even in the face of death.

Facing an uncertain future and creatures of anticipated hostility in a given situation, religious language, genuinely and personally used, making present my confidence in being, evokes the resources to embrace rather than defend against the present situation. The faithfulness of being, expressible and embodied in the use of religious language, eliciting faith, enables me to assimilate within what I had rejected in the world and repressed in myself: the whole of being and its direction. As I expand my context to the circumambient community of being and extend my duration toward the ambience of resurrection, I am being integrated; I am attaining a coherence in relation to myself, to the world, and to that radical action which originates and sustains me and all reality. My life is undergoing conversion.

In his earlier writings "conversionism" meant transformation through the recognition of the pattern of divine meaning inherent in being. In THE MEANING OF REVELATION the power and reality of God is not that of a supernatural being outside the world but the power and reality of the world itself. The value of God is not some abstract ideal beyond the world but the everyday goodness of love. The unity of God is not that of the one beyond the many, the unification of the ideals of beauty, truth, and goodness, but of the One who is active in and through all things.[2] Through revelation our expectations are met but in ways we had not anticipated: "But though the Father of our Lord Jesus Christ met that expectation he fulfilled it in another manner than we anticipated, and made necessary a change in all our thinking."[3] We are being converted by a change in our thinking, by the recognition that God is not an ideal outside the world but a present reality in the world. Similarly, in CHRIST AND CULTURE we are being converted by recognizing the presence of the inherent pattern of divine action. Creation is not some event of earlier times but is the present origin and foundation of all that is. The fall is not a past event, but a present falling away from God. Judgment of the world is not in some distant future, but is now. Eternal life is not some future state but a quality of existence in the here and now. Conversion in this book, however, is expressed more in terms of personal being than of thinking: we

[2] See MR p. 186 on God's power, MR p. 189 on God's value, and MR pp. 183–185 on God's unity.
[3] MR p. 183.

are being converted by a "new beginning" taking place "in each living, existential moment" through the present action of God.[4]

From Niebuhr's perspective in THE RESPONSIBLE SELF our speaking and being is undergoing continuing transformation by bringing that pattern of divine meaning inherent in existence to expression in religious language. The pattern of divine meaning in being, the pattern of being which is the pattern of divine goodness, is the pattern of divine faithfulness we encounter in the first person dialogue between God and self occurring through the use of religious language.

I am being integrated by discovering the presence of God within my being in the world. Through the faithfulness I discern in being, I increasingly find confidence to name everything in the world as part of *my* world and there to exercise capacities and dimensions within myself, such as the everyday goodness of love, in this present place and this given moment—the space and time of my present renewal and God's present action. Not only do I expand myself and the world so as to encompass the totality of being, I find a center in myself and the world. The faithfulness I am able to recover and consolidate through my use and personal endorsement of religious language is not only indefatigable loyalty to the entire realm of being; it is the presence of One action and One intention within every event in being. In response to this One action and intention in every event I not only can trust every situation, I can find developing within myself an integrity as I find a constancy of response in my relation to the One in the many. Only because I meet the same action and intention in every event am I able to be my central self in every situation.

For Niebuhr the small seed of integrity begins to grow as I participate in dialogue with God. The ineradicable dialogical nature of self comes to full expression in religious language. For the self to speak in the first person with a God who speaks in the first person is to live at the most fundamental level in dialogue. As we have seen, Niebuhr at the end of his career takes dialogue as the model for all our response-relations to being. I am born into a dialogue already going on in my society and my natural environment; I live in dialogue with compresences living, dead, and anticipated; I am unable to make decisions or to know my mind, body, or emotions apart from this ongoing conversation; and now we see that at the most fundamental level of personal being, I exist as a committed and irreducible "I" in dialogue.

Niebuhr understands the self's interaction with God as dialogical because this linguistic metaphor illumines certain aspects of the divine-human interrelation otherwise not visible. The logic of God's encounter with the self is not that of abstract reasoning but of everyday talk. Dialogue is always situated, never floating in abstraction from a concrete circumstance. It thus

---

[4]CC p. 201; see CC pp. 192–195 & 200–201.

has a history, both a past out of which it comes and a future into which it moves, and its origin like its end is imprecise, issuing out of that beyond memory and moving uncompleted into the future unknown. Not only are the beginning and end unknown, the full context of present conversation extends beyond our ken, as it includes much that is unsaid and unsayable. In the midst of such a situation where I am in touch with much beyond my conscious awareness, I must make a fitting response to my fellow participant in dialogue. To do so I must not only be sensitive to the entire context, I must listen to what he or she says and discern within what is said, what is meant. As I make what I consider a fitting response, I stand committed to it and expect my dialogist to take me as standing responsible for it, so he or she can make a fitting response in turn, not only to the meaning of what I said in the given context, but to the importance in which I hold it.

In the midst of this divine-human dialogue I achieve self-definition. I attain a continuity of self in response to One action and intention, not only because I respond constantly to the same reality, but as well because dialogue incarnates my commitments. In dialogue I show myself to be *this* self; seen by the other as this self, I see myself in the other's eyes as *just this*, and not something else. Prior to dialogue I can retreat into my hopes and fears, my dreams and illusions, as to who I am. But in meeting another in dialogue my real commitments are expressed and heard by the other, so I am, as it were, held fast in his or her eyes, and therefore in my own, as this particular self. Thus I am changed; through conversation I am drawn out of the relative indeterminateness of my as yet unarticulated, unformed self into the relative determinateness of articulate self-disclosure.[5]

As I become more determinate, more an individuated self, in dialogue with God through using religious language, I can now respond to the various systems of action in the world (which I relate to through my mind, body, and emotions) as ingredient in one ongoing conversation, as I carry into every situation my continuing dialogue with the One present there, and respond out of the increasingly centered and comprehensive self I am becoming.

Beyond the alternatives of objectivism or subjectivism of the critical age, the grammatical method emergent in Niebuhr's theology points a way towards a postcritical world. Through a sensitivity to the grammar of language, especially religious language—the guardian of the central self—we can transcend the dichotomies of critical thinking. But this does not mean the loss of all duality; a duality, indeed a multiplicity, remains. The duality of first and non-first person speech, the multiplicity of first, second, and third person speech, remains. In attending to the grammar of the first person we have come to see the presence of commitments and a self-transcending self in dialogue. Recognizing all our relations to being as ingredient in dialogue, we

[5] See MR pp. 146–147.

have come to see the presence of the committed "I" in all our relations to
being, whether in scientific knowing or religious talk. We can see then that
the objectivism of the third person mood is an illusion, is a theoretical
construct unbefitting the "theory" present in our living. Third person, and
with it second person, are spoken by a person, and are dependent upon the
first person. While not evident because the "I" does not appear in non-first
person speech, the self in its commitments and irreducibility stands behind,
is responsible for, what it says. But we have needed a linguistic method that
would draw our attention to the grammar of the first person to see this.
Having explored the grammar of first person speech, we can now see that
even articulation in the third person is not "objective." All speech, even that
in the third person, is *speech*, the endorsement of our own words by us as
speakers. Expression in the first person makes obvious what is less manifest
in other forms: viz., that the self is present in and stands behind what it says.
A proper understanding of the grammar of religious language can recall us
from the apparent objectivism of the third person forms to recover and take
seriously the grammatical mode by means of which we express our existence
as integrated selves. We now can see the indispensability of religious language in preserving inviolate that dimension in personal being of the central
self and to evoke within that dimension the integration of all its relations to
the real and shared world and its ground. Religious language is the language
of integrity and, as such, the indispensable medium for recovering the
personal.

Reflexiveness: Referential Language and the Objective Self—A Critical Recalcitrance

A tension remains, however, in Niebuhr's theology up until the last.
Articulate as his linguistic method has become in THE RESPONSIBLE
SELF, it is never fully explicit. The postcritical thrust of his entire theology
exists in tension with residual commitments to critical thought. He has over
and over again defined the task of theology as describing the pattern emerging in our actual being in the world, illuminating the theory present in
practice.[6] What he finds in our actual being is a self committed in its
dialogue with world and God, yet, correlatively, irreducibly elusive within
these commitments. Nevertheless there are places in some of his explicit
theorizing about the nature of the self (divine and human) and religious
language where he speaks from a critical perspective. While he had earlier
embraced such a point of view, he had sought to leave it behind, but
evidently not with complete success. In these instances he fails to illumine
the pattern actually, though unacknowledgedly, present, but rather imposes
an alien order. He conceives of the self as *objective* and of religious language
as *referential*.

[6] See RS p. 135.

This critical recalcitrance is present, in the first place, in the manner in which Niebuhr conceives of the self as "reflexive." Following George Herbert Mead's way of speaking of the ineradicable social nature of self, he defines reflexiveness as the self's ability to make itself an object for itself by embracing, through dialogue, another's understanding of itself. Secondly, religious language used by such an objective self is referential. In the passage calling for a theology of religious grammar, he concludes by saying "language refers."[7] In an essay appended to RADICAL MONOTHEISM he makes it clear that we refer to a being which is our god in the very act of believing that life is worth living. Not only is belief referential; all language, except expressions of love and hate, is communication about things.[8]

Referential language and objective self are correlative terms within a critical framework. Dealt with in the third person, God is an object to which we can refer through religious language; the self is reflexively an object to itself, upon which it can reflect. In the meeting of God and self through using religious language, the self knows itself, not merely as its own object of knowing; in referring to God, it knows itself as the object of God's knowing. God is then the counterpart of faith, as the knower of us; in revelation "we know ourselves to be known."[9] Referential language is correlative with an objective self, because the self, divine or human, is an object, and we know it, as language refers to it, as an object.

The objective self in Niebuhr's thought exists in tension, however, with the elusive self, as referential language exists in tension with expressive language. To know myself as the object of another's knowing, even of God's, is to know myself in the third person as an object, rather than to know myself in the first person in act. I only know myself as "looked at" rather than being aware of myself as I "look with" others at something else.[10] Niebuhr has used objective reflexiveness—the self knowing itself through God knowing it—to affirm the central self's transcendence beyond its relations to the world and to its own mind, body, and emotions, but has as a result denied the central self's irreducibility, the inexhaustible depths of the self in which I stand elusively in and behind my commitments to God, self, and world, which depths can only show themselves in the first person.

Language, understood as referential, similarly exists in tension with language as expressive of forms of life. The linguistic act of referring can be construed as a piece of behavior and therefore as a form of life, one among many others. But when it is taken as definitive of the nature of language as

---

[7] MR p. 18; see RS pp. 71–72.

[8] See H. Richard Niebuhr, "Faith in Gods and in God," in RMWC p. 119; (originally published as "The Nature and Existence of God: A Protestant's View," in *Motive*, IV [1943]); and see RS p. 80.

[9] MR p. 152.

[10] See MR p. 73 for distinction between "looking at" and "looking with."

such, it is not acknowledged as a form of life. The meaning of words understood paradigmatically as reference assumes that some inherent bond, independent of speech-acts, binds a word to a thing, that the object is the meaning of the word apart from the act of a speaker using words so as to bear on the object. As Wittgenstein describes this view, "the individual words in language name objects. . . . Every word has a meaning. This meaning is correlated with the world. It is the object for which the word stands."[11] And as Niebuhr himself describes it in his own attack upon the copy theory of truth: it is a view "not primarily concerned with words but with things signified." It is a "magic fallacy that believes that there is an objective reality corresponding to every word."[12] But Niebuhr, like Wittgenstein, rejects this view of the meaning of language: the meaning of words is not in the object they name but in their use, in the setting of human life in its whole ambience of living speakers, in the setting, in short, of a form of life. As we have seen Niebuhr say, words have meaning as they perform their meaning-giving function in a context.[13] The comparative method of metaphor-analysis presupposes subtle differences in the use of words, in the inherent patterns of meaning they bring to expression in particular situations, which can only be gotten at through comparing the words in use. Meaning is emergent from the depths of our existence in the world; divine meaning is emergent from the pattern of being itself, which becomes articulate through using language.

If the meaning of words lies, independently of their use in the act of speech, in the objects to which they refer, words are emptied of their power and meaning; they become meaningless abstractions pointing to the meaning-bearing objects. Niebuhr's view of language as referential is consonant with his view, criticized above, that words are interpretative symbols imposing order on otherwise chaotic and meaningless reality. If there is no meaningful pattern of tacit commitments to beings beneath language the object to which we refer recedes beyond our grasp as an unknowable *ding an sich*, knowable only as the symbolic form we impose on it. Words would have the power of forming an otherwise formless reality, but they would not have the power of bringing being to expression. Words would not be evocative of being, being would not be manifest in speaking; we would be precipitated back into the scepticism and solipsism of modernity, unable to know whether language bears on reality, unable to know our words as anything other than sibilant emissions, reverberating within the privacy of our minds. Words would not entice forth a dimension of already existent personal being but would simply refer to some unknowable object; words would not, where

---

[11] Wittgenstein, PHILOSOPHICAL INVESTIGATIONS, par. #1.

[12] Niebuhr, "An Introductory Essay on Language and Theology," p. 1.

[13] See Wittgenstein, PHILOSOPHICAL INVESTIGATIONS, pars. #19 &43; and see MR p. 141.

before there had been distrust, evoke confidence in being in their hearers; they would simply refer to the idea of confidence.

Niebuhr's view of language most fundamentally, as we have seen above, is, however, that language is expressive, evocative, of prelingual meaning. Without this affirmation of emergent meaning, we cannot recover a real and shared world. Nor can we recover the self in its agency, for if words themselves essentially refer,[14] they do not need a refer*er*—a self using words in order to make reference. As we have seen, however, first person talk is performed by an agent self, and entices forth the central self in its prelingual commitments to beings; religious language, enacted by a self, brings to expression the prelingual pattern of divine faithfulness inherent in our being in the world.

Not only his emergent view of language, his own use of language displays this expressive significance of religious language. When he speaks, for instance, of our image of the metahistory of death within which we ordinarily dwell, as "everlasting winter lying on the frozen wastes of existence" or as the "all-destroying fire raging before and after the brief interval of . . . life," or when he speaks of being reconciled to being—

> we were blind in our distrust of being, now we begin to
> see; we were aliens and alienated in a strange, empty world,
> now we begin sometimes to feel at home; we were in love with
> ourselves and all our little cities, now we are falling in love, we
> think, with being itself, with the city of God, the universal
> community of which God is the source and governor[15]—

he is not referring to an object, death or being, nor imposing a symbolic form upon an unknowable and therefore formless reality, but is using language to express our distrust and confidence in being, and to evoke in the hearer a felt-knowledge of these. The density of metaphoric richness lures us forth from our defenses into first person dialogue with others, where we achieve understanding and definition of ourselves in action.

Niebuhr has embraced Mead's objectifying view of the reflexive self in his concern to affirm the irrefrangibly dialogical nature of the self. We are born into a world of persons as well as subhuman realities and grow into maturity, our full humanity, in the compresence of others. We exist in dialogue with the world, and underlying that we live in or seek to ignore dialogue with the radical action creating, sustaining, and concluding our lives. To see the self's relationship to the entirety of being and its ground as

---

[14] Niebuhr is ambiguous on this: sometimes it is words that refer (see MR p. 18), sometimes it is we who refer with words (see Niebuhr, "Faith in Gods and in God," p. 119).

[15] RS pp. 106 & 177–178.

dialogical is one of Niebuhr's most fruitful insights. It can be affirmed, however, without this encumbering objective self, a mortgage to his critical past. The whole thrust of *homo dialogicus* is towards imaging the self as elusive rather than objective, as fundamentally first rather than third personal.

The reason Niebuhr appropriates Mead's objective sense of reflexive is to affirm the dialogical nature of self: a self is a being capable of becoming an object to itself, and it only becomes so through taking toward itself the attitude of other selves—through dialogue. And yet the selves we are as we participate in dialogue are not objective but elusive—manifesting our commitment and irreducibility. While there is no doubt we become more ourselves as we see ourselves through others' eyes, we do so by internalizing their external views. Assimilating the other's second or third person statements about me, so that I can say them in the first person, I may become aware of my unacknowledged elusive commitments or be confirmed in those of which I am already consciously aware, and thus become more fully a self.

Dialogical Transformation

Because of the self-transcendence and commitment of an elusive self, to engage in dialogue is to participate in ongoing self-transformation. Only where the self can take up an attitude toward things, committing itself in a multiplicity of ways, as in the elusive, dialogical self, can the self become more itself as it deepens and broadens its commitments and the ways it stands both within and behind them.

In spite of the tension between critical and postcritical perspectives on the nature of the self and its reflexiveness, Niebuhr is very clear that the dialogical self undergoes a continuing processes of self-transformation. As we have seen in RADICAL MONOTHEISM, language, whether poem or scientific inquiry, "brings before us a self." The self that is brought forth through dialogical response to God is one engaged in "the development of integrated selfhood." Only as I participate in the dialogical response to God of confidence and loyalty as I respond in dialogue to every event does that radical faith become incarnate within me.[16] In THE RESPONSIBLE SELF we see this same thrust towards dialogical self-transformation more fully developed. Through the use of religious symbols in dialogue "we grope for understanding of ourselves and toward definition of ourselves in action." Through the use of "great images, metaphors, and analogies" the self "grasps and shapes . . . the actuality of his own existence." Specifically "In religious language . . . I am one within myself" as I engage in "dialogue with the circumambient world" within the dialogical response to God. By engaging in dialogue with God, in "explicit responsiveness to the deed by which it is a

[16] RMWC pp. 46–48.

self," and "to one action in all the actions to which it is subjected, . . . the responsible self finds its unity."[17]

We find unity in dialogue with God because within that dialogue we begin to trust, to trust the fate that lowers over us, to trust the world in all of its uncontrollable might, and to trust ourselves in all the fragility and mystery of being human. For Christians it is especially through the symbol of Jesus Christ that this faith is elicited. To employ this "*Gestalt* of grace" in our ongoing dialogue with God and world is to begin "a great relearning which is never completed" in our lives. This is to take up the "central work of revising our mythology of death into a history of life." Revising our mythological language involves a transformation of ourselves through the transforming of our language inasmuch as to change our responses is to change ourselves, for the revising of our mythology is "the redefining for us of what is fitting response"—response within "a lifetime and a history surrounded by eternal life, as well as by the universal society of being."[18]

The transformation of self is central to Niebuhr's view of dialogical responsibility, and flows as a natural consequence from the affirmation of an elusive self. Through the use of religious language we are transformed towards increasing trust and integrity. The residual tension between objective and elusive selves keeps him, however, from further clarity about the postcritical process of self-transformation through the use of religious language. Beyond any explicit recognition of Niebuhr's, but evident in the whole movement of his thought, we can say: dialogue makes more determinate what before articulation was less determinate. The elusiveness I exist in before I speak takes on a particular configuration as I stand behind a particular statement. I exist in a multiplicity of tacit commitments to being. When I speak in dialogue in the first person, I identify myself with one of these commitments. I stand behind it, and in giving my personal backing to it, I disclose myself as standing in *this* way behind *this* commitment. Thus through dialogue I achieve self-definition. Speaking is not simply a matter of making visible what was before invisible; it is rather a making determinate what before was relatively indeterminate in its prelingual state. In drawing more of the self into determinateness through speech we undergo transformation; we achieve definition of self.

Elusive God and Elicited Faith

If a person is not a passive thing in God's eyes but a responsible self achieving self-definition, God and self interact in terms of elusiveness. Tempted at points to make a person into an objective self, Niebuhr is

---

[17]RS pp. 48, 161, 122, 151, & 125, respectively.
[18]See RS pp. 175–176 & 107.

similarly inclined sometimes to make God into an objective self. When he speaks of God as divine Self, it is possible to take this as a statement in the third person, as if deity is an object, a discrete person. The personal nature of God as it comes to expression in religious language is essential to Niebuhr's entire view, but not that God is *a* Person. He is not a person but, as he elsewhere makes clear, is person*like*.[19] As we have seen, to say God is personlike is to affirm the elusiveness and committedness of being itself. There is in being an inexhaustible richness of meaning like a self standing behind its words in concrete situations. There is in being an indefectible loyalty and irrefragable trustworthiness toward selves and the entire realm of being like a self standing committed in its words.

From this perspective faith in being is *elicited* from the complex of commitments to being we dwell within, rather than given from without, as one self gives to another an object which it did not before possess. Nowhere does Niebuhr make the direct connection between animal faith and faith in being. He does speak of animal faith coming to be "attached" to being itself within the monotheistic religions,[20] and understands the Christian to be affirming faith in being, but does not identify the two. The difference between these two types of faith should be, on Niebuhr's own terms, that Christian faith penetrates through our defensive layers, protecting us from hostile being and all-destroying death, to open and to enable us to live more fully out of animal faith in being. Transformation of the self occurs not through a Divine Self bestowing what the human self does not have, but through that faith in being, obscured in our depths, becoming the focus of our lives through religious expression.

Recovering the Personal

By speaking in the first person grammar of religious language, the central self is brought into dialogue with its own deep-lying commitment to being, as it experiences the faithfulness of being towards it in the first person expression of God addressed to the self. Manifesting its elusiveness and commitment in act as it speaks religiously, the self gives its personal backing to this commitment. In whatever diverse ways it actually stands behind this commitment brought to expression in religious language, the self is achieving definition. It is becoming determinate, expressing this commitment and

---

[19] See MR pp. 152–154 & RMWC pp. 45 & 47.

[20] "In the faith of Judaism, Christianity, and Mohamedanism, animal belief in life's meaning attaches itself at last to the final and infinite Being, to the 'I am that I am,' the creative and destructive power, whence all things come and to which they all must return" (H. Richard Niebuhr, "Life Is Worth Living," *Intercollegian and Far Horizons*, LVII [October, 1939], p. 22).

standing behind it. Unexpressed commitments, the entirety of response-relations, are reordered in the light of expressed commitments to which the self has now given its backing.

While there are tendencies in Niebuhr's theology, recalcitrant elements from his critical past, to make God, as well as self, objective and to conceive all language as object-referential, these stand in opposition to the overwhelming (though not wholly unambiguous, because not wholly explicit) postcritical thrust of his theology. God most fundamentally and most fruitfully is not an objective self but is the pattern of faithfulness in being, inviolably sovereign like an elusive self in its irreducibly transcendent mystery and its irrepressibly immanent commitment to being. Religious language most fundamentally, with intimations of as yet unrecognized suggestiveness, is not referential but expressive, manifesting the pattern of our being in the world and within this the pattern of divine faithfulness.

To speak of God in this fashion is to understand that divine reality forever eludes our explicit grasp. The mystery at the heart of the world, at the root of my personal being in the world, can never be grasped so as exhaustively to explain and define it. There are things to be said about divinity but like a self it is ultimately not "something that can be known" but "something lived."[21] God is the pattern of meaning present within our being in the world, coming to expression in forms of life. To speak of religious language as expressive of forms of life is similarly to understand that language's ground forever eludes our explicit grasp. As forms of life religious language is not grounded in objects or propositions to which it can refer; rather it is grounded in ways of acting, forms of being, that reach beyond our knowing into the mysterious depths of personal existence. This does not mean, however, that religious language is more uncertain than other forms of speech, for all language has its meaning in its use and is therefore forms of life coming to expression as they are used in particular circumstances. No use of language has greater certainty than that founded upon commitment to particular ways of being human. We speak as we live—by faith.[22] And in that faith we have brought to articulation an entire world of human habitation through which we have been in touch with reality, whose inexhaustible richness sustains us yet transcends our grasp and surprises us in unanticipated ways. Religious language differs from non-religious language, not in being any more uncertain, but in embodying in its frankly first person emphases—thereby enabling us to express—this underlying faith which elsewhere lies veiled.

While all the more rich and radical for them, Niebuhr's theology con-

---

[21] Niebuhr, "Sören Kirkegaard," p. 33.

[22] Poteat speaks tellingly of the fiduciary grounding of all language in our living, and thus not in absolute certainty but in hope, which has proved itself fruitful beyond expectation, in "Myths, Stories, History, Eschatology and Action: Some Polanyian Meditations," pp. 230–231.

tains tensions between a critical perspective and the postcritical orientation emerging within it which have made understanding more difficult. Nevertheless, we have been able to discern, underlying the critical categories, coming now and again to direct consciousness, and emerging into unmistakable explicitness at the end of his career, the effort to cope with the modern problem of integrity through a postcritical theology of religious grammar.

Wrestling throughout his career in the heuristic metaphors of history, value, faith, and feeling with nothing less than the foundations of modernity, Niebuhr arrives in the life form of responsibility at a linguistic resolution for the linguistic problem. We have lost a real and shared world and are divided in ourselves because we have been seduced to live and speak, when we are expected to be intellectually alert and serious, in a third person mood. Through the use of religious language we find the confidence to speak in the first person and find a world inhabitable by persons. Within religious language functioning in concrete situations we discover a world faithful to the essential commitment and irreducibility of our dialogical nature. We are thus able to recover a real and shared world and to integrate within the parts formerly alienated; we are able to embrace those parts of ourselves existing in relation to beings we believed hostile, as we discover the principle of being to be trustworthy and loyal to us and to its cause, the totality of being.

Niebuhr's theology is extraordinarily rich, the metaphorically dense presentation of a radical resolution of the deeply rooted problem in modernity of integration. Since modernity took its rise in the seventeenth century, we have become increasingly enamored with the world of objects. Loving objects, there is something in being we have not loved—ourselves. Throughout the critical age we have sought to make ourselves over in the image of our love, to disembody ourselves of all that is idiosyncratically and inviolably personal. Through an emergent postcritical theology focused on the first person grammar of religious language, Niebuhr has sought to return us to ourselves, to love that being we have sought to ignore.

To embrace the first person grammar of religious language is to undergo a revolution in theological method. Theology must become confessional, that is, first personal. We must do in our religious reflections what Niebuhr has shown Michael Polanyi doing in science: I must state the "ultimate belief, which I find myself holding."[23] To reflect on our religious existence, as on the scientific enterprise, is to come upon beliefs—not that we ought to hold but—that we have been holding unawares. Theology should attempt to uncover these commitments fundamental to living as selves and especially to the unique self each of us is.

Rather than engaging in polemical attack upon other's theologies in defense of our own, we should enter into dialogue with our companions.

---

[23] Polanyi, PERSONAL KNOWLEDGE, p. 299, quoted in Niebuhr, "Science in Conflict with Morality?," p. 133.

Speaking of the unequivocally great theologians of the past, Niebuhr says they have participated in

> conversation with each other, learning from each other even while protesting and correcting each other where they feel they must. Almost entirely, the great chapters of Christian ethical theory have been written in a confessional rather than a polemical mood. That is, they are written with the disposition of one who says, I have found this or this to be true of the Christian life, rather than as attempts to refute another's claim.[24]

Whereas polemic precipitates a defensive posture that loses sight of the evanescent dimension of commitment and irreducibility, dialogical sharing in the first person of what each of us has found true, of what we believe, makes present the realities upon which theology rightly reflects.

Relying upon prelingual commitments in our being in the world coming to speech in dialogue brings to articulation what before had been inarticulate. Entering dialogue can become a way of discovering what in fact we are adhering to in the tacit depths of our being. While giving a lecture may not express anything new we had not earlier known, talking in ordinary conversation with another can bring us unwittingly upon unanticipated novelty. In dialogue we engage in self-discovery as we come upon both unsuspected convictions and unimagined ways of holding them. To bring aspects of self to focus in language is to achieve the ongoing transformation of self.

Through dialogue Niebuhr, in his theopoetic quest to recover the personal, has been led to the emergence of a postcritical linguistic theology centered in the first person grammar of religious language. Emergent out of his being in the world, Niebuhr's religious reflection seeks to return us to the world and within it to ourselves. Reaching beyond the self-alienating dichotomies of the critical age that ignore the "I" and fragment the world, matrix of self-integrity, the theology of H. Richard Niebuhr seeks to draw us toward love of the being of a real and shared world inhabitable by selves and love of our own being, coming to expression in the grammar of the first person.

On the first page of his first published essay Niebuhr speaks of the need for God to make the world "a livable home for man."[25] On the last two pages of his posthumously published THE RESPONSIBLE SELF he again speaks of being at home in the world, no longer simply as a need, but as an

---

[24] H. Richard Niebuhr, "Introduction," to Waldo Beach and H. Richard Niebuhr, eds., CHRISTIAN ETHICS: SOURCES OF THE LIVING TRADITION (New York: The Ronald Press Company, 1955), p. 8.

[25] Niebuhr, "An Aspect of the Idea of God in Recent Thought," p. 39.

emergent actuality. Recovering the personal through the emergence of a postcritical theology of the first person grammar of religious language leads to this incredible affirmation: "we were aliens and alienated in a strange, empty world, now we begin sometimes to feel at home." Through the use of religious language we can begin now, as selves coming to expression in the first person, to feel at home in the world, for "now we are falling in love, we think, with being itself."[26]

[26] RS pp. 177–178.

BIBLIOGRAPHY

I. H. Richard Niebuhr's Works Cited

"Adumbrations." Unpublished fragment written in connection with "Faith on Earth." Probably after 1958, Niebuhr Folder III-P-A.

"An Aspect of the Idea of God in Recent Thought." *Theological Magazine of the Evangelical Synod of North America*, XLCIII (1920).

"Can German and American Christians Understand Each Other?" *Christian Century*, XLVII (July 23, 1930).

"The Center of Value." RADICAL MONOTHEISM AND WESTERN CULTURE, WITH SUPPLEMENTARY ESSAYS. New York: Harper & Brothers, 1960. Originally published in MORAL PRINCIPLES OF ACTION: MAN'S ETHICAL IMPERATIVE. Edited by Ruth Nanda Anshen. New York: Harper & Brothers, 1952.

CHRIST AND CULTURE. Harper Torchbooks. New York: Harper & Brothers, 1956. Originally published New York: Harper & Brothers, 1951.

"Christian Ethics." Student lecture notes, handwritten by R. Melvin Keiser, delivered at Yale Divinity School, spring semester, 1961.

"Christian Ethics." Student lecture notes, transcribed by Robert Yetter, Gene Canestrari, and Ed Elliott, delivered at Yale Divinity School, spring semester, 1952.

"Christian Ethics Lectures." Niebuhr's lecture notes, handwritten, for class in "Christian Ethics" at Yale Divinity School, spring semester, 1961, Niebuhr Folder X.

CHRISTIAN ETHICS: SOURCES OF THE LIVING TRADITION. Edited with introductions by Waldo Beach and H. Richard Niebuhr. New York: The Ronald Press Company, 1955.

"Christian Theory of Sin." Student seminar notes, handwritten by R. Melvin Keiser, taught at Yale Divinity School, fall semester, 1961.

THE CHURCH AGAINST THE WORLD. By H. Richard Niebuhr, Wilhelm Pauck, and Francis P. Miller. Chicago, New York: Willett, Clark & Co., 1935. Niebuhr's contributions, "The Question of the Church" and "Toward the Independence of the Church," reprinted in THEOLOGY IN AMERICA: THE MAJOR PROTESTANT VOICES FROM PURITANISM TO NEO-ORTHODOXY. Edited by Sydney E. Ahlstrom. Indianapolis and New York: The Bobbs-Merrill Company, 1967.

"A Communication: The Only Way into the Kingdom of God." THE

CHRISTIAN CENTURY READER. Edited by Harold E. Fey and Margaret Frakes. New York: Associated Press, 1962. Originally published in *Christian Century*, XLIX (April 6, 1932).

"The Ego-Alter Dialectic and the Conscience." *Journal of Philosophy*, LXII (1945).

"Faith as Virtue." Student seminar notes, handwritten by R. Melvin Keiser, taught at Yale Divinity School, fall semester, 1960.

"Faith in Gods and in God." RADICAL MONOTHEISM AND WESTERN CULTURE, WITH SUPPLEMENTARY ESSAYS. New York: Harper & Brothers, 1960. Originally published as "The Nature and Existence of God: A Protestant's View." *Motive*, IV (1943).

"Faith on Earth." Unpublished booklength manuscript originally titled, according to Richard R. Niebuhr, "Knowledge of Faith," later titled "Faith on Earth: An Inquiry into the Structure of Faith," begun in 1950, intended for a time prior to the publication of RADICAL MONOTHEISM in 1960 to be published with it under the altered title "Faith on Earth: Essays on Human Confidence and Loyalty," Niebuhr Folder III-B.

"Introduction to Theological Study." Student lecture notes, handwritten by Elizabeth B. Keiser, delivered at Yale Divinity School, fall semester, 1960.

"An Introductory Essay on Language and Theology." Unpublished fragment, intended at one time, according to Richard R. Niebuhr, as introduction to "Faith on Earth: An Inquiry into the Structure of Faith," probably 1960, Niebuhr Folder III-C.

THE KINGDOM OF GOD IN AMERICA. Harper Torchbooks. New York: Harper & Brothers, 1959. Originally published New York: Harper & Brothers, 1937.

"Language and Theology." Seminar syllabus in possession of, and student lecture notes, handwritten by, Libertus A. Hoedemaker, taught at Yale Divinity School, spring semester, 1960.

"Life is Worth Living." *Intercollegian and Far Horizons*, LVII (October, 1939).

THE MEANING OF REVELATION. New York: The Macmillan Company, 1941.

"Memphis Lectures." Niebuhr's lecture notes, handwritten, in Niebuhr Folder III-AP-2, titled by Richard R. Niebuhr "Faith—Miscellanies," n.d.

"Moral Relativism and the Christian Ethic." New York: International Missionary Council, 1929. Address given at a Conference of Theological Seminaries, meeting at Drew Theological Seminary, Madison, New Jersey, November 29–December 1, 1929, on "Theological Education and the World Mission of Christianity."

"On the Nature of Faith." RELIGIOUS EXPERIENCE AND TRUTH: A SYMPOSIUM. Edited by Sidney Hook. New York: New York University

Press, 1961. Delivered at the New York University Institute of Philosophy, held at Washington Square, New York, October 21–22, 1960.

"Next Steps in Theology." Unpublished Cole Lectures delivered at Vanderbilt University, April 10–12, 1961. Four lectures transcribed from tape recording: I. "Toward the Future," II. "Toward New Symbols," III. "Toward the Recovery of Feeling," IV. "Toward the Service of Christendom."

"The Problem of the Individual in Richard Dehmel." By Helmut Niebuhr. Unpublished M.A. thesis in the Department of Germanics, Washington University, June, 1917.

"Protestant Theology Since Schleiermacher." Student lecture notes, handwritten by Joe E. Elmore, delivered at Yale Divinity School, fall semester, 1951.

THE PURPOSE OF THE CHURCH AND ITS MINISTRY: REFLECTIONS ON THE AIMS OF THEOLOGICAL EDUCATION. H. Richard Niebuhr, in collaboration with Daniel Day Williams and James M. Gustafson. New York: Harper & Brothers, 1956.

"Questions about Faith in Many Contexts." Unpublished fragment in Niebuhr Folder III-AP-2, titled by Richard R. Niebuhr "Faith—Miscellanies," among untitled batch beginning "Intro.—Questions about faith in many contexts . . ." from 1958 or later.

RADICAL MONOTHEISM AND WESTERN CULTURE, WITH SUPPLEMENTARY ESSAYS. New York: Harper & Brothers, 1960.

"Reformation: Continuing Imperative." HOW MY MIND HAS CHANGED. Edited with an Introduction by Harold E. Fey. Meridian Books. New York: World Publishing Company, 1961. Originally published in *Christian Century*, LXXVII (1960).

"The Religious Emotions." Student seminar notes, handwritten by R. Melvin Keiser, taught at Yale Divinity School, spring semester, 1962.

"Religious Realism in the Twentieth Century." RELIGIOUS REALISM. Edited by D. C. Macintosh. New York: The Macmillan Company, 1931.

THE RESPONSIBLE SELF: AN ESSAY IN CHRISTIAN MORAL PHILOSOPHY. By H. Richard Niebuhr, with a Preface by Richard R. Niebuhr, and an Introduction by James M. Gustafson. New York, Evanston, and London: Harper & Row, 1963.

"Science in Conflict with Morality?" RADICAL MONOTHEISM AND WESTERN CULTURE, WITH SUPPLEMENTARY ESSAYS, New York: Harper & Brothers, 1960. Lecture delivered at St. John's College, Annapolis, Maryland, February 28, 1959, as part of a symposium on the theme, "The Scientist as Philosopher."

"The Social Gospel and the Mind of Jesus." Unpublished lecture, handwritten, read before the American Theological Society, in New York City, April 21, 1933, in Niebuhr Folder VIII.

THE SOCIAL SOURCES OF DENOMINATIONALISM. Living Age Books. New York: Meridian Books, 1957. Originally published New York: Henry Holt and Company, 1929.

"Sören Kierkegaard." CHRISTIANITY AND THE EXISTEN-TIALISTS. Edited by Carl D. Michalson. New York: Scribner, 1956.

"The Structure of Faith." Unpublished fragment in Niebuhr Folder III-AP-2, titled by Richard R. Niebuhr "Faith-Miscellanies," from 1958 or later.

"Translator's Preface." THE RELIGIOUS SITUATION. By Paul Tillich. Living Age Edition. New York: Meridian Books, 1956. Originally published New York: Henry Holt & Co., 1932.

"Value Theory and Theology." THE NATURE OF RELIGIOUS EXPE-RIENCE: ESSAYS IN HONOR OF DOUGLAS CLYDE MACINTOSH. Edited by J. S. Bixler, R. L. Calhoun, H. R. Niebuhr. New York: Harper & Brothers, 1937.

"Wach, SOCIOLOGY OF RELIGION." *Theology Today*, II, No. 3 (1945).

II. Other Works Cited

Ahlstrom, Sydney E. A RELIGIOUS HISTORY OF THE AMERICAN PEOPLE. New Haven: Yale University Press, 1972.

Ahlstrom, Sydney E., ed. THEOLOGY IN AMERICA: THE MAJOR PROTESTANT VOICES FROM PURITANISM TO NEO-ORTHODOXY. New York: The Bobbs-Merrill Company,1967.

Auden, W. H. SECONDARY WORLDS. New York: Random House, 1968.

Auerbach, Erich. MIMESIS: THE REPRESENTATION OF REALITY IN WESTERN LITERATURE. Translated by Willard Trask. Anchor Books. New York: Doubleday and Company, 1957.

Barth, Karl. CHURCH DOGMATICS. Vol. I, THE DOCTRINE OF THE WORD OF GOD. Part 1. Translated by G. T. Thomson. Edinburgh: T. & T. Clark, 1936. Part 2. Translated by G. T. Thomson and Harold Knight. Edinburgh: T. & T. Clark, 1956.

Bultmann, Rudolf. KERYGMA AND MYTH: A THEOLOGICAL DE-BATE. Edited by Hans Werner Bartsch. Harper Torchbooks. New York: Harper & Brothers, 1961.

Campbell, Joseph. THE MASKS OF GOD. Vol. 1, PRIMITIVE MY-THOLOGY. Vol. 4, CREATIVE MYTHOLOGY. Viking Compass Edition. New York: The Viking Press, 1970.

Campbell, Joseph. "Mythological Themes in Creative Literature and Art." MYTHS, DREAMS, AND RELIGION. Edited by Joseph Campbell. New York: E. P. Dutton & Co., 1970.

Cassirer, Ernst. LANGUAGE AND MYTH. Translated by Susanne K. Langer. New York: Harper & Brothers, 1946.

Cassirer, Ernst. THE PHILOSOPHY OF SYMBOLIC FORMS. Vol. 1, LANGUAGE. Vol. 2, MYTHICAL THOUGHT. Translated by Ralph Manheim. New Haven and London: Yale University Press, 1953 and 1955.

Cobb, John B., Jr. LIVING OPTIONS IN PROTESTANT THEOLOGY: A SURVEY OF METHODS. Philadelphia: The Westminster Press, 1962.

Eliade, Mircea. PATTERNS IN COMPARATIVE RELIGION. Translated by Rosemary Sheed. Meridian Books. Cleveland and New York: The World Publishing Company, 1970.

Feidelson, Charles, Jr. SYMBOLISM AND AMERICAN LITERATURE. Phoenix Books. Chicago: The University of Chicago Press, 1953.

Fowler, James W. TO SEE THE KINGDOM: THE THEOLOGICAL VISION OF H. RICHARD NIEBUHR. Nashville & New York: Abingdon Press, 1974.

Frei, Hans W. "The Theology of H. Richard Niebuhr." FAITH AND ETHICS: THE THEOLOGY OF H. RICHARD NIEBUHR. Edited by Paul Ramsey. Harper Torchbooks. New York: Harper & Row, 1965.

Gombrich, E. H. ART AND ILLUSION: A STUDY IN THE PSYCHOLOGY OF PICTORIAL REPRESENTATION. London: Phaidon Press, 1960.

Harvey, Van Austin. THE HISTORIAN AND THE BELIEVER: THE MORALITY OF HISTORICAL KNOWLEDGE AND CHRISTIAN BELIEF. New York: The Macmillan Company, 1966.

High, Dallas M. LANGUAGE, PERSONS, AND BELIEF: STUDIES IN WITTGENSTEIN'S PHILOSOPHICAL INVESTIGATIONS AND RELIGIOUS USES OF LANGUAGE. New York: Oxford University Press, 1967.

Hoedemaker, Libertus A. THE THEOLOGY OF H. RICHARD NIEBUHR. Philadelphia and Boston: Pilgrim Press, 1970.

Hopper, Stanley Romaine. "Myth, Dream, and Imagination." MYTHS, DREAMS, AND RELIGION. Edited by Joseph Campbell. New York: E. P. Dutton & Co., 1970.

Kirk, Elizabeth D. THE DREAM THOUGHT OF PIERS PLOWMAN. New Haven and London: Yale University Press, 1972.

Langland, William. PIERS PLOWMAN: THE A VERSION. Edited by George Kane. London: Athlone Press, 1960.

Macmurray, John. THE FORM OF THE PERSONAL. Vol. 1, SELF AS AGENT. Vol. 2, PERSONS IN RELATION. London: Faber and Faber Limited, 1957 and 1961.

Marcel, Gabriel. HOMO VIATOR: INTRODUCTION TO A METAPHYSIC OF HOPE. Translated by Emma Craufurd. Chicago: Henry Regnery Company, 1951.

Merleau-Ponty, Maurice. PHENOMENOLOGY OF PERCEPTION. Translated by Colin Smith. London: Routledge & Kegan Paul, 1962.

Niebuhr, Reinhold. "The Truth in Myths." THE NATURE OF RELI-

GIOUS EXPERIENCE: ESSAYS IN HONOR OF DOUGLAS CLYDE MACINTOSH. Edited by J. S. Bixler, R. L. Calhoun, H. R. Niebuhr. New York: Harper & Brothers, 1937.

Pepper, Stephen. WORLD HYPOTHESES. Berkeley: University of California Press, 1961.

Polanyi, Michael. PERSONAL KNOWLEDGE: TOWARDS A POSTCRITICAL PHILOSOPHY. London: Routledge & Kegan Paul, 1958.

Polanyi, Michael. THE TACIT DIMENSION. Anchor Books. New York: Doubleday & Company, 1967.

Poteat, William H. "Birth, Suicide, and the Doctrine of Creation: An Exploration of Analogies." NEW ESSAYS ON RELIGIOUS LANGUAGE. Edited by Dallas M. High. New York: Oxford University Press, 1969.

Poteat, William H. "God and the 'Private-I'." NEW ESSAYS ON RELIGIOUS LANGUAGE. Edited by Dallas M. High. New York: Oxford University Press, 1969.

Poteat, William H. "Myths, Stories, History, Eschatology and Action: Some Polanyian Meditations." INTELLECT AND HOPE: ESSAYS IN THE THOUGHT OF MICHAEL POLANYI. Edited, with an Introduction, by Thomas A. Langford and William H. Poteat. Durham: Duke University Press, 1968.

Ramsey, Paul. "The Transformation of Ethics." FAITH AND ETHICS: THE THEOLOGY OF H. RICHARD NIEBUHR. Edited by Paul Ramsey. Harper Torchbooks. New York: Harper & Row, 1965.

Ricoeur, Paul. INTERPRETATION THEORY: DISCOURSE AND THE SURPLUS OF MEANING. Fort Worth: The Texas Christian University Press, 1976.

Sewell, Elizabeth. THE ORPHIC VOICE: POETRY AND NATURAL HISTORY. London: Routledge & Kegan Paul, 1960.

Tillich, Paul. SYSTEMATIC THEOLOGY. Vol. 1–3. Chicago: The University of Chicago Press, 1951, 1957, and 1963,

Wilder, Amos. THEOPOETIC: THEOLOGY AND THE RELIGIOUS IMAGINATION. Philadelphia: Fortress Press, 1976.

Wittgenstein, Ludwig. ON CERTAINTY. Edited by G. E. M. Anscombe and G. H. von Wright. Translated by Denis Paul and G. E. M. Anscombe. New York and Evanston: J. & J. Harper Editions, 1969.

Wittgenstein, Ludwig. PHILOSOPHICAL INVESTIGATIONS. Translated by G. E. M. Anscombe. New York: Macmillan Company, 1953.